HUEY

SPIRIT OF THE PANTHER

Bobby Seale (left) wearing a Colt. 45 and Huey with bandoleer and shotgun. (AP Photo / San Francisco Examiner)

HUEY
SPIRIT OF THE PANTHER

DAVID HILLIARD

with

KEITH and KENT ZIMMERMAN

THUNDER'S MOUTH PRESS

NEW YORK

HUEY
SPIRIT OF THE PANTHER

Published by
Thunder's Mouth Press
An Imprint of Avalon Publishing Group Inc.
245 West 17th Street, 11th Floor
New York, NY 10011

AVALON
publishing group incorporated

First printing January 2006

Library of Congress Cataloging-in-Publication Data is available.

ISBN: 1-56025-837-3
ISBN 13: 978-1-56025-837-7

9 8 7 6 5 4 3 2 1

Book design by Sara E. Stemen
Printed in the United States of America
Distributed by Publishers Group West

CONTENTS

FOREWORD

Huey Newton and the Black Panther Party he created have passed out of existence, as all things do. Like all things, the man and his organization leave behind memories, sadly destined to be weaned out of history with each new generation. But they also have left behind tangible references to lives lived and life works. Their legacy is a humane one that is a beacon from the past.

I came to know and embrace the best of Huey Newton—first from the distance of a Black Panther Party youth member beginning in 1970, then many years later from a wife's intimate, firsthand perspective after we were married in 1981. I was therefore witness to the enlightened dreams he dreamed and to the agony of the dreamer. I came to know that Huey was the truest revolutionary, seeking always to bring harmony between the nature of things and the state of things, to transform dark into light, to challenge fear and hate with courage and love.

As Huey's former wife and comrade, I am also uniquely situated to attest to the common humanity of the man who struggled always with the trappings of his international celebrity. To many observers, admirers, and detractors alike, Huey was the embodiment of the black liberation struggle in America. His 1967 arrest in connection with the shooting death of an Oakland police officer thrust him into headline news around the world. Of course, he had already achieved tremendous local notoriety in the San Francisco Bay Area when he founded the Black Panther Party in 1966. However, the landmark trial that followed forever elevated Huey to the iconic status that at once rightly celebrated his role as an African American freedom fighter while enshrouding the man in the myths and falsehoods that have obscured his legacy for decades.

In order to bring truth and clarity to the historical record, I launched the Huey P. Newton Foundation, along with former party members David Hilliard and Elaine Brown in 1993. The foundation is the repository of the Black Panther Party archives, including hundreds of papers, photographs, correspondence, and personal documents. A primary component of our work has been highlighting Huey's intellectual contributions, especially his eloquent, far-sighted political philosophies that remain as relevant to world affairs today as when they were written some thirty years ago.

I am therefore thrilled by the publication of *Huey: Spirit of the Panther*, the first-ever authoritative biography of Huey P. Newton. This long-overdue, much-needed book represents the definitive account of his life, work, and legacy. Meticulously researched and involving the participation of dozens of insiders from Huey's private and public lives—many of them never before having shared their recollections of Huey and the Black Panther Party—this groundbreaking biography opens new windows onto the past. Just as importantly, however, *Huey: Spirit of the Panther* presents new avenues for future scholarly endeavors that seek to enlighten our understanding of the party, its founder, and the black liberation era.

History is witness to the fact that Huey acted on his vision by inventing an instrument for enlightenment and freedom called the Black Panther Party. This was his essence and his life's work, and its spirit lives on as his personal legacy. The Black Panther Party has left behind a legacy, a foundation laid, a seed sown that flowers the barren fields of today.

—Fredrika Newton
Oakland, California
March 28, 2005

ACKNOWLEDGMENTS

This book was made possible by the contributions of many people, including family, friends, and colleagues from Huey's life.

Foremost, I would like to acknowledge Fredrika Newton, whose love, strength, and trenchant wit inspired me to carry on my life's work of restoring truth to the historical record by reclaiming the original vision of the Black Panther Party as it was set down by founder Huey P. Newton.

This book was also made possible by contributions from the Newton family, particularly Demetra Gayle, who brought new, firsthand accounts of Huey's family life to light. Without the encouragement, belief, and foresight of Keith and Kent Zimmerman to collaborate with Fredrika and me, this book would be nothing more than an idea. "You guys made it happen!"

I owe thanks to Professor Robert Trivers of Rutgers University and Professor Triloki N. Pandey of the University of California, Santa Cruz, for sharing their recollections of Huey's academic life. Their words are valuable testimonies to Huey's intellectual might.

Special thanks to George Robinson, Ericka Huggins, Andrea Jones-Dunham, John Oakes, Donald Freed, Charlie Winton, Bobby Seale, Jim Fitzgerald, Pat Richartz, Billy "Che" Brooks, and Stan McKinney.

Very special thanks to Don Weise for his work at the Huey P. Newton Foundation, including his contributions as coeditor of the *Huey P. Newton Reader.*

Former Oakland mayor Elihu Harris has my gratitude for introducing the Black Panther Party into the curriculum of the Peralta Colleges, where Huey and Bobby Seale met as students before going on to found the party in 1966.

CHAPTER 1

"LET ME DIE RIGHT HERE."

On October 18, 1967, Bobby Seale sat in jail. Five months earlier, the Sacramento state legislature had been visited by a group of gun-toting members of the Black Panther Party. Bobby was still locked up on gun charges after a compromise enabled the remaining members arrested in Sacramento to go free. Sacramento put the Black Panther Party on the map, just as Huey had planned. Immediately afterward, we were deluged with publicity and press from all over the world. Black Panther Party memberships came rolling in from all across the country. We went from being a small neighborhood Oakland organization to a nationwide phenomenon. Huey's plan had worked beautifully. Sacramento was the "colossal event" that sent shock waves throughout the country; black men and women in forty cities were prepared to defend their own people with their lives.

When Bobby Seale and Huey came together to form the Black Panther Party, they observed many political groups. Many seemed steeped in rhetoric, withdrawn from reality, with no practical programs for the people. The actions the BPP engaged in were purely strategic for political purposes designed to mobilize the community.

The situation was desperate, and some of our rhetoric became as inflamed as that used against us by politicians and media. The press painted us as wild, gun-toting animals. We had picked up the gun, now we could not put it down; the media froze us in this agonizing posture.

Bobby, the cofounder of the Black Panther Party, was incarcerated, and Huey wanted him out of the Santa Rita Jail. Huey didn't have a job. Today marked the end of his probation. I had a job and a car, a family, and very little money. The young Black Panther Party was experiencing one of its very first lows.

I would go over to Huey's house, and it might be two o'clock in the afternoon. He'd still be lying in his bed, reading a magazine or a book. Thinking. Huey was always thinking, and I knew what was on his mind. I could see the wheels turning. How were we going to raise the bail to get Bobby out of Santa Rita? How were we going to top Sacramento in terms of another "colossal event"?

A windfall came our way in the form of a paid speaking engagement across the Bay at San Francisco State College. Like many colleges and universities, San Francisco State was already a hotbed of debate and radical politics. A year later the college would be the site of student riots, tear gas, strikes, and demonstrations under the tumultuous administration of S. I. Hayakawa, a conservative and feisty semantics professor–turned–campus president and later a Republican U.S. senator.

Huey and I jumped into my car and rode over to the campus, on the foggy side of San Francisco, to the student union, where Huey was scheduled to speak that day. After the speech, we looked at one another. Five hundred dollars. It was enough money, I figured. Now we could maybe parlay it into something bigger to help get Bobby out. At the very least, we'd have ourselves a small reserve.

"What do you think we should do?" Huey asked me.

Before I had started my job at the longshoreman union hall, my best way of making money came from the street. I knew that weed was one of the easiest commodities to buy and sell quickly.

"I know these guys who've got bricks," I suggested to Huey. "Let's buy a couple, break them down, and sell them. I'll bet we can triple our money." I knew people who sold large quantities of weed. I figured we could break the stuff down and sell matchboxes full of it for five bucks apiece to raise money for Bobby's bail.

Gene McKinney had been my junior high school friend since the eighth grade. We grew up together in West Oakland, along with his four brothers and two sisters. A couple of those brothers were basketball players. Another brother, Bull McKinney, was built like a football player. They were all tough guys. Gene's father held gambling parties at his house, and Gene's mother would cook up a mountain of fried chicken and ribs and bake cakes. Gene was my big-brother, right-hand partner. The events of October 1967 brought Gene into the inner circle of the Black Panther Party.

Gene was a ladies' man, a handsome guy. All the girls liked him. Plus, he was a good street fighter. He came out of the Codornices Village housing projects in Berkeley along with Bobby Seale.

"We've got to get Gene involved in this," I said to Huey.

Gene was an asset. Just about anytime during the week, you could go over to Gene's house, especially during the weekends, and Gene's daddy would be running his gambling parties, the biggest in West Oakland. My idea was that we would throw our own gambling party and raise enough money to bail Bobby out of Santa Rita.

Gene and my brother June agreed to help Huey and me out. Later, after we broke down the weed, we still had a few dollars left to buy food, hamburgers, and chicken for our party. June agreed to cook. We would "pay the house." That meant the house could take a piece of all the gambling action. That way everybody wins. Players would pay us to come to the house and play. With the weed, food, and our gambling cut, we'd all make money, Bobby would be out of Santa Rita, and we might even have enough left over for a three-hundred-dollar reserve. It was all set. Our gambling fund-raiser would be held at my house on Thirty-second Street and Magnolia. By two in the morning, we were doing all right. My place was packed. The house was jumping with winners and losers.

Then Huey had an idea. About a week earlier, he and I had been riding down Seventh Street. Seventh Street in Oakland was where all the street action was. We called it the "Hoe Stroll." Huey recalled seeing a pretty young girl standing on the street with a pad of paper and a clipboard. She said she was conducting a sociology study for her college class. Huey liked what he saw.

"I'd like to be *your* student," Huey mused.

"Here," the girl says, handing him the clipboard. "Sign your name on this."

I had already forgotten about the girl, but apparently Huey hadn't. Now, here it was, two in the morning, and Huey turned to Gene.

"I think I want to go down to Seventh Street and find my fine little sociology student."

"Huey," I said, "I really think that girl was a student. Besides, it's two AM."

"I think she's a prostitute," he said, "and I'm going to go out and look for her."

As Huey and Gene left the house, I was thinking, "Man, they're wasting their time; the girl was a legitimate student." But Huey was convinced she was running a game. That was how Huey typically thought. Everybody had his or her game. Besides looking for the girl, Huey went out to get more food, some barbecue. Huey loved to eat.

"We've got plenty of food in the house," I said. Besides, the place was still jumping, crowded with gamblers, and our food and weed supply were still holding up. Nevertheless Huey and Gene split.

An hour later, there was a loud banging at the door. Everybody froze. The room turned dead silent. Somebody opened the door and Huey fell crumpled onto the floor, a huge gaping hole in his stomach. He hit the floor with a thud, unconscious. Gene was out of breath, hollering, saying something about the cops and how they shot Huey. One cop was dead. The other was shot. Thanks to Sacramento, every man in blue knew Huey and who he was, and what organization he stood for: the Black Panther Party for Self-Defense. The guys suddenly grew nervous about being in the same house with Huey. Huey was lying on the floor, a massive hole in his gut, bleeding like a dog. Everybody broke for the door, and the house immediately emptied.

I was frantic.

"What are we going to do?"

Huey came to, long enough to ask the same question.

"I'm going to take you to the hospital," I decided.

Huey protested. "Let me die right here. All they're going to do is give me the gas chamber. They're going to kill me anyway, so let me die right here."

"I can't," I stammered. "I can't do that."

I ran frantically around the house, gathering towels to soak up the blood streaming from Huey's stomach. Then we lifted Huey into my car. June, Huey, and I raced down MacArthur Boulevard toward Kaiser-Permanente Medical Center. As we drove up onto the emergency-room ramp, I assumed Huey was already dead. I blew my horn and revved up the engine. June jumped out and opened the car door. We now had Huey by both legs. I saw a nurse run out of the emergency room toward us just as we set Huey down on the hard concrete ramp.

"He's shot, he's shot, he's shot," I yelled out to the nurses as I headed back to my car.

As the nurse ran back inside to grab a gurney, June and I took off in the car. I burned rubber, and in seconds we'd gotten the hell out of there.

The next day, Huey stared back at me from the front page of the *Oakland Tribune*. In fact, he was on the front page of almost every metro newspaper across the country. He was not dead after all. In the press photo, Huey is wounded and manacled to a gurney in the Kaiser Oakland emergency room. In the forefront of the picture a fat Oakland cop stares sternly into the camera lens. Huey is lying on his back in the ER, his hands cuffed to the gurney. He is stretched out, in an oddly Christlike position, a man about to be executed.

CHAPTER 2

THE OAKLAND STREETS

I first met Huey when we moved from West Oakland to North Oakland in the fifties. Every morning we'd hurry off together to Woodrow Wilson Junior High School, a racially mixed school where black students were in the minority. Huey and I were the same age, same grade, and would attend many of the same schools, although we never shared a single class.

While neither of us played sports, Huey admired the boxers. Joe Louis, the Brown Bomber. Kid Gavilan. Sugar Ray Robinson. Jersey Joe Walcott. Athletes like Joe Louis and Jackie Robinson instilled pride and courage.

Huey's physical appearance was always tidy. His face was oiled and shined; he looked like a piece of jade. He was compulsive about cleanliness and brushed his teeth incessantly, several times a day. Huey loved classical music. His mother had furnished him with piano lessons, so he introduced me to the music of Tchaikovsky. He loved the *Nutcracker*. One of his favorite songs was Rimsky-Korsakov's "Flight of the Bumblebee."

Huey was shy and introverted. He couldn't talk much to the girls. The way he'd get their attention was to recite poetry. Although Huey had learning and reading disabilities in the classroom, he had no problems memorizing epic poems. "The Bells" or "The Raven" by Edgar Allen Poe, T. S. Eliot's "Love Song of J. Alfred Prufrock," the *Rubaiyat of Omar Khayyam,* and *Macbeth* were all part of his spoken repertoire. That was how he impressed the girls.

Huey's father, Walter Newton, was born in Alabama. His mother, Armelia Johnson, was born in Louisiana. The couple lived in Arkansas for seven years before moving to Louisiana, where Walter held jobs in a gravel pit, carbon plant, sugarcane mill, and sawmill, and served briefly as a brakeman. A deeply religious man, he preached regularly at the Bethel Baptist Church in Monroe, Louisiana. When Walter decided to pull up stakes and eventually settle in Oakland in 1944, he sought work at the naval air station in Alameda County. By 1945 the entire family had relocated westward. Walter Newton worked multiple jobs to see to it his family never went hungry. Walter strictly forbade his wife to take on a job, particularly as a domestic worker for any of the white Oakland households.

Huey P. Newton, the youngest child of the Newton family, was born in Monroe, Louisiana, on February 17, 1942, the last of seven children. Lee Edward, the eldest son, was old enough to be Huey's father. After Lee was Walter Jr. (nicknamed Sonny Man), whose innate street sense would later have a tremendous impact on Huey while growing up. Next came Melvin. There were three sisters: Myrtle, Leola, and Doris. To his mother and sisters, Huey was the little prince. He was named after Louisiana governor Huey Pierce Long, a politician Walter admired because of Long's talent to cleverly and simultaneously cater to the area's white patricians while passing programs that also helped Louisiana's black communities through the back door.

Huey struggled as a boy and as a young student. He hid his learning disabilities by constantly behaving in ways that got him kicked out of class. Because his mother always insisted on Huey using the initial "P" in his name, some of the kids at school made fun ("Huey P. goes wee, wee, wee"), which only sharpened and honed his fighting skills on the playground.

When we first met, Huey was attending sixth grade at Santa Fe Elementary. I lived on Forty-seventh and West, while Huey lived around the corner on Forty-seventh Street. Our neighborhood was working class and integrated. Soon the Newton family spread out. Nearly all the daughters had grown and moved away, as did the older sons. Lee Edward moved to the San Francisco Peninsula, toward Menlo Park. Walter Jr., Sonny Man, was in Southern California. That left four Newtons in the household— Walter, Armelia, Melvin, and Huey.

While growing up, Huey was greatly influenced by four strong male role models. He would eventually become an amalgam of all four figures. Walter, the strict disciplinarian, had a strong sense of moral character and was deeply rooted in Old Testament values. Oldest brother, Lee Edward, was the first of the family to see the inside of the Oakland County Jail, and he taught Huey the meaning of standing up and holding his ground, even if it meant a fight. Walter Jr. represented the excitement of the street to Huey. Hanging out at the racetrack or being kept by a woman made Sonny Man a player in Huey's eyes. For the rest of his life, a part of Huey would always emulate Sonny Man. Melvin would influence Huey on the importance of education. Melvin steered away from any trouble on the streets with the police. Instead, he studiously attended Oakland City College. It was Melvin who tutored Huey when Huey was ready to settle down and apply himself scholastically. Throughout his life, Huey maintained a delicate balance of all four figureheads—Walter's values, brother Lee's strength, Sonny Man's street smarts, and Melvin's intellectual prowess.

The tenth grade at Oakland Technical High School was a tough year for Huey. He rarely got along with his teachers and was constantly thrown out of class for challenging their authority. But he continued to memorize literary passages from books and LP records. "I remember Huey in the eleventh or twelfth grade," Melvin Newton recalled. "He brings me this notebook and says, 'Help me.' Then he says, 'Turn the page.' He knew everything on the page, verbatim. I was shocked."[1]

Besides his studies, Huey picked up another talent from Melvin: hypnosis. Huey was able to hypnotize people into various deep and comical trances. His subjects barked like dogs or ate grass on command.

By the summer of 1959, after Huey graduated from Oakland Technical High School, he began to admire certain political figures. First it was blacklisted actor and orator Paul Robeson, then Fidel Castro and the Cuban Revolution.

After Oakland Tech, Huey grew increasingly restless and confused about the course of his life. He had suffered the sting of being labeled an illiterate in high school with an IQ of 79, and he had not yet developed full confidence in his own intellectual abilities. He also witnessed with disdain his father working two and three jobs. The man rarely enjoyed any time off. Huey loathed the fact that Walter Sr. could barely pay the interest on his bills, let alone the principal.

By the fall of 1959, while I worked on the docks, Huey enrolled as a freshman in Oakland City College. Like a few young black males during that time period, he was casually drawn to the bohemian tenets of the Beat Generation. He grew a short, stubbly beard. His unkempt appearance caused havoc and loud arguments in the Newton household. Finally, in his stubbornness and rage, Huey left the family's house and moved out on his own.

During his first semester at Oakland City College (now called Merritt College), Huey moved into a flat near the campus with a friend named William Brumfield. Brumfield had plans to write three books about his avid philosophies of love and sex and changed his name to Richard Thorne. To Thorne, men and women had no need to "own" each other and permanently bond in traditional fashion. Marriage was a rigid tool of bourgeois society. Thorne was later to become a major proponent of the prehippie, "Free Love" movement that grew out of the Bay Area and went on to cofound the Sexual Freedom League. Although Huey found Thorne's ideas controversial and radical (and they certainly were at the time), he was much more impressed that Thorne usually kept a small stable of adoring and attractive females and college coeds around the house at all hours.

The Free Speech Movement and other human potential groups were taking shape just across the city line in Berkeley and would soon spread into Oakland. Huey delved deeply into the writings of W. E. B. DuBois, Frantz Fanon, and Booker T. Washington. Volumes like Ralph Ellison's *The Invisible Man, The Fire Next Time* by James Baldwin, Danish philosopher Soren Kierkegaard, and French novelists Albert Camus and Jean-Paul Sartre made a deep impression. The early 1960s proved to be a fertile period for Huey. College made him less insecure, and his learning processes unfolded at a rapid pace.

It was during this time frame when the lexicon of Afro-American (and later Afro-centrism) threaded their way through the campus social set. Subjects like institutional racism, civil disobedience, and civil rights became fair-game topics of dialogue in the classrooms, fraternities, and student lounges. Huey was among the first dozen charter members of the Afro-American Association (AAA). The association discussed various works by notable black authors of the time and regularly sponsored rallies on the Oakland City College campus in order to promote black awareness and various other causes.

Through Afro-American Association rallies and events, Huey applied some of the viewpoints and beliefs he had accumulated and sharpened his skills as a street-corner debater. He had a talent to captivate his fellow students. The more Huey read and learned, the greater his powers of observation, analysis, and discourse.

Unlike most college students, Huey lived a double life, both as an academic and a petty criminal. He maintained ties among a lot of our lumpen friends for extra cash. He scammed pocket money as a quick-change artist. Huey and his burglar friends also cruised the wealthier neighborhoods in broad daylight and sold stolen merchandise picked up through stolen credit card transactions. Unlocked cars that held valuables were fair game for Huey and his friends. Throughout his life, Huey would maintain close contact with the street. Whether he excelled as an academic, a leader, or a philosopher, he would not stray far from the people and the streets.

In the spring semester of 1962, Richard Thorne met up with a past family acquaintance, a twenty-six-year-old City College engineering student who had just finished a four-year hitch in the air force. His name was Bobby Seale. Seale lived in his parents' house on nearby Fifty-seventh Street, a stone's throw from the four-block City College campus. Toting his drafting board, an armload of books, and precision drawing instruments, Seale approached an impromptu rally sponsored by the Afro-American Association.

Thorne introduced Seale to members of the Afro-American Association. He motioned over toward Huey, who at the time was engaged in a deep discussion with a young lady who seemed as taken with Huey's good looks as she was with the rhetoric he was laying down. "Bobby," Richard said, interrupting Huey's rap, "this is Huey Newton. Huey's a good friend of mine."

A few weeks later, Seale saw Huey a second time. He was debating intensely with another campus colleague. Huey was articulating various passages from a book by E. Franklin Frazier called *Black Bourgeoisie*. Seale watched in amazement as Huey's opponent pointed out certain general passages in the book, only to be corrected by Huey, who then referred verbatim to the actual page numbers and paragraphs of the points made in Frazier's book. Seale was astounded by Huey's disarming debating skills.

As the two walked down the street together, Huey told Bobby about a scuffle he had had with a character outside a nearby liquor store over a bottle of wine. The matter had turned into fisticuffs.

"Well, if it had been me," Bobby said matter-of-factly, "I would have shot that dude."

Huey's eyes lit up again. "You got a gun?"

"I've got three or four guns. C'mon, I'll show them to you." Seale led Huey through the back door of his house only a block away. In Seale's bedroom, posters of a B-52 bomber and a Gemini missile hung alongside placards of Martin Luther King Jr. and Malcolm X.

"I thought you had a pistol," Huey said to Bobby. Seale proudly showed Huey a .38 pistol housed in a tooled leather holster.

Upon leaving Seale's house, Huey invited Bobby to a party he planned to attend that night. Seale turned him down, citing a prior commitment. A few days later, Huey showed up at the doorway of one of Seale's engineering classes.

"What's up?"

"Remember that party I invited you to?"

"Yeah."

"Well, I was at the party and, uh, I had to defend myself."

"What do you mean?"

"This guy threatened to kill me. So I wanted to know, could I borrow your pistol?"[2]

Bobby arranged for Huey to meet him back at his house later, but on the way, Huey was picked up and handcuffed by the police.

The incident evolved from an altercation Huey had at the party with a dude named Odell Lee. The two exchanged heated words at the party, and Lee challenged Huey's views on Afro-Americans. After Huey turned his back, Lee grabbed Huey and a fight ensued. Huey stabbed Lee repeatedly with a steak knife.

Sonny Man came up from Los Angeles and raised Huey's bail after he was arrested. After the trial a couple of months later, Huey was convicted of felonious assault.

Huey would spend the next six months in the Santa Rita Jail, a long way from the comforts of academia. Prior to being dispatched to Santa Rita, Huey was housed in the Alameda County Jail and was sent into solitary confinement after taking part in a food strike. At the age of twenty-two, Huey spent nearly three weeks in solitary in a four-by-six-foot cell that had been nicknamed "the soul-breaker" by the other inmates.

After Huey was moved to Santa Rita, he incited another skirmish in the mess hall by bashing a steel tray over a food worker's head. Already a veteran of the soul-breaker, Huey was taken to Greystone in Santa Rita's nearby "cooler" section. It was then that Huey learned through discipline and strength how to endure prison isolation and punishment.

CHAPTER 3

THE SEEKER

Between 1959 and 1965 Huey attended Oakland City College on an on-and-off basis. As he had told Bobby Seale, higher education entertained his mind, and unlike high school, he wasn't forced to attend each and every class. It was worthwhile because he could stay politically active on campus and pursue (at his own depth and pace) highly complex academic subjects like biological behaviorism and stimulus response (studying the works of B. F. Skinner and Pavlov), existentialism, and logical positivism through the works of A. J. Ayer, a philosopher from the 1930s who explored the inner meanings of reality, perception, and knowledge.

In 1964, after serving out his six months in the Alameda County and Santa Rita jails, Huey's relationship with Donald Warden and the Afro-American Association was gradually deteriorating. Although he couldn't verbalize it at the time, Huey thirsted for a form of organized social activism that went beyond the campus teach-ins and discussion groups. He yearned for something that could reach out to poor and working-class blacks and all oppressed people in order to help improve their social and economic conditions and to end institutional racism.

The Afro-American Association did not have the answers Huey was seeking.

In addition, Huey perceived Warden's leadership as more opportunistic than activist. Warden was a local lawyer who was eager to bolster his practice through his latest political contacts. The matter finally came to a head when the Oakland City Council publicly criticized the Afro-American Association for being a radical organization. Warden responded immediately by putting himself on the agenda at the next city council meeting to denounce his detractors. Huey sat in the audience with twenty other association members and watched with annoyance as Warden was unceremoniously squeezed off the agenda by the council, in favor of a last-minute presentation by an all-white business group from the nearby upscale hamlet of Piedmont. When Warden finally got his chance to address the council, he back-pedaled on his Afro-American advocacy and acquiesced to Mayor John Houlihan. He told the mayor that he too agreed that Oakland blacks needed to get off the welfare and unemployment rolls and start improving their own social standing in the city. The Afro-American Association, Warden assured the council, wanted to help achieve those goals.

Huey interpreted Warden's performance as a lack of backbone and bolted from the association ranks. Although it was Huey who had first reached out to Warden in the early 1960s, and although he had enjoyed the literary discussion groups, the street-corner debates condemning the white racist system, and the early campus rallies, in Huey's eyes Warden's accomplishments fell short. Deep down, Huey knew that organizations like the AAA would not move beyond their own rhetoric and they did not represent the downtrodden masses.

And besides, Warden was no street brawler like Huey. Once when the group was meeting in San Francisco, a handful of white youths yelled out racial epithets at association members. Huey ran out onto the street, fighting and throwing punches. Warden was seen running down the street, distancing himself from the imminent fracas.

In the final analysis, Warden talked a great game about instilling pride among black Americans. He introduced the term "Afro-American" into Huey's lexicon. But when the AAA leader extolled the virtues of Black Power and black capitalism, he avoided the vital issues of capitalist exploitation and racism, and this was the central contradiction affecting blacks in America.

On an interpersonal level, Huey was more deeply influenced by his friend Richard Thorne than by Don Warden. When Huey finally moved into his own apartment, he enjoyed the company of several young women. He espoused Thorne's views of open arrangements and "mutual honesty and the elimination of jealousy" to his own new love interests. Together Huey and Richard elucidated their philosophies of nonbinding love, and their female counterparts responded with wide-eyed curiosity.

"We would all be together at my house at the same time," Huey wrote in his 1973 book, *Revolutionary Suicide*. "Richard would bring his friends over, too. Together we became almost a cult. We spread our ideas around Oakland City College and Berkeley before group living and communalism became popular. I might even say that this was the origin of the Sexual Freedom League, since Thorne went on from this to start that organization. The girls found our experiments unusual and romantic and thought we were very exciting."[3]

Throughout his college days, Huey was a self-professed seeker. While he was still active with the Afro-American Association, Huey took the opportunity to see Malcolm X speak live at Oakland's McClymonds High School at a function sponsored by the AAA. He was inherently impressed with Malcolm's ability to articulate black folks' problems. "Here was a man," Huey used to tell me, "who combined the world of the street and the world of the scholar."

Malcolm's poise reminded Huey of some of his toughest street-corner friends who hung out on the block. Later on, Huey noticed a similar attitude among some of the Santa Rita Jail inmates out on the prison yard. As it turned out, Malcolm X served seven years of a ten-year prison sentence, which might have explained the indescribable aura Huey felt emanated from the man.

Also appearing at the McClymonds event was a successful young professional heavyweight boxer named Cassius Clay. Clay, soon to be renamed Muhammad Ali, had just joined the Black Muslims and voiced his support for brother Malcolm on the stage. During that time, Huey attended a few Muslim services, and although he did not ultimately embrace the teachings of Muslim founder Elijah Muhammad, Huey was attracted to the Muslims' mental toughness and their regimentation and sense of discipline. He kept up with their movement by reading *Muhammad Speaks*, a communication vehicle that Huey would soon find to be quite effective in spreading his own future organization's messages to potential followers on the street.

As always, Huey sharpened his contacts with "the brothers on the block." He even tried his hand at pimping for about nine months. Although Huey felt comfortable with the fringe lifestyle, his intellectual side could not logically justify the notion of a man controlling a woman for his own monetary gains. The pimping game too closely resembled the oppressive role of master and slave, where a human being became somebody else's private property.

Right up to the time before he was sent off to jail, Huey had finally broken off a lingering, five-year, on-and-off relationship with a lively young woman named Dolores. "Dolores," Huey wrote, "was a beautiful Afro-Filipino free-spirit child-woman who lived with a passionate intensity. Life with her was spontaneous, unpredictable, and filled with surprises, for she had the unself-consciousness of an impulsive and mischievous child."[4]

During his stormy relationship with Dolores from 1960 to 1964, Huey realized that, unlike most of his peers, he would have trouble committing to a long-term relationship. He decided that, unlike his father, he was not the typical guy who could settle down, find a job, and start up a family. Huey's hesitance to make such commitments made his relationship with Dolores a tempestuous one. It caused the two to break up and make up on a regular basis, until one day Dolores showed up at Huey's parents' house to find him accompanied by another woman. Hours later, when Huey checked in on Dolores at her apartment, he found her unconscious on the floor. She had taken a few dozen sleeping pills. An ambulance was called and showed up just in time. Dolores survived the suicide attempt, but her relationship with Huey was over for good.

It was after his breakup with Dolores in 1965 when Huey renewed his friendship with Bobby Seale. It had been over a year since the two had last spoken. Huey was out of jail, and Bobby was about to be married and needed to buy a new bedroom set. Huey, on the outs with Dolores at the time, had sold his old bed to Bobby. The exchange rekindled their friendship. Over the next few months, Huey and Bobby would continue a close association in and out of various local political organizations around the East Bay.

Just like the days when they first met, Huey borrowed Seale's pistols on a few occasions. Walking through the neighborhood one day, Bobby approached Huey, who was standing on the corner near his house.

"Huey," he asked. "What's up?"

"Just waiting here."

Bobby was curious as to what his friend was up to.

"Huey, you got my pistol?" he said.

"Yeah."

"Let me see."

Huey opened his coat, exposing Bobby's 9-millimeter.

"Huey, you ain't gonna shoot nobody, are you?"

"If they bother me, I will."

"How long have you been standing here?"

"A couple of hours. Look, you don't understand—"

"Huey, please, man. Don't shoot nobody if you don't have to."

Seale walked back home. Huey came by the next day and returned the borrowed firearm, but there had been no shooting incident.[5] Still, the connection with guns remained as Bobby and Huey became closer friends.

Between Seale, Cal Berkeley student activist Richard Aoki, and another military-trained hunting friend of Bobby's, named Elbert "Big Man" Howard, Huey enjoyed wide access to firearms. Seale was a good teacher for Richard and Huey. He was an expert shot with an M-I carbine. After a rigorous course at military basic training, he could dismantle and reassemble his M-I weapon blindfolded. As a result, Huey, too, became more and more gun savvy around his friends.

After Huey had resigned from the Afro-American Association, Seale stuck around the organization for a short while longer before departing himself. Not long after their disassociation from the AAA, an East Coast leftist organization called the Revolutionary Action Movement (RAM) made plans to start up a West Coast Bay Area chapter. Not a sanctioned City College campus organization, RAM promoted itself as an underground revolutionary group. Seale was intrigued and became a charter member, along with a few undercover cops who surreptitiously joined the group in order to keep an eye on Oakland and Berkeley's burgeoning student radical activities.

At Seale's urging, Huey was poised to join RAM, too. But strangely, the organization rejected Huey's bid to become a member of the small group of leftist intellectuals. They ludicrously dismissed him as being too "bourgeoisie," simply because his family had a home closer to the upper class Oakland Hills as opposed to living in the working class Oakland flatlands. Dismissing the group as phony armchair revolutionaries, Huey shed no tears over his rejection. Still, he was dismayed that his friend Bobby, who was more of a public speaker than a reader, was allowed to join, while he himself, who was geared more toward literature and philosophy than public speaking, had been turned down.

Regardless, Huey was humored by Bobby's latest attempts to become a professional comedian and an actor. Certainly not an animated public speaker in the league of Bobby, even Huey the activist intellectual cracked up as Seale performed his act on a comedy stage that included comedic impressions of James Cagney, Martin Luther King Jr., and "Chester" from the television western *Gunsmoke*. If Huey was considered introverted, then his comrade Bobby was surely the extrovert of the two.

On February 21, 1965, when the news erupted that three gunmen had assassinated black nationalist leader Malcolm X outside a Manhattan ballroom, Seale, sullen with grief over the loss of his hero, lashed out at his Revolutionary Action Movement brethren. He talked about seeking out Huey.

"Not a good idea," his cohorts warned Seale. "Don't you know the guy's shaky?"

"Shaky my ass," Seale responded hotly. "You guys ain't nothing but a bunch of armchairs. You sit and talk, but you don't do anything. Yeah, that's right. I'm gonna go find my friend Huey. We're going to start something, and I'll make a fucking Malcolm out of my own goddamned self."

Within hours of Malcolm's death, Seale banished his RAM comrades from the living room of his house, where the group regularly met. He resigned from the group immediately, packed up his camping gear, and headed into the Berkeley hills for three days with his friend Steve Brumfield. Upon his return, still needing someone with whom to vent his frustration, he sought out Huey through a mutual student friend, an ex-Muslim named Lawrence White.

The intellectual posturing of the Revolutionary Action Movement turned out not to be an altogether futile situation. A fortuitous chain of events occurred as a result. A RAM associate (and former AAA member) named Kenny Freeman formed a spin-off group called the Soul Students Advisory Council (SSAC). Originally it was intended to be RAM's connection to the City College campus. But unlike RAM, the SSAC showed a spark of activist potential. Huey and Bobby attended meetings sporadically, often upsetting the rank and file by engaging in protracted debates over issues and policies. They challenged Freeman and the SSAC ranks to venture beyond their usual base of college-educated black students and try to appeal to the younger working-class blacks in the outlying Oakland neighborhoods.

Luckily for the SSAC, two new burning issues had raged through the Oakland City College campus, galvanizing the various student movements. The campus was awash in speculation; efforts were being made to petition City College to add a black history class to the general education curriculum. In addition, the SSAC rallied against certain incidents of police brutality that occurred recently within the area. At last, here were two hot issues that could unify all the radical political forces on campus.

Clearly, the dominant issue of the two involved the new black history course. Kenny Freeman, Huey, Bobby, and the SSAC met with the school administration heads, who offered weak excuses as to why the college had not yet offered such a class. Soon the activist students scored a major victory: City College enacted the area's first fully credited Afro-American history college course.

In their fervor, Huey and Bobby continued to press the SSAC leadership to expand their black constituency on the streets. Huey had read about how a group of African-American veterans of World War II and the Korean War from Louisiana had formed a disciplined and secretive neighborhood patrol group in July of 1964. They were called the Deacons for Defense and Justice, and each man had summarily armed himself against white racists like the Ku Klux Klan. The Deacons for Defense and Justice adopted a fearless stance of self-defense in order to preserve and secure their newly passed voters' rights statutes.

Fueled by the momentum of their on-campus political victory, Huey and Bobby envisioned the SSAC becoming even more of a powerhouse group. Huey once again approached the leadership of the SSAC with his latest controversial idea. What if, in future demonstrations, the SSAC showed up armed with weapons and firearms? Such a bold stance, he argued, would be the ultimate gesture of self-defense in the eyes of oppressed blacks in the Oakland community. Huey pointed out that since local police and highway patrolmen now began to prominently display *their* shotguns in the front seat of their cars, what if an armed cadre of SSAC members responded in kind with guns of their own, just like the Deacons for Defense and Justice?

The SSAC leadership reacted to Huey's revolutionary suggestions with utter shock. It was a foolhardy course of action, they pointed out. Huey then suggested that armed members of the

SSAC could also patrol the streets of Oakland and Berkeley and help forestall the growing incidents of police brutality among the black citizenry. The SSAC officers were once again astonished by Huey's audacious suggestions. According to Freeman and the SSAC, no group of young black men could ever hope to survive one single patrol. If the Oakland cops were ever met with young black men wielding pistols, rifles, and shotguns, that would only lead to complete destruction of the entire organization. It was an option that the SSAC would never be willing to consider.

CHAPTER 4

THE FOUNDING OF THE
BLACK PANTHER PARTY AND
THE TEN-POINT PROGRAM

n October 1966 Huey was back at school studying the law. It was another subject that he delved into to feed his personal desires merely because of a thirst for knowledge as opposed to vocational reasons such as becoming a lawyer. Throughout his life, Huey was fascinated with the finer points of law, and his knowledge of the subject would come in handy as his life began to unfold. Knowing the law also contributed to Huey's skills as a debater.

> I began to study police science in school to learn more about the thinking of police and how to out-maneuver them. I learned how they conducted investigations. I also began to study law.
>
> My mother had always urged me to do this, even in high school, because I was good at arguing points and she thought I would be a good lawyer. I studied law, first at City College, and later at San Francisco Law School, not so much to become a lawyer, but to be able to deal with the police. I was doing the unexpected.[6]

Bobby had gotten himself a full-time position working at the North Oakland Neighborhood Services Center as a community liaison with the War on Poverty. Since the grant application budget provided for an assistant, he handed the six-month position over to Huey. Although Bobby would technically be Huey's supervisor, he'd give his friend more than ample leeway to show up whenever he needed or wanted to.

During this time, Huey and Bobby had no plan to start a new organization, let alone a party. Watts had exploded the year prior. More significantly, Huey and Bobby noticed how Martin Luther King Jr.'s nonviolent philosophy had fallen on deaf ears. As Huey wrote: "What good, however, was nonviolence when the police were determined to rule by force? We had seen the Oakland police and the California Highway Patrol begin to carry their shotguns in full view as another way of striking fear in the community. We had seen all this, and we recognized that the rising consciousness of Black people was almost to the point of explosion. One must relate to the history of one's community and to its future. Everything we had seen convinced us that our time had come."[7] What Huey and Bobby needed to do was to create an organization that related to the people on the streets, or in Huey's words, "involve the lower-class brother."

As Huey and Bobby's ideas of self-defense estranged them from organizations like the Afro-American Association, Revolutionary Action Movement, and the Soul Students Advisory Council, they began to hang out more often in Bobby's living room, not far from the City College campus. Huey pored over Bobby's collection of Malcolm X speeches collected from issues of *The Militant* and *Muhammad Speaks*. Malcolm X's spirit began to seep more and more into Huey and Bobby's discussions and plans to start a brand-new type of political action organization. "We worked it out in conversations and discussions," Huey wrote. "Most of the talk was casual. Bobby lived near the campus, and his living room became a sort of headquarters. Although we were still involved with Soul Students, we attended few meetings, and when we did go, our presence was mostly disruptive; we raised questions that upset people."[8]

Between classes, Huey and Bobby had ideological debates over the current political landscape, correlating it with the past black achievements. Besides talking, Huey was doing a lot more reading. He became immersed in the works of Frantz Fanon, particularly *The Wretched of the Earth,* as well as four volumes of Chairman Mao Tse-tung, and Che Guevara's *Guerrilla Warfare.* These sessions were the genesis of what would later be our political education classes, focusing not only on problems, but solutions.

Besides books by Mao, Che, and Fanon, the writings of Robert Williams, a president of the National Association for the Advancement of Colored People (NAACP) out of Monroe, North Carolina, inspired Huey deeper in the direction of self-defense. Williams was one of the first modern Afro-American advocates who armed his supporters. He urged his members to carry guns as protection against the white racist groups who terrorized black community neighborhoods. In 1961, while fleeing a kidnapping charge involving a police harassment dispute, Williams traveled to Cuba, China, and Tanzania as a fugitive before returning to the United States in 1969. Williams's 1962 book, *Negroes with Guns,* influenced Huey greatly. It told of Williams's program of self-defense in Monroe, North Carolina. The biggest difference was that Williams and his supporters demanded government assistance. Huey clearly saw the government as the enemy and as ruling agents of the country and the upper class.

Besides William's NAACP chapter, there were other black self-defense organizations operating, especially in and around the southern United States. The Deacons for Defense and Justice in Louisiana, who defended civil rights marchers and pressured local sheriff and police, inspired Huey further when he heard one of their leaders speak during a Deacons fund-raising trip through the Bay Area.

It was mid-October 1966 when Huey and Bobby met up at the Oakland War on Poverty office, around the corner from the North Oakland Services Center, where Bobby worked and not far from where he lived. Huey and Bobby's organization and "political party" was about to be officially unveiled. Unlike any other association, this would be an organization founded on action, not merely on talk and debate. The two young men were eager to construct a first draft of a document that would eventually define their new organization's goals and demands. A specific ten-point program would soon emerge, reading like a bill of rights, with its political and economic agenda, partly constitutional, and partly inspired by the Declaration of Independence.

A few nights after hashing out a rough draft, Huey and Bobby met again at the Seale home. Sitting at the dining-room table, they continued to hone their document. After Bobby's wife, Artie, typed up the results, the two took the paper over to Huey's brother Melvin's place at University Village for an inspection. Melvin was doing graduate work at the nearby University of California, Berkeley. He would correct the document's grammatical structure. Once their new "platform program" was nearly complete, Artie Seale retyped their collaboration, this time onto a blank oil stencil so that several copies could be run off at the War on Poverty office's mimeograph machine and passed out into the community.

Huey and Bobby's organization now had a manifesto. But it still needed a name to fill the blank space Artie Seale had left at the top of the stencil. For Huey and Bobby, the tricky part was finding the most suitable name—one that was dynamic and colorful enough, but one that promoted action instead of political armchair discourse.

On October 21, 1966, Bobby received an intriguing piece of mail from a black political organization in Mississippi. It was a voter registration pamphlet from a group who called themselves the Lowndes County Freedom Organization. Bobby had written to the group earlier, asking for more information after reading about them. The next day, when Huey dropped by, Bobby showed him the pamphlet. The Lowndes County Freedom Organization had even adopted a striking logo for their group, a dark black panther.

"What do you suppose this black panther means?" Bobby asked.

"Must be a political party or something," Huey said. "Something like how the Republicans and Democrats use an elephant and a donkey."

"Well, a black panther kicks a donkey's and elephant's ass any day." The two laughed.

"I suggested that we use the Black Panther as our symbol," Huey wrote, "and call our political vehicle the Black Panther Party. The Black Panther is a fierce animal, but he will not attack until he is backed into a corner; then he will strike out. The image seemed appropriate and Bobby agreed without discussion."9

"Black Panther Party for Self-Defense," Huey declared.

Huey and Bobby had just agreed upon the name when Li'l Bobby Hutton walked up to the front door. Bobby Seale had met Li'l Bobby at the Oakland Services Center. Li'l Bobby was only fifteen, yet he was wise beyond his years. He was the last of seven children in a family who had settled in Oakland from Arkansas when Li'l Bobby was just three years old. Li'l Bobby grew up fast, poor, but with a thirst for knowledge. After he was kicked out of school, he'd come around to Seale's house to talk and learn to read.

"What's happening?" Li'l Bobby asked.

"The Black Panther Party," Huey said to Li'l Bobby. "We just named the organization."

"Black Panther Party?"

"Black Panther Party for Self-Defense," Bobby added proudly.

Li'l Bobby became Huey and Bobby's first official member, and later the party's first treasurer. That day, as the trio hit the street together, Huey stopped and turned to both Bobbys and offered his bold prediction: "When the Panther roars, the world trembles." "Black Power," all three said in unison.[10]

Later that night at the War on Poverty office, the blank space at the top of the oil stencil was officially filled in. Copies of the new organization's ten-point program platform were ready to be run off. Bobby's brother John stopped by as Huey and Bobby were stapling the first copies off the press. John Seale was an East Bay Transit driver. Still in uniform, he had just completed his evening shift. It was ten o'clock at night when he noticed Bobby's Mercury still parked outside the War on Poverty office. Huey and Bobby now had three full boxes containing the first copies of their 10-Point Platform Program. They headed toward Bobby's house so they could stash two of the boxes in Bobby's garage and leave one in the car in order to pass around copies.

"The party sprang out of the education that was received by visionaries like Huey and Bobby Seale," Melvin Newton recalled later. "But it began with people—if you're talking about leadership in this area—who had a cultural, nationalist perspective. Huey and Bobby went further than that. They became revolutionary nationalists. That's what Malcolm was teaching, and that was what the Black Muslims were teaching."[11]

"At this point," Huey wrote, "we knew it was time to stop talking and begin organizing. Although we always wanted to get away from the intellectualizing and rhetoric characteristic of other groups, at times we were as inactive as they were. The time had come for action."[12]

Inside the boxes that were stacked in Bobby Seale's garage, Huey's ten-point program read:

THE BLACK PANTHER PARTY
Ten Point Platform & Program
October 1966
WHAT WE WANT
WHAT WE BELIEVE

1. **WE WANT** freedom. We want power to determine the destiny of our Black Community.
   WE BELIEVE that black people will not be free until we are able to determine our destiny.

2. **WE WANT** full employment for our people.
   WE BELIEVE that the federal government is responsible and obligated to give every man employment or a guaranteed income. We believe that if the white American businessmen will not give full employment, then the means of production should be taken from the businessmen and placed in the community so that the people of the community can organize and employ all of its people and give a high standard of living.

3. **WE WANT** an end to the robbery by the **CAPITALIST** of our Black Community.
   WE BELIEVE that this racist government has robbed us and now we are demanding the overdue debt of forty acres and two mules. Forty acres and two mules was promised

100 years ago as restitution for slave labor and mass murder of black people. We will accept the payment in currency, which will be distributed, to our many communities. The Germans are now aiding the Jews in Israel for the genocide of the Jewish people. The Germans murdered six million Jews. The American racist has taken part in the slaughter of over fifty million black people; therefore, we feel that this is a modest demand that we make.

4. **WE WANT** decent housing, fit for the shelter of human beings.
WE BELIEVE that if the white landlords will not give decent housing to our black community, then the housing and the land should be made into cooperatives so that our community, with government aid, can build and make decent housing for its people.

5. **WE WANT** education for our people that exposes the true nature of this decadent American society. We want education that teaches us our true history and our role in the present-day society.
WE BELIEVE in an educational system that will give to our people knowledge of self. If a man does not have knowledge of himself and his position in society and the world, then he has little chance to relate to anything else.

6. **WE WANT** all black men to be exempt from military service.
WE BELIEVE that Black people should not be forced to fight in the military service to defend a racist government that does not protect us. We will not fight and kill other people of color in the world who, like black people, are being victimized by the white racist government of

America. We will protect ourselves from the force and violence of the racist police and the racist military, by whatever means necessary.

7. **WE WANT** an immediate end to **POLICE BRUTALITY** and **MURDER** of black people.

    WE BELIEVE we can end police brutality in our black community by organizing black self-defense groups that are dedicated to defending our black community from racist police oppression and brutality. The Second Amendment to the Constitution of the United States gives a right to bear arms. We therefore believe that all black people should arm themselves for self-defense.

8. **WE WANT** freedom for all black men held in federal, state, county and city prisons and jails.

    WE BELIEVE that all black people should be released from the many jails and prisons because they have not received a fair and impartial trial.

9. **WE WANT** all black people when brought to trial to be tried in court by a jury of their peer group or people from their black communities, as defined by the Constitution of the United States.

    WE BELIEVE that the courts should follow the United States Constitution so that black people will receive fair trials. The 14th Amendment of the U.S. Constitution gives a man a right to be tried by his peer group. A peer is a person from a similar economic, social, religious, geographical, environmental, historical and racial background. To do this the court will be forced to select a jury from the black community from which the black defendant came. We have been, and are being tried by all-white juries that have no understanding of the "average reasoning man" of the black community.

10. **WE WANT** land, bread, housing, education, clothing, justice and peace. And as our major political objective, a United Nations–supervised plebiscite to be held throughout the black colony in which only black colonial subjects will be allowed to participate, for the purpose of determining the will of black people as to their national destiny.

WHEN, in the course of human events, it becomes necessary for one people to dissolve the political bonds which have connected them with another, and to assume, among the powers of the earth, the separate and equal station to which the laws of nature and nature's God entitle them, a decent respect to the opinions of mankind requires that they should declare the causes which impel them to the separation.

WE HOLD these truths to be self-evident, that all men are created equal; that they are endowed by their Creator with certain inalienable rights; that among these are life, liberty, and the pursuit of happiness. *That, to secure these rights, governments are instituted among men, deriving their just powers from the consent of the governed; that, whenever any form of government becomes destructive of these ends, it is the right of the people to alter or abolish it, and to institute a new government, laying its foundation on such principles, and organizing its powers in such form, as to them shall seem most likely to effect their safety and happiness.* Prudence, indeed, will dictate that governments long established should not be changed for light and transient causes; and, accordingly, all experience hath shown, that mankind are more disposed to suffer, while evils are sufferable, than to right themselves by abolishing the forms to which they are accustomed. *But, when a long train of abuses and usurpations, pursuing invariably the same object, evinces a design to reduce them under absolute despotism, it is their right, it is their duty, to throw off such government, and to provide new guards for their future security.*

CHAPTER 5

THE FIRST ARMED PATROLS
AND BADGE 206

The formation of the Black Panther Party for Self-Defense in 1966 was, in the context of the times, an extremely dangerous undertaking. "My big concern was the guns," said Melvin Newton. "There was the right to bear arms. Of course we knew that in California you could bear weapons, as long as they weren't concealed. But I had concerns about that, and I saw graveyards being dug, and I told Huey that then."[13]

Huey's response was to continue on with his program, specifically Point 7, calling for an immediate end to police brutality. Like Huey always said, the party armed themselves in the name of self-defense of their homes and communities against the Oakland Police Department (OPD). As a result of years of recruitment of officers in the southern states, there were very few, if any, black members on the force. The OPD was considered by Huey to be a white occupying force of the black community. "You have to remember the times," said Melvin Newton. "This was the sixties. You had the Vietnam War going on. You had black nationalism going on. You had cultural nationalism going on. You had leftist youth that had their movements going on. You had the hippie movement. A lot of things. But anything could happen. [The question was] how much blood is going to be shed, and how soon?"[14]

Huey put his life on the line from the first day the Black Panther Party was formed. He would walk a thin line between the hearts of the black community and the wrath of the Oakland Police Department. Historically, the police killed black folk with impunity. Huey would attempt to stop that by becoming the example of how to foil and resist fear. He became the first to try to remove the stigma of fear from the young Afro-American's mind when it came to dealing with the police. In his way, Huey civilized the police by humanizing them, showing us that the only difference between the police and the people they oppressed was the great equalizer—the gun. And once we mastered that, that's when the image of the police as outlaws with control over our destinies disappeared. That was the message that shot fear into the local, state, and federal governments and all of its law enforcement agencies. Consequently, the government could not allow black youth to follow Huey and the example that he was about to set, a standard that black men and women still embrace and respect. With their ten-point program, one of the Black Panthers' most immediate goals was to eliminate fear of the police inside our neighborhoods.

After the murders of Malcolm X and Martin Luther King Jr., no other black leader—not H. Rap Brown or Stokely Carmichael—would ever come as close to being shot on a daily basis as Huey P. Newton. Prior to Huey, political confrontation with the police meant being beaten while standing on a picket line. Huey chose to face the police on the streets differently—head-on, and not with a picket sign, but with a shotgun exactly like theirs in one hand and a law book in the other. He'd stand there with his gun and his book, reciting the law, careful not to step outside the limits of the law, but rather, using the law and the gun as a means for legitimizing the rights for black citizens to protect themselves in the name of self-defense. Huey knew exactly where the line of the law was drawn. He had a strategy.

Huey never left home without his law book. Much has been written about the gun in association with the Black Panther. However, Huey's fixation with the law, and the law book, is rarely mentioned. Whenever he came across a policeman harassing a citizen, he would stand off to the side and recite relevant passages and penal codes within earshot of the cop. Members of the black community were shocked. Never had black men, much less *armed* black men, stood up to the police for the people. As a result, two things happened: many brothers came right out of jail and joined the party; but more importantly, murder and police brutality statistics fell sharply.

Huey demonstrated intrepid courage by meeting the cops on their terms, because he now knew and felt their fears. "If you shoot, I'm shooting back," he'd tell them, "and you'll die just like I do." The cops realized that they would be met with the reciprocity of retaliation, which evened the score. For the first time, the playing field was getting level.

The night after they printed off their ten-point program, Huey and Bobby took a copy over to Richard Aoki's house. Over beer and wine, Huey discussed the need for a functional definition of power. According to Huey, they needed to temporarily set the word "black" aside and come up with just the right definition.

"Power," Huey used to say to me, "is the ability to define phenomenon and then in turn, make it act in a desired manner."

"Okay," Bobby said, "if you're going to go out onto the streets, and you're going to break this down to the brothers on the block, how would you say it? That when a racist cop is beating you, you can define him for what he is, a racist brutal cop. But if you want to make it an action 'in the desired manner,' you've

got to get a hold of his boot, flip him on his ass, take his goddamned billy club and make his ass act 'in a desired manner.' "[15]

Everybody cracked up as Bobby continued to reinterpret
Huey's definition of power with his own analogies.

During the early days of the Black Panther Party we first
became famous for our neighborhood street patrols. Upstairs
from the War on Poverty office was a legal aid office. Huey had
gotten to know the lawyers who were furnishing free legal aid
services to the black community. During the six months that
Huey worked with Bobby, and while he studied law at Oakland
City College and San Francisco Law School, quite often Huey
could be found upstairs, late at night, researching. "Research
and find a ruling" was how his instructors responded to his
many questions.

The legal aid office gave Huey unlimited access to its law
library, though most of the books pertained more to civil and not
criminal law. Still, one night Huey struck gold. He found an
obscure California State Supreme Court ruling stating that
indeed all citizens had the right to stand and observe a police
officer carrying out his or her duty. It was an old ruling, but
nonetheless valid.

Huey's idea of setting up neighborhood patrols grew out of
what had happened a year prior in Southern California, in
August of 1965 during the uprisings of Watts. A month or two following the rebellion, the Community Alert Patrol (CAP) was
formed, made up of a group of citizens from the black community who drove and walked around their neighborhoods with
armbands, law books, and tape recorders. The CAP was an organization designed to simply observe the police. They carried no
guns whatsoever.

Huey followed their progress in the newspapers and noticed
that within a couple of months CAP members wound up getting

their law books taken away and torn up, their tape recorders smashed, and their heads beaten before eventually being dragged downtown and locked up. Such conduct, in Huey's eyes and according to his newfound California State Supreme Court ruling, was a clear violation of CAP's constitutional right to peacefully observe the police and address their grievances.

The first official Black Panther patrols didn't take place until Huey had accumulated a large enough crew of people who underwent training. The patrolling process couldn't start by merely sticking a gun in somebody's hand. There had to be training and political education involved in the process. If everything was to be carried out to the letter of the law, there had to be rules, regulations, and instruction. Learning to break a weapon down. Cleaning the weapon. Never pointing the weapon at a person.

Huey's methodology was fastidiously legal, and to the people of the black community, empowering. He understood the law and had done his research and homework. According to Huey, the party could objectively patrol the police, but they could not pull out a weapon unless they were truly defending themselves. And if they had to defend themselves, they would have to prove it in court. So he came up with the basic rules for patrolling. Number one: you cannot ride in the car with a live round in the chamber of a shotgun or a rifle. A loaded weapon under California law meant a live round in the chamber. However, that did not apply to a handgun. Huey was careful to point out such distinctions. Whether or not there was any intention to shoot, if someone merely pointed a weapon at another person, even inadvertently, under California law that constituted assault with a deadly weapon. No member of the Black Panther Party could afford to step even slightly out of line. According to Huey, the gun was a tool to be used in a very particular situation to the strict letter of the law.

In order to increase the Black Panther Party membership, Huey spent most of 1966 circulating in the pool halls and bars of the black communities of Oakland and Berkeley. He immersed himself in the day-to-day activities of the black community. The Bosn's Locker, a bar-restaurant in North Oakland, became his office, sometimes until it closed at 2:00 AM, his shotgun lying on the bar unless the owners objected. If they did, he left it in his car.

"Wherever brothers gathered, we talked with them about their right to arm," Huey wrote. "In general, they were interested but skeptical about the weapons idea. They could not see anyone walking around with a gun in full view. To recruit any sizable number of street brothers, we would obviously have to do more than talk. We needed to give practical applications of our theory, show them that we were not afraid of weapons and not afraid of death. The way we finally won the brothers over was by patrolling the police with arms."[16]

Even before the patrols were officially instituted, Huey and Bobby had already hit the streets with their guns a couple of times. One night they went to a party. "We shouldn't have," Bobby Seale remembered, "but we had to learn. We thought we would observe the police while going to a party. Then we'd check our guns, party, and observe the police coming back from the party. It was only Huey and I. I had a forty-five I got from Richard Aoki, because I had pawned my other gun. Then we got an M-1 carbine from Richard."[17]

Huey and Bobby, however, found most black residents still apprehensive about the guns. A woman at one party called the police as Huey and Bobby left the house. As they argued with the police, Huey pointed out that under California law, as long as their weapons were not concealed, they were entirely legal. As a result, no one was arrested and Huey and Bobby went home that night, guns intact.

It was soon time for the Black Panthers to implement their ten-point program, specifically Point 7. Since a few communities had already tried (and failed) to create civilian review boards in order to supervise the behavior of the police, Huey and the Black Panthers proposed a different, more direct approach. According to Huey's logic, what good did it do to report police brutality to the police? Huey's plan was to patrol the neighborhoods and the police with arms. The results would be multifold. The neighborhoods would benefit by the party's presence, the police would change their behavior, and the organization now had a powerful means of recruiting.

As the party grew in membership, the first thing Huey did was to double, and then triple, the patrols in Oakland. Patrols were scheduled randomly, so that the police could not anticipate them. Huey knew in practical terms that no particular area could be totally defended. Only the community itself could accomplish that. His aim was to teach, to pass out literature—specifically, the ten-point programs—discuss community defense, and educate the people regarding their rights concerning arms. As a result, party membership steadily enlarged.

By the first week of January 1967, fourteen Black Panthers hit the streets for their first organized neighborhood patrol. Huey had his father's car. Bobby drove an old Chevrolet. Seven people to a car—thirteen men, one woman—all armed with long guns and pistols in plain sight, never concealed. It was nighttime. Bobby followed Huey, who was headed down Seventh Street toward Oakland's red-light district. Huey spotted a police car and stopped.

"Let's park," Huey signaled to Bobby. Fourteen Black Panthers piled out of the two cars to observe the police.

"When we patrol the police," Huey had reminded them, "only one person talks. You can't have a bunch of people talking in case you have to go to court. The police have to say we're under arrest, and we will take the arrest if they say we are under arrest. Then we can demand to know what we're being arrested for."

Fourteen Black Panthers walked to the red-light district corner. Nearby was a liquor store and bar. As they approached the corner, there were ten to fifteen people standing outside. A police officer was sitting in his passenger seat with his car door open, writing out a ticket, while his suspect was standing in the back with his hands on the trunk of the patrol car. The group of Black Panthers stopped about twenty feet shy of the scene. They began observing.

Somebody came out of the liquor store, spied the Panthers and yelled out, "What the fuck have they got in their hands? Sticks or something?"

Someone else responded, "Man, they ain't no damn sticks. Them goddamned guns."

The word "guns" caught the policeman's attention.

"I'm getting out of here," someone else said.

Huey turned around.

"No one leaves," he announced to the people on the corner. "Everyone stays here. We're a new organization called the Black Panther Party."

He pointed to the cop.

"We're here to observe these policemen who have been brutalizing us in the community. Everyone stay. We've researched the law, and just like us, you have the right to stand and observe."

The policeman stepped out of his car.

"You have no right to observe me," he said, approaching the Black Panthers.

Huey responded by quoting the California Supreme Court ruling that stated, "Every citizen has a right to stand and observe a police officer carrying out their duty as long as they stand a reasonable distance away."

"That particular rule says eight to ten feet," said Huey, "I'm standing approximately twenty feet from you. We'll observe you whether you like it or not."

One of the street corner women shouted out encouragement, "Well, go ahead on and tell it."

An older black man asked, "Man, what kind of Negroes are these?"

"Is that gun loaded?" the cop finally asked.

Huey had his answers. "If I know it's loaded, that's good enough." Then he quoted more state rulings, one to the effect that the police could not remove his property—not even a gun—without due process of law.

"Step back," warned Huey. "You cannot touch my weapon."

The people on the corner all stepped back.

"Like I said," Huey repeated, "If I know it's loaded, that's good enough." Huey jacked a round into the shotgun's chamber. There were six Black Panthers, all with long guns. Li'l Bobby Hutton jacked a round into the chamber of his rifle. It was an unmistakable sound, the sound that caught everybody's attention that night. When all the weapons were jacked, the policeman, shocked and out of his car, noticed that one of the Black Panthers was actually a woman wearing long earrings and a big Afro.

"The gun is my equalizer," Huey told the cop. "I can now debate you, whether you like it or not."

The policeman grabbed his suspect, opened his car door, and put his suspect into the backseat, walked around to the driver's side, then shook his head as he got into the car and drove off.

"Brothers and sisters," announced Bobby Seale to the growing crowd on the street corner, "this is brother Huey P. Newton, the minister of defense for the Black Panther Party. I'm Bobby Seale, chairman of the Black Panther Party. We're a new organization, a political organization. When you join the Black Panther

Party, you do not necessarily have to carry a gun, because we have a lot of programs we're going to work on in the community to help organize community power."

Just then, a kid ran up with a dozen of his friends.

"See? I told you."

"We will capture the imagination of the people," Huey said to Bobby and the others, noticing the young boys.

Back at Bobby's house, over a big pot of Bobby's hickory sirloin chili, cornbread, and shotguns, everybody talked about what had just happened. Bobby's mother and father were in the front room. Huey stood over them, pleased. He had finally had his chance to articulate the law, which was very important.

That was the very first Black Panther patrol.[18]

When I went on my first patrol, Huey and I rode in my red and white 1964 Oldsmobile. I had an M-1 next to me. Huey had his shotgun. We had often talked about our plan to organize the streets, which included the prostitutes, the pimps, and the drug dealers. Our plan was to politicize these people into our ranks, something that had never been done before. The focus would be on the brothers and sisters of the block, a tough undertaking in that although they might shoot at each other, they hadn't yet mustered the courage or the consciousness to stand up to the oppressor who oppressed everyone—the government. The way Huey saw it, sooner or later the brothers on the street corners would have to pay homage to the liberation struggle. "Recruiting had an interesting ramification," Huey wrote, "in that we tried to transform many of the so-called criminal activities going on in the street into something political, although this had to be done gradually."[19]

The Black Panthers were a party and a movement, not a gang. By challenging the whole state apparatus, we were slowly gaining recognition, first in the black communities. The players and the criminals on the streets were beginning to notice us. Huey saw an infrastructure that he called "illegitimate capitalism." Prostitutes were pimped by the pimps, who were pimped by the system. Our goal was to control the destiny of our community by politicizing the underworld and demanding support for our programs. Our goals included establishing a defense fund for the pimps and the prostitutes. We wanted to furnish them with bail and legal representation.

As we rode down the street, I looked in my rearview mirror. "Huey, the cops are behind us."

Huey sat up in his seat. "That cop better pray he doesn't stop this car, because we won't ever give our guns up," said Huey looking over at me. "Especially you and I."

I was gripped with fear and my stomach was turning flips. I thought I was prepared, but I'd never had to face something like this before. This was the moment of truth. That was Huey's style. He dealt with situations using a Buddhist reference he studied called "the deep flow of play." "When you deal with a man," Huey used to say, "deal with his most valuable possession, his life. There's play and there's the deep flow. I like to take things to the deep flow of play, because everything is a game, serious and nonserious at the same time. So play life like it's a game."

Huey's words and actions were synonymous. Huey did exactly what he talked about, and he never ran. If Huey exemplified fear, I never saw it.

Luckily those cops didn't pull us over that night. Judging from Huey's mood, if they had, there might have been a couple of dead cops.

Another early patrol happened just around the corner, two or three blocks from Bobby's house. Huey was out to test the law. When we patrolled police officers, we seldom rode up behind them. However, when Huey saw a police car two or three blocks away, he would stop, but only if they'd pulled someone over. That way he could legally observe the police at work under the California State Supreme Court ruling.

Driving up the avenue, Huey saw a police car turn a couple of blocks ahead, so he turned down the same street. Two blocks over, the same cop was now sitting on the corner in back of a stop sign. As Huey drove alongside the police car, he carefully stopped at the stop sign and turned in front of him. Just then, the cop turned his lights on. Bobby was in the front seat, holding Huey's shotgun in plain sight, armed with .45-caliber army pistol. Li'l Bobby Hutton sat in the back. As the cop turned on his lights, Huey drove another twenty feet and turned down Fifty-eighth Street. As he turned, Huey could see the cop's flashing lights coming up behind him.

Bobby turned to Huey and said, "He has his red lights on. We might as well stop now."

Huey shook his head. "I want to test the law."

"What are you talking about?"

"Technically, I could be color-blind. Let's wait until he turns on his siren."

As soon as he heard the "whoop" of the siren, Huey stopped the car. The cop's car stopped two car-lengths behind.

"Out of the car with them guns," screamed a fat, sloppy, burly white cop. "Who do you goddamn niggers think you are with them goddamn guns? Now get the fuck out of the car."

Bobby was holding the barrel of Huey's shotgun. Huey cracked the window and slipped his license through the crack at the top of the window. Huey was always meticulous about presenting his ID and never rolling his window all the way down.

Grabbing the license, the cop made his way back to his car, then walked back toward Huey, Bobby, and Li'l Bobby Hutton.

"Is this your current address?"

"Yes," Huey answered patiently.

"This automobile is not registered to you. What is your phone number?"

"Five," Huey replied.

"Five what?" the cop asked.

"Five," Huey answered. "The Fifth Amendment. Have you ever heard of the Fifth Amendment? I've already properly identified myself. I've given you my license. You now know my address and my name. I don't have to say anything else to you. You still want to know my phone number? Five."

"You think you're smart," the cop said. "You some kind of Marxist?"

"Are you a fascist?" Huey responded.

Soon everyone was out of the car, spread around the vehicle, still arguing.

"Are you a Marxist?" the cop persisted in asking.

"Are you a fascist?" Huey retorted.

"I asked you first."

"I asked you second."[20]

While out on patrol, Huey was pulled over and arrested several times. One time Huey, Bobby, and Li'l Bobby Hutton were pulled over by OPD Badge 206 not far from the Oakland City College parking lot. Once again Huey slid his license through a slightly cracked window. After Badge 206 slapped the license out of Huey's hand, he angrily grabbed the car door and pulled it open. Eyeing the shotgun, he reached over Huey and grabbed for the top of the barrel. Bobby held on tightly, pulling the shotgun back in a tug of war. Meanwhile, Huey was hitting the cop while Li'l Bobby Hutton joined in, wielding the butt of his M-1 rifle. After Huey hit the cop again, he pushed Badge 206 away and grabbed his shotgun just as Bobby was getting out of the car. The cop stumbled back, and by the time he got back up to draw his weapon, Huey stood over him.

"Go for it and I'll blow your brains out right where you stand. I'll kill you."

Most of the street's residents were now out on their porches. One little kid yelled out, "Oooh, it's the Black Panthers. They're gonna shoot the police."

Another woman shouted out, "Now don't you all shoot the police."

"We aren't going to shoot him," Huey replied to the woman, "and he ain't gonna shoot us."

"Who do you think you are?" Huey asked the cop as he got up and backed away.

Badge 206 staggered back to his car and called for backup. It was now 9:45 at night. Students were just leaving the Oakland City College night classes. A crowd gathered as more police, students, and even an assistant district attorney arrived on the scene.

"We need to get the serial numbers off of these guns," one cop said.

"You do not need to get *any* serial numbers off of *anything*," Bobby replied defiantly.

"You cannot remove our weapons without due process," Huey argued calmly. "You had no reasonable cause to stop us in the first place."

The cops and the assistant DA consulted each other. It had been about two months since the very first Black Panther patrols. By then, undoubtedly the police and the district attorney were already aware of the Black Panthers.

"The guns are not illegal," the assistant DA muttered to Badge 206.

"We have to get them on something," insisted Badge 206.

Bobby was handed a ticket for attaching his license plate with a coat hanger.[21]

The legality of the guns and the armed Black Panther neighborhood patrols would continue to heat up Oakland and the Bay Area streets until the next "colossal event" organized by Huey, involving the Sacramento State Legislature, blew open the entire gun issue. Soon the Black Panther Party would enjoy an unprecedented, overnight, worldwide notoriety.

CHAPTER 6

THE KILLING OF DENZIL DOWELL

During the earliest days of the party's formation, East Bay police departments routinely recruited police officers from far-off southern states such as Georgia, Mississippi, Louisiana, and the Carolinas. Little wonder Oakland and the surrounding East Bay cities had a reputation for employing the meanest and most racist cops. There was no such thing as outreach programs that recruited minorities to become police officers in their own black neighborhoods. Rather, during the late sixties, parts of Oakland, Berkeley, and nearby Richmond were occupied by a tight-fisted and aggressive white police presence.

We invented the term "pigs" in reference to the cops in order to rhetorically reduce the police force to its lowest common denominator. Although "pigs" was a harsh and contemptuous term, we felt that anybody who so flagrantly ignored the civil liberties of black people deserved such a scurrilous description, especially, Huey insisted, one devoid of profanity. He tried the reverse of god, "dog." Beast. Brute. Animal. None of those caught on. Then one day Eldridge Cleaver showed us a postcard from Beverly Axelrod, his lawyer. On the front of the card was the tired slogan "Support Your Local Police," with a sheriff's star. There it was, in the middle of the star. A grinning, slobbering pig. The perfect word, racially neutral. "Pig" immediately entered our lexicon. White kids on college campuses protesting the draft and the Vietnam War also picked up on it.

When twenty-two-year-old Denzil Dowell was shot to death by the Martinez Sheriff's Department during the early hours of April Fool's Day 1967 in North Richmond, he had purportedly been involved in the act of stealing a car. Little did the Dowell family or the surrounding black communities of North Richmond realize that his death would become an important catalyst, a linchpin to the burgeoning black liberation movement. As a result, Denzil Dowell would not die in vain.

Mark Comfort, a well-known East Bay Afro-American activist, introduced Huey to the plight of the Dowell family. When the Black Panther Party showed an active interest in the Dowell case, it became one of the very first high-profile community causes the party took on outside the Oakland city limits.

Huey and Bobby made the ten-mile drive over to Richmond carrying their guns. They met with the Dowell family and sympathized with the mother's tragic grief over the murder of one of her sons by the police. As a result, the entire Dowell family considered themselves members of the Black Panthers. "Mrs. Dowell, a beautiful and noble Black woman," Huey wrote, "told us about her son's life. She had spent much of her time and energy trying to survive in North Richmond, supporting her family and raising the children right. She was terribly upset about Denzil's death and over the indifferent and contemptuous way the authorities treated it. She knew her son had been murdered in cold blood."[22]

The evidence surrounding Denzil's death was confusing and contradictory. His body was blown apart from police shotgun blasts. The coroner's office originally declared that he had been shot nine or ten times. Then the police department and the press amended the story. They now said Denzil had been shot once or twice. According to Denzil's brothers, Carl and George Dowell, the police knew Denzil well, even by name. He'd been arrested a number of times, and there were threats made by the police that they would eventually "get" him. Plus, Denzil wasn't the only one in the area caught in police crossfire. Only a few months before, others had been shot down, some in the armpits, suggesting they died with their hands up. Two black men were shot dead in Richmond just a week before Christmas 1966. Another black woman was brutally beaten. A fourteen-year-old girl was beaten in East Oakland. These were only a few of the murders and the brutal beatings by East Bay racist cops that had occurred and had been reported on in the newspaper or were known about in the black community.

The specific details surrounding the Dowell case didn't make much sense to Huey. Also, a doctor who examined the body told the family that the wounds showed that Dowell had been shot while his hands were up. So Huey and ten Black Panthers staged their own investigation. The story from the police was that Denzil was shot and killed after fleeing, then jumping one fence and attempting to scale another. Yet he could have hardly run, because he had suffered a hip injury in a recent automobile accident. Police claimed Denzil had bled to death, but there was no pool of blood at the fence site where Denzil was supposedly gunned down. And if Denzil had been shot while jumping a fence, why was there blood found twenty yards from the fence in two different places? Dowell's family and friends also questioned why no medical assistance had been summoned after the gunfire.

The scene of the Panther investigation and the sight of Huey and the Black Panthers carrying their guns drew an immediate crowd of about 150 people. Especially curious were the younger kids, who weren't shy about asking specific questions about Huey and the Panther organization. Suddenly a woman in the crowd hollered out, "Uh-oh, here come the cops." Huey looked up and jacked a round into his shotgun. Bobby unhitched the strap that held the hammer down on his holstered .45 pistol. As most of the people moved back anticipating a shoot-out, Huey and the Black Panthers lurched forward and held their ground. The cops kept driving.

During the days after Denzil Dowell's death, the police habitually returned and continued to search and intimidate the Dowell household at will. As Huey and Bobby sat with Mrs. Dowell, a policeman knocked on the door and walked inside uninvited, insisting on searching the premises again. Huey stood up, grabbed his shotgun, jacked a round into the chamber, and asked the officer to produce his warrant or leave right then. The Richmond policeman quickly walked out of the house, got into his patrol car, and drove off.

Huey immediately called for a rally that Saturday, to be held on the corner of Third and Chesley streets. Twenty Black Panthers arrived, armed and in uniform. Huey dispersed the members across the intersection, each about thirty feet apart, while he and Bobby addressed the crowd about the plight of the Dowell family. While the community was at first timid, they were nonetheless proud of our presence. They asked questions about the guns. Were they legal? Were they loaded? Then we saw a remarkable thing happen. The people went home, grabbed their guns, and joined us. One old sister, about seventy years old, came back toting a shotgun.

Bobby worked the crowd as the rally proceeded, while police cars patrolled the perimeters. "The Black Panther Party has come to North Richmond to serve the people," Huey addressed the crowd. Two to three hundred members of the community had turned out to hear what Huey and members of the Dowell family had to say.

"Run it down about the pigs, Bobby," Huey told Bobby. "About how we're going to hold this street rally, and how we're going to exercise our right to free speech. Tell them about the reason why no pig's going to stop it because we've got guns and force here to protect ourselves, and to protect the people."

As the Black Panthers stood at parade rest around the intersection, four members walked over and confronted an approaching patrol car. Standing nine or ten feet away, Panther member Warren Tucker had a .38 pistol hanging on him, while Reginald Forte held a 9-mm pistol. As the cops drove away, there were yells and shrieks from the crowd. Huey's message of self-defense and Black Power was starting to resonate to the people. Huey and the Black Panthers immediately scheduled another rally.

The second rally was held in Richmond, drawing a few hundred more in front of a Dowell relative's residence at 1717 Second Street. Because of the huge turnout, Second Street was entirely blocked off. The whole street was cluttered with cars, and people stood on top of their cars up and down the long street. A police helicopter circled overhead as Huey shook his fist skyward and shouted out to the people, "Always remember that the spirit of the people is greater than the man's technology." That day the Black Panthers collected three hundred new applications for party membership.

Getting to the bottom of the shooting details behind Denzil's death became a struggle between Huey and the Dowell family and the Richmond police and the Contra Costa County Sheriff's Department. Because Richmond was a hopelessly gerrymandered community, the jurisdictions between city and county were confusing. Since the shooting had occurred outside the Richmond city limits, after a meeting the City of Richmond's DA instructed Huey and the Dowells to present their grievances to the Contra Costa Sheriff's Department, located in the city of Martinez, the county seat.

A few days later, a couple of carloads of North Richmond community members and Black Panthers headed for Martinez. Huey, Bobby, a writer who was interested in the party named Eldridge Cleaver, and the Black Panthers accompanied the Dowell family to meet with county law enforcement officials. They arrived armed with shotguns and M-1s. Huey carried his pump-action shotgun with double-O buckshot, the same weapon used by the California Highway Patrol. Once the police saw the rifles, six burly sheriffs sprung into action and attempted to intervene when Huey, the Black Panthers, and the Dowells entered the county building.

"You can't go in with no gun," one officer ordered Huey.

"What do you mean we can't go in with a gun?" Huey demanded. "This is public property. We have a constitutional right to carry guns anywhere on public property. So we're going to go in with these guns."

"If you go in, we're going to arrest you."

Huey knew the law regarding weaponry. "Tell you what we do," Huey said. "We'll take one brother, and he's going to volunteer to go in and take the arrest, because we're going to make this a test case."

Panther Reginald Forte, carrying a shotgun, stepped forward. "Here I am, brother."

As Forte approached the elevator, a wall of six cops stood between Forte and the elevator doors, resulting in a shoving match. As Forte, shotgun in hand, bumped and pushed his way into the line of cops, one of the cops stepped on Huey's feet. Huey pushed him off and said, "Get off my feet. Who do you think you are?"

"I think that all these people are disturbing the peace," the cop answered. "We're just going to have to place somebody under arrest."

Huey was livid. *"You're* disturbing the peace," he shouted back.[23]

They had reached an impasse: the deputies wouldn't arrest anyone, and the Black Panthers wouldn't disarm. At the insistence of Ms. Dowell, Huey reluctantly agreed to lock up their weapons inside one of the cars.

Once inside the county offices, Huey, the Black Panthers, and the Dowells were shuffled around until they secured a meeting with the sheriff, which turned out to be fruitless. Not only would the sheriff not charge or suspend the officer who had killed Denzil, he also refused to discuss the department's policy regarding shooting suspects. The sheriff argued "reasonable cause," meaning that whether or not Denzil was armed (and he was not), the officers had the right to shoot and kill him. "That's the law," said Sheriff Young. "If you don't like it, only the legislature can help you."

Huey knew a bureaucratic stonewall and whitewash when he ran up against one. In response to Denzil's murder, Huey had "indicted" the police for murder. But he wasn't going to stop in Martinez. He had plans to carry the Dowell case to the next plateau.

To Huey, the Black Panthers' guns were starting to serve their purpose by attracting the attention of the community and the press. By explaining the legality of self-defense, Huey and the party were making inroads toward raising the political consciousness of the Richmond and Oakland's communities. The word was spreading quickly. Soon, the group would find an even more powerful avenue to spread the word on their movement—the written word.

Huey and the party had done as much as they could in dealing with the authorities. They would now take it to the next stop, unveiling an even more powerful weapon. "Bobby suggested that we put out a leaflet describing the rally and what the Black Panther Party was trying to do for the Dowell family," wrote Huey. "The boldly headlined leaflet dealt with all the aspects of the murder. This was our first newspaper, and when we held it in our hands, it seemed we had taken down another barrier between the Black Panthers and the community."[24]

The *Black Panther* newspaper was born during the height of the counterculture revolution and the hippie underground newspaper movement. We used to put together the newspaper to the strains of Bob Dylan's *Highway 61 Revisited*. Huey's favorite song was "Ballad of a Thin Man." Publishers who were sympathetic to the Black Panthers and their ten-point program regularly printed weekly editions of various alternative press, circulating everything from leaflets to full-blown newsprint periodicals such as the *San Francisco Oracle* and the *Berkeley Barb*. Consequently, one publication offered Huey and the Black Panthers use of their mimeograph machines. If Huey and the party provided the necessary paper, ink, and staples, they could assemble their own leaflets.

According to plan, this "leaflet" needed to be strategically distributed throughout the Richmond community. By enlisting a small army of young kids and local paperboys who already distributed the *Richmond Independent,* the *Oakland Tribune,* and the *San Francisco Chronicle* to assist them, Huey and the Black Panthers passed out their headlined leaflet primarily on foot throughout North Richmond, Parchester Village (a mile farther north), and into the black sections of South Richmond. The group presented quite a sight. Black leather jackets, black berets and gloves, carrying shotguns over their shoulders. Bobby never left home without his .45 pistol strapped to his side. People constantly stopped them on the street and asked, "What are you distributing?" Huey's response was "armed propaganda."

The Black Panther newspaper was responsible for the mass appeal success of early Black Revolutionary Cinema, specifically Melvin Van Peebles's *Sweet Sweetback's Baad Assss Song.*

Volume 1, issue number 1 of the *Black Panther,* dated April 25, 1967, marked an important milestone for the young Black Panther Party. It was well written and had a strong immediate impact. The headlines were hand-printed, the story texts typewritten. "Why Was Denzil Dowell Killed, April First 3:50 a.m.?" asked the banner headline of the first issue. San Francisco artist Emory Douglass's hand-drawn black panther, ready to strike, stalked the masthead next to some hand lettering proclaiming the birth of the "Black Community News Service." The two-paged, double-sided legal-sized "leaflet" offered eleven facts and observations surrounding Denzil's death. On the front page below a hazy snapshot of Denzil Dowell was a call for united community action, advertising the second Dowell rally. "WE BLACK PEOPLE ARE MEETING SATURDAY 1:30 AT 1717 SECOND STREET. LET US SUPPORT THE DOWELL FAMILY. EVERY BLACK BROTHER AND SISTER MUST UNITE FOR REAL POLITICAL ACTION." The rest of the pages stayed on message as more typewritten text ran down the concepts of black political power, carefully centered on the Dowell cause. And although the layout of the *Black Panther*'s first issue was crude and simple, the writing was clear, concise, and free of typographical errors. The front-page story read: "There are too many unanswered questions that have been raised by the Dowell family and other neighbors in the North Richmond community. Questions that don't meet the satisfaction of the killing of Denzil. The Richmond Police, the Martinez Sheriff's Department, and the Richmond Independent would have us black people believe something contrary to Mrs.

Dowell's accusation. That is, her son was '*un*justifiably' murdered by a racist cop."

Page 2 read: "Let Us Organize To Defend Ourselves. 'We believe we can end police brutality in our black community by organizing black self-defense groups that are dedicated to defending our black community from racist police oppression and brutality. The second Amendment of the Constitution of the United States gives a right to bear arms.' "[25]

The party's walk through the streets of Richmond was powerful propaganda. The party set out to publicize the Dowell family's plight, and succeeded. We gained respect and also aroused considerable interest in the party. Huey and the early party members were then able to communicate one-on-one the necessity for armed self-defense.

In the months to come, the Panthers' mimeographed leaflet would soon be propelled into something bigger—a full-fledged newspaper and news service for the community. On the heels of the first leaflet that was passed out in North Richmond, the *Black Panther* would go on to serve many purposes on several levels. Local causes and cases like that of Denzil Dowell could be publicized. Hard news items relevant to the black community and not reported in the mainstream press would be crammed inside the pages of the *Black Panther*. In addition, the philosophies of the Black Panther Party and a dialogue between politicians like Assemblyman Ron Dellums, and members of the surrounding communities could be established. The *Black Panther* would soon become a vehicle that promoted the party's ideals by getting the word out. Plus, people eagerly read and anticipated each issue that hit the streets.

Meanwhile, Huey and the Black Panthers were creating a striking visual image that was spreading and starting to gain the attention of the conventional metro press. The *San Francisco*

Examiner came down to the Black Panthers' offices at Grove and Fifty-sixth for a Sunday edition feature. The resulting article turned out to be disappointing and biased. Nevertheless, the group's profile was growing. "Everywhere we went we caused traffic jams," Huey wrote. "People constantly stopped us to say how much they respected our courage. The idea of armed self-defense as a community policy was still new and a little intimidating to them; but it also made them think. More important, it created a feeling of solidarity. When we saw how Black citizens reacted to our movement, we were greatly encouraged. Despite the ever-present danger of retaliation, the risks were more than worth it. At that time, however, our activities were confined to a small area, and we wanted Black people throughout the country to know the Oakland story."[26]

But how? Huey was adamant about getting the entire Black Panther Ten-Point Program printed in the establishment press. In order for the Black Panther Party to maintain momentum, he reasoned, they needed regular exposure not only in the black communities, but also through the mass media—radio and television, in addition to newspapers. But again, how? Even if press and exposure in the ordinary media turned out to be a double-edged sword and a mixed blessing, at this point Huey had no choice. He needed to find a way to keep the message and the party alive. His next move would be to take the Contra Costa Sheriff's advice literally and press on to Sacramento, to the steps of the state capitol. Huey's aim was to launch "a colossal event." Just how colossal would exceed everyone's wildest expectations.

CHAPTER 7

WHY SACRAMENTO?

After the days spent productively in North Richmond, Huey was invited to appear on a local radio talk show to field questions from curious listeners. He took the opportunity to read through the ten-point program, particularly to explain the significance of Point 7 and the necessity for black people to arm themselves. Caller response was overwhelming. Hundreds of calls poured in, including one from Donald Mulford, a conservative Republican state assemblyman who represented the 16th Assembly District located in Piedmont, the wealthiest section of Oakland and Alameda County. Mulford was irate and threatened to introduce a bill in the state assembly that would make it illegal for the Black Panthers to engage in any further armed patrols of their neighborhoods.

Mulford's call was no surprise to Huey. He knew that once the party played by the rules, the rules would soon change. Despite the constitutional right to bear arms, as well as state and local fish and game regulations that allowed citizens to possess and carry firearms, Mulford had reportedly been asked by the Oakland police to introduce his bill.

When the stories of the bill hit the newspapers a few days later, Huey jumped up and picked up the phone. "Bobby, come over to the house right quick."

"Look here," Huey said, holding up a newspaper. "Mulford is up in the legislature now, trying to get a bill passed against us. I've been thinking. Remember when I told you we have to go in front of a city hall, in front of a jail, and do something like we did in Martinez, to get more publicity, so we can get a message over to the people? You know what we're going to do?"

"What?" Bobby was ready for anything.

"We're going to the capitol."

"The *capitol*?" This was the popular Governor Ronald Reagan's turf. "For what?"

"Mulford's there," Huey continued, "and they're trying to pass a law against our guns, and we're going to the capitol steps. We're going to take the best Black Panthers we've got, and we're going to the capitol steps with our guns and forces, loaded down to the gills. And we're going to read a message to the world, because all the press is going to be up there. The press is always there. They'll listen to the message, and they'll probably blast it all across the country. I know they'll blast it all the way across California. We've got to get a message over to the people. We've got to create a colossal event."[27]

The next day, the plan to send a delegation to Sacramento was implemented, timed on the day the California Assembly would begin debate over Mulford's bill. The Black Panthers needed to be there. Their presence was required. But the mission also needed to be kept quiet; otherwise the delegation would undoubtedly be met by an army of cops and state troopers.

That night Huey and Bobby met in San Francisco at a cultural center called the Black House, in the office of Eldridge Cleaver. Leroy Eldridge Cleaver was a bright and charismatic reporter for *Ramparts* magazine, a respected politically progressive monthly publication. Huey and the Black Panther Party intrigued Cleaver. He observed them and later covered their activities for *Ramparts*. Cleaver, who spent most of his adult life incarcerated, was out on parole, which restricted his travel and the amount of high-profile time he could associate with party members, since they had guns. Yet he and a friend, Emory Douglass, were interested in helping evolve the *Black Panther* (or the *Black Community News Service*) from the four-sheet mimeograph passed out in Richmond into a real newspaper that could be circulated and peddled on the streets.

Mulford's bill was big news. It would outlaw carrying a loaded firearm on one's person or inside a vehicle. It would also ban an ordinary citizen from having a loaded firearm in or near the state capitol building, any other state or government building, and certain other restricted areas.

It was agreed that the Black Panthers would send an armed contingent to Sacramento the very next morning. It was also decided in advance that Huey would not make the trip, as he was still on probation from the Odell incident. There were sure to be arrests, and Huey, as minister of defense, was selected to stay behind in order to spearhead the task of raising bail. "The brothers felt we could not risk Huey getting shot or anything, so we voted that he would stay behind in Oakland," Bobby recalled. "We voted Huey down and wouldn't let him come. We couldn't risk losing him."[28]

Upon giving Bobby his instructions, Huey stressed that his main purpose was to deliver a message to the people. In doing so, Huey said, if Bobby was fired upon, he should shoot back. If a gun was drawn on him, he was to defend himself by whatever means necessary. He was not to take the offensive unless there was imminent danger. If they attempted to arrest him, he was to take the arrest, so long as he delivered the message, whether inside the legislature, or if that was against the rules, on the capitol steps.

But first, a message had to be drafted. Huey prepared and wrote "Executive Mandate Number One," designed as the Black Panther's first official message to the American people and more specifically, the black communities of California. It read in part:

The Black Panther Party for Self-Defense calls upon the American People in general and the Black People in particular to take careful note of the racist California Legislature now considering legislation aimed at keeping the Black People disarmed and powerless at the very same time that racist police agencies throughout the country intensify the terror, brutality, murder, and repression of Black People....

The enslavement of Black people at the very founding of this country, the genocide practiced on the American Indians and the confinement of the survivors on reservations, the savage lynching of thousands of Black men and women, the dropping of atomic bombs on Hiroshima, Nagasaki, and now the cowardly massacre in Vietnam all testify to the fact that toward people of color the racist power structure of America has but one policy: repression, genocide, terror, and the big stick.

Black people have begged, prayed, petitioned, and demonstrated, among other things, to get the racist power structure of America to right the wrongs which have historically been perpetrated against Black people. All of these efforts have been answered by more repression, deceit, and hypocrisy. As the aggression of the racist American Government escalates in Vietnam, the police agencies of America escalate the repression of Black people throughout the ghettos of America. Vicious police dogs, cattle prods, and increased patrols have become familiar sights in Black communities. City Hall turns a deaf ear to the pleas of Black people for relief from this increasing terror.

The Black Panther Party for Self-Defense believes that the time has come for Black people to arm themselves against this terror before it is too late. The pending Mulford Act brings the hour of doom one step nearer. . . .

On the morning of Tuesday, May 2, 1967, Bobby lent his car out to a fellow Black Panther, then borrowed his brother John's car and drove to Richmond to pick up the Dowell brothers and members of their crew. Mark Comfort, a respected East Bay activist, brought his people over to Bobby's. Writer Eldridge Cleaver and artist Emory Douglass showed up in another car with a woman. Five more women were recruited. A total of thirty people in six cars headed to Sacramento that morning, twenty of whom were armed. Since Bobby hadn't stressed the importance of wearing matching black berets, black leather jackets, and blue shirts, he was the only one in Black Panther uniform.

After the car caravan made the two-hour trip to Sacramento, they parked and the contingent assembled, armed with shotguns and sidearms (Bobby wore his .45 pistol). Since it was a felony to point a gun at anyone, the shotguns and M-1 rifles were carefully pointed to the ground or straight up, everything perfectly legal.

"All right, brothers," Bobby ordered, "Let's roll."

"We started walking and moving," Bobby recalled, "We didn't walk in military form or anything like that. We were scattered across the sidewalk. We were not in any rank, but we held our guns straight up, because Huey had taught us not to point a gun at anyone, because not only was it unsafe, but at the same time, there was a law against just the pointing of a gun."

As the contingent walked about thirty feet into the capitol area, around a grove of trees not fifty feet away was Governor Ronald Reagan addressing approximately one hundred young boys. As the Black Panthers walked by, one of the kids exclaimed, "Wow! A gun club."

"One of the brothers," Bobby said, "saw Reagan turn around and start trotting away from the whole scene, because here come all these hard-faced brothers. Their ages ranged anywhere from sixteen—which was about the youngest we had there, that was Bobby Hutton—all the way up to myself, thirty-one. I guess I was about the oldest."

About twenty of the kids rushed toward the Black Panthers, followed by a cadre of press who were routinely stationed outside the capitol building hoping for a hot news story. Well, they got one. As the press quickly set up their cameras and tape recorders, Bobby did his job and read Huey's statement aloud.

"Read it again," one member of the press asked. Bobby repeated it verbatim.

As Bobby and the Black Panther members stood on the stairs, Bobby made up his mind about whether to enter the capitol or not. A group of security guards were gathered nearby. Bobby overheard one say, "You aren't violating anything with your gun, so if you want to, you can go inside."

That made up Bobby's mind. He waved to the contingent. "All right, brothers, come on, we're going in here. We're going inside."

A cameraman approached the contingent. "Are you going inside the capitol?" he asked.

Bobby, with one of our earliest members, Warren Tucker, on his left and Li'l Bobby Hutton with his 12-gauge shotgun on his right, opened the door and walked down a long hall.

"We're looking for the assembly," Bobby said to some of the passing people, whose expressions showed shock and awe.

"Where the hell's the assembly?" he asked. "Anybody in here know where you go in and observe the assembly making these laws?" At first nobody said anything. Then someone hollered, "It's upstairs on the next floor."

As Bobby and the contingent made it to the second floor,

they continued their stride to the flash of bulbs. Bobby asked one of the reporters, "Could you please tell me where I go to observe the assembly? I want to see Mulford supposedly making this law against us black people."

"Straight ahead, sir," a reporter replied.

Six feet from the gate, the cops finally stopped Bobby. "Where the hell are you going?"

"I'm going to observe the assembly. What about it?"

"You can't come in here!"

"What the hell you mean I can't come in here? You gonna deny me my constitutional right? What's wrong with you?"

Meanwhile more reporters were crowding the gate, creating just the right diversion for Bobby to slip by and make his way toward the assembly floor. He approached a large door. Standing in front was a doorman. Looking scared, like a servant, the doorman opened the door and in walked Bobby. Already inside, Eldridge Cleaver was standing among the reporters. Panther Warren Tucker was already halfway up the assembly aisle with a .357 Magnum strapped to his side.

As Bobby was trying to decide whether to stay in the well or proceed upstairs, Li'l Bobby Hutton passed him, cussing out a cop who had snatched his shotgun.

"What the hell you got my gun for?" Li'l Bobby yelled, recalling Huey's instructions. "Am I under arrest or something? If I'm not under arrest, you give me my gun back."

Bobby ran up to the commotion between the cop and Li'l Bobby. "Is the man under arrest? What the hell you taking his gun for?"

"You're not supposed to be in here."

As Bobby walked out the big doors, the cop and Li'l Bobby Hutton followed, Hutton still raving and angry. Then someone grabbed Bobby by the shoulder and pushed him into the elevator.

Back on the first floor, Bobby was ready to take the arrest. Then he remembered the mandate. He was momentarily confused. Had he read it? Bobby took his group into a small adjoining room, followed by a flock of reporters and read and reread the rolled-up copy of Huey's mandate a few more times. In the background he could still hear Bobby Hutton arguing with the cop. After reading the mandate for the third time, a black cop entered the room.

"Look man, are we under arrest or not?" Bobby asked him.

"No," the cop answered, "you're not under arrest."

"Then, dammit, give these black brothers back their guns."

On the way out, another cameraman approached Bobby, who asked him to reread the mandate yet again. As Bobby and the contingent found their way back to the parked cars, a jubilant Eldridge Cleaver came up behind him.

"Brother, we did it. We did it, man. We put it over."

"That's right," Bobby said. "We sure did." Bobby turned to the contingent and shouted, "Let's get out of this town. I'm hungry and it's hot here."[29]

As soon as the group left for Sacramento, Huey went over to his mother's house. He had promised his mother that he would mow her lawn that morning. Before starting, he turned on a portable radio and placed it on the porch. He asked his mother to turn on the television and to listen for the news. When a noon bulletin interrupted the radio programming, Huey's mother ran outside to alert him that all the television channels were covering the incident in Sacramento. Huey ran into the house. There was Bobby on the television reading "Executive Mandate Number One." Huey's "colossal event" had turned out exactly as he'd planned: the message was out. Huey had hoped that after the weapons gained the attention, the press would focus on the message. But the press was interested only in sensationalism.

Militancy, not ideology was what they wanted. The Black Panthers' presence, particularly the weapons, upstaged us. As a result, the Black Panther Party became a household word, resulting in millions of dollars worth of publicity.

With their mission accomplished, the Black Panther contingent was preparing to leave town. Shotguns and rifles were being emptied and loaded into the cars. As Bobby was about to get into the car, he noticed a single cop with a gun in his hand walking toward him on the sidewalk. Bobby's strategy was to meet the cop head-on. Just as Huey had advised, Bobby would take the arrest.

"Now wait a minute," Bobby said to the cop. "First thing you have to do is put that gun away. Put it back in the holster. If you want to make an arrest, you can make an arrest, but put that gun away." All around him, Bobby heard the sound of the surrounding Black Panthers jacking rounds into their shotguns. Then another cop drove up and parked his motorcycle. After muttering into his radio, he demanded Bobby's identification. Just as Huey had told him to do, he willingly handed it over. Soon more police drove up. State troopers. Plainclothesmen. All wanting to see ID.

"Arrest them all. On anything. Where have you been?"

"To the capitol," Bobby answered. "Why? What about it?"

"What are you?" another cop asked. "A gun club?"

"No, we're the Black Panther Party. We're black people with guns. What about it?"

More cops arrived as members of the contingent were rounded up and arrested. Two cops grabbed hold of Sherwin Forte, Reginald's brother. As Bobby reached for his wallet to present his ID again, he was seized. "You're under arrest for carrying a concealed weapon," referring to his holstered .45 pistol.[30]

Bobby was driven to the Sacramento Police Station, where he was tightly cuffed and shoved face-first up against a wall.

Huey made contact with a member of the Black Panther contingent, one of the women, who updated him on the situation. It was time for him to initiate the next phase of the plan, raising bail money. That night, Huey appeared on another radio talk show to field calls and to dispel some of the misinformation that was going out over the airwaves. Most assumed that Huey was in jail, including the radio station's program director. On the air, Huey tried to explain the Sacramento incident as best he could, though the results were frustrating. Callers had trouble communicating the issues and staying on track. However, Huey managed to make an appeal for money. The party was faced with fifty thousand dollars in bail bonds. Within twenty-four hours, the necessary five thousand dollars was raised in order to get the "troops back on the streets." A bail bondsman by the name of Glen Holmes arranged bail for Mark Comfort and Bobby. Back in Oakland, it was now time to raise bail for Eldridge and the remaining Black Panthers who were still locked up.

The next day, in Sacramento, Huey held an early-morning press conference. He talked about the white power structure and the need for the guns. He addressed the accusation of reverse racism. "No, I'm not anti-white. I don't hate a person because of the color of his skin," Huey told the reporters. "Because I wouldn't stoop to the level of the Ku Klux Klan, to hate a person because of the color of his skin."[31]

By nine that morning, there was a court hearing concerning the lowering of the bail bonds. Eldridge Cleaver's attorney, Beverly Axelrod, argued her case persuasively. When they arrested Eldridge, he was automatically placed on parole hold, bond withheld. As the cops brought him in, they told him, "You've had it now. You'll never get out." However, thanks to Cleaver's own foresight, Axelrod had a strong case to argue. It seemed that Cleaver had previously informed his parole officer, Officer R. L. Bilideau, that he was indeed making the trip to

Sacramento to cover a story for *Ramparts* magazine, not as a
Black Panther Party member, but as a member of the press. After
going through the television news footage, it was also revealed
that Eldridge was filmed holding a camera, not a gun, and that he
was standing always with the press and not alongside the gun-
toting Panther contingent. As a result, his parole was not
revoked. He was, however, sternly ordered to limit his travel to
seven miles from San Francisco, was forbidden to write anything
critical of the California Department of Corrections (CDC) or
any state programs or politicians, and was not to appear on television. Eldridge played it cool, but eventually challenged the
press restrictions on his writing on the grounds of censorship.

By six o'clock that evening, after Huey persuaded bondsman
Glen Holmes to bail out the remainder of the delegation, most of
the Black Panthers were free and greeted by Huey as revolutionary heroes as they each walked out of the jailhouse.

"Brother, are you glad you did it?" Huey asked between hugs
and strong pats on the back.

"Right on."

The only contingent members who remained in jail were the
juveniles like Li'l Bobby Hutton, a young member named
Oleander Harrison, as well as an acquaintance of Bobby's who
worked with him on the poverty program, and two of Mark
Comfort's friends.

The May 2 edition of the *Sacramento Bee* carried huge banner
block headlines: "Capitol Is Invaded." Underneath, a secondary
headline read "State Police Halt Armed Negro Band."

Governor Ronald Reagan called the Black Panthers' actions,
"A ridiculous way to solve problems that have to be solved by
people of good will. There's no reason why on the street today the
citizen should be carrying loaded weapons."

Further, according to the *Sacramento Bee*, "it was later determined the Black Panthers had broken no laws since they hadn't concealed their loaded weapons. Six Black Panthers, including Seale, ultimately received short jail terms for 'creating a hazard to public safety.' "

A deal was made in order to spring the remaining Black Panthers still in jail. Unfortunately it called for Bobby's being arrested for carrying a concealed weapon, even though his customary .45 pistol was holstered on his hip in plain sight. Others were charged for failing to remove the round from the chambers of their guns when they put their weapons back in the car. Bail was set for fifty thousand dollars. That meant Huey needed five thousand in cash, 10 percent of the bond, in order to spring Bobby out of Santa Rita, where he was being held for the charges stemming from the Sacramento "colossal event."

Later reflecting on what happened in Sacramento, Huey wrote:

Looking back, I think our tactic at Sacramento was correct at that time, but it was also a mistake in a way. It was the first time in our brief existence that an armed group of Black Panthers had been arrested, and it was a turning point in police perceptions. We took the arrests because we had a higher purpose. But it was not until then that the police started attempting to disarm the Party. They leveled shotguns on the brothers, handcuffed them, and generally pushed them around. I had given orders not to fire unless fired upon. Maybe the order should have been to fire on everybody in there; then they would have realized we were serious.

But our purpose was not to kill; it was to inform, to let the nation know where the Party stood. The police, however, took it to mean that the Party was only a front with weapons, that we would not defend ourselves. This attitude caused a number of problems for us, and it took some time to restore caution to the police after Sacramento. . . .

Sacramento was certainly a success in attracting national attention; even those who did not hear the complete message saw the arms, and this conveyed enough to Black people. The Bay Area became more aware of the Party, and soon we had more members than we could handle. From all across the country, calls came to us about establishing chapters and branches; we could hardly keep track of the questions. In a matter of months, we went from a small Bay Area group to a national organization, and we began moving to implement our ten-point program."[32]

The Mulford Bill passed by a huge majority to become law as California Penal Codes 12031 and 171c. Once the laws took effect, Huey reacted. As soon as it was illegal to carry loaded weapons, Huey halted the armed patrols. But the police read the move as submission, and stepped up their campaign of harassment.

Huey still needed to somehow raise more bail money in order to free Chairman Bobby, and more importantly, he needed to maintain momentum for the party. What would happen next, however, would be yet another set of spectacular circumstances that would spring Huey and the party once again into the world-wide spotlight.

CHAPTER 8

HUEY AND THE KILLING OF OFFICER JOHN FREY

Midmorning, Friday, October 27, 1967, was shaping up to be a good day. Huey woke up and enjoyed a breakfast with his mother and father at their home in North Oakland. There was a good reason for Huey to be cheerful. This was his last day of a three-year probation stemming from the Odell Lee party incident with the steak knife back in 1964. After spending six months in county jail, Huey had been assigned to report regularly to his probation officer. October 28 would officially mark the end of three years of reporting. Later that day, Huey proposed celebrating his freedom with his girlfriend, LaVerne Williams.

October 27 also presented a bonus in the form of a paid speaking engagement at San Francisco State College. Thanks to the Sacramento incident, a number of campus groups were calling regularly, interested in the Black Panthers' ideas and liberation philosophies. With Bobby Seale behind bars, the onus of performing speaking engagements rested on Huey's shoulders, a task he didn't particularly relish, preferring to leave the speeches and fiery oratory to Bobby and Eldridge, who had become the voices of the party. Still, Huey never passed on a chance to talk up the party and its ten-point program and other topical events. The students wanted to know why we opposed "spontaneous rebellions" and what our stand was on the recent riots in Newark and Detroit. Since Bobby was in jail, Huey was taking over the speaking engagements, something he neither enjoyed nor felt he was good at. Abstract and theoretical ideas were more his style. Huey was never a fiery speaker. But we went to San Francisco State anyway. Huey felt that contact with black college students was important.

I drove Huey over the Bay Bridge to the foggy San Francisco State campus, where he spoke for about two hours to a predominately black student audience. Because he couldn't be counted on to espouse a typical left-wing militant viewpoint, the discussions after the address between Huey and the black students were spirited and full of disagreement.

After the speech, an informal discussion broke out. Huey took a lot of heat because of the Black Panthers' willingness to work in coalition with white groups. Huey felt that as long as we controlled the programs, we could work with any group. The black students opposed this view. Huey saw their position as emotional without principle, and they failed to take into consideration the reality regarding black limitations in power. We needed allies, according to Huey, and the color of their skin was irrelevant. Coalitions were worth the risk.

Huey saw the value of incorporating the young, disenfranchised white students into the liberation movement. Oddly, while on one hand Huey was branded a black racist by critics, white politicians, and some reporters, the younger black students of San Francisco State opposed him because of his open-mindedness toward working with whites. Everywhere he went in 1967, he was attacked for this stand. Later he wrote, "I agree that some white people could act like devils, but we could not blind ourselves to a common humanity."[33]

Once we returned to the East Bay, I dropped Huey off at his parents' home. We would meet up later that night at the gambling party we'd organized that would be held at my house on Magnolia Street. Our plan was to throw a party in an effort to raise the five thousand in bail money to supplement the five hundred dollars we'd already earned that day at San Francisco State, to help get Bobby out of Santa Rita.

After a family dinner of mustard greens and corn bread, Huey made his way over to LaVerne Williams's house on foot. That night they would drive her car, a 1958 gold Volkswagen Beetle, and head out to a couple of Huey's favorite places for a few celebratory drinks before joining me, my brother June, and Gene McKinney at the gambling party later that night. Unfortunately, LaVerne was ill and Huey's celebration would have to wait. No, she insisted, handing Huey the keys to the Volkswagen bug. He should go on ahead without her. It was close to ten o'clock, still plenty of time for Huey to make his rounds at his favorite nightspots on his own.

Especially on a weekend night, Huey could still almost *always* be found at the Bosn's Locker at Fifty-eighth and Shattuck. The night of October 27 was no exception. It was his favorite place to drink his favorite drink, Cuba Libres—a concoction of lime, a shot of Coca-Cola, and plenty of Bacardi rum served over ice in a highball glass. Usually Huey downed them in honor of Fidel Castro's revolution. Tonight, he was celebrating no more probation.

After a few drinks at the Bosn's Locker, at 10:30 Huey jumped into LaVerne's Volkswagen and drove over to the Congregational church on Forty-second and Grove, where on Friday nights and weekends the church often held socials that included dancing and card-playing. As usual, Huey opted to do neither. Instead he talked about the Black Panthers to anyone who would listen, including Fritz Pointer, who taught Afro-American history and another friend, Dave Patterson.

After leaving the church, Huey joined us at our gambling party, still going strong at my place. We had a packed house and "the house" was racking up. Our food supply was holding up well, too. Fried chicken. Cakes. Spaghetti. Pies. At this rate it looked like we would raise enough money for the bail we needed and would still have a little left over for our war chest.

Just after 4:00 AM Huey talked about going "down on the Stem," to Seventh Street, and possibly running into the girl we'd seen with the clipboard. Gene was game to go along. They would head down together to Seventh Street, a West Oakland nightclub and nightlife district. There was a famous nightclub owned by Slim Jenkins on Willow. Esther's Orbit Room was a half block west of Willow on Seventh. There were barbeque joints, pool halls, gambling joints, nightclubs, soul food and burger places, and plenty of underworld activity and vice, especially at the Arcadia Hotel, a block west of Willow and Seventh, on the corner of Seventh and Campbell, where pimps, prostitutes, and hustlers, attracting a steady stream of black and white patrons, operated as late as 8:00 or 9:00 on a Saturday morning. Also on the corner of Seventh and Willow was a Union 76 gas station.

It was a little after 4:30 in the morning when Huey and Gene rounded the corner of Willow and Seventh. Huey was still driving LaVerne's gold Volkswagen, although he was not exactly savvy when it came to navigating Oakland's streets. He took a left off Willow onto Seventh.

Officer John Frey was sitting in his car at Willow and Seventh, the engine turned off, as a "tan-colored" Volkswagen passed him, turning left onto Seventh. Frey was about halfway through his shift. It had been a relatively quiet morning. At 4:25 AM, he'd just finished a routine arrest for drunkenness. After pulling the man into his car, he radioed for a wagon, which arrived quickly. Frey handed over the drunk to Officer Gilbert DeHoyos, who deposited him into the Oakland drunk tank downtown.

After the wagon left, Frey remained on the corner for a few more minutes, sitting in his car and listening in on the morning's calls over the police radio. Frey was athletically built, twenty-three years old.

At Frey's fingertips on the console was a "hot list," a register of stolen and suspicious vehicles he might encounter. Next to that was another list of approximately twenty cars, "known Black Panther" vehicles. Among them was listed "Dodge—1963—Registered Newton, Huey, Percy, MN—25, 821 or 881 47th St. AXP921." The second to the last, on the bottom of the list was "Volkswagen, 1958, sedan, tan, AZM-489." The registered owner was unknown.

Frey instinctively glanced at the plate on the passing Volkswagen. Then he started his car up and called in his ID on the radio to request a license check. "I'd like a quick rolling three-six on Adam Zebra Mary 489."

The time was 4:51 AM on Saturday morning, October 28. Huey had been officially off probation for almost five hours.

As Huey turned onto Seventh Street in search of a parking space, he saw the red light of a police car in his rearview mirror. He hadn't realized a cop was following him. "Here we go again," he must have thought. More harassment. Having been stopped so many times, he was ready. He knew the police kept a list handy of "Black Panther cars." That's why he kept his law book handy, between the Volkswagen's bucket seats. He figured that once he started reading to the cop, he would have to let him go since Huey had obeyed all the traffic regulations.

On Seventh Street, after seeing the red light, Huey pulled the car over to the curb as the OPD patrol car pulled up directly behind him. Officer Frey remained in his car for a minute or so, then got out and ambled up to the window on the driver's side. After getting a good look at Huey, he stuck his head further into the car, six inches from Huey's face.

"Well, well, well, what do we have here? The great, *great* Huey P. Newton," Huey would later recall in court.

Huey remained silent, looking Frey squarely in the eyes. The officer asked for Huey's driver's license, which he handed over.

"Who does this car belong to?" Officer Frey asked.

"It belongs to Miss LaVerne Williams," Huey answered, offering the registration as well. Frey compared the license with the registration, then handed back the license and bounded back to his patrol car. As Huey and Gene sat in the Volkswagen waiting for Frey to finish running his check on the vehicle, a second squad car, driven by Officer Herbert Heanes, pulled up and parked behind Frey's car on Seventh. Both officers talked for a moment, then Heanes walked up to Huey, who was still sitting behind the wheel inside the Volkswagen.

"Mr. Williams, do you have any further identification?"

"What do you mean 'Mr. Williams'? My name is Huey P. Newton, and I have already shown my driver's license to the first officer."

Heanes nodded his head. "Yes, I know who you are."

Frey walked back to the Volkswagen and ordered Huey out, while the second officer walked to the passenger side and ordered Gene out. Heanes walked Gene to the street side of the Volkswagen.

Huey grabbed his law book from between the seats and started to get out. He believed he was holding his book about criminal evidence and the laws dealing with reasonable cause for arrest and search and seizure laws. But he was wrong. That night, Huey mistakenly picked up the wrong book, one on criminal law.

"Am I under arrest?" Huey asked Frey.

"No, you're not under arrest; just lean on the car."

Huey leaned on the top of the Volkswagen with both hands clutching the law book.

The officer searched Huey in an especially degrading manner, pulling out his shirttail, feeling his body, pat-searching his legs, and bringing his hands up into his genitalia.

"Go to the back of my car. I want to talk to you," Frey told Huey, taking Huey's left arm in his right hand. The two began walking toward Frey's car. Then Frey pushed Huey harder toward the car. The pushing continued until Huey reached the back door of Heanes's police car. Huey opened his law book. Frey was to Huey's left, just slightly behind him.

"You have no reasonable cause to arrest me," he told Frey.

"You can take that book and shove it up your ass, nigger," Frey snarled.

Huey later recalled what happened next:

With that, he stepped slightly in front of me and brought his left hand up into my face, hooking me with a smear that was not a direct blow, but more like a solid straight-arm. This momentarily dazed me, and I stumbled back four or five feet and went down on one knee, still holding on to my book. As I started to rise, I saw the officer draw his service revolver, point it at me, and fire. My stomach seemed to explode, as if someone had poured a pot of boiling soup all over me, and the world went hazy.

There were some shots, a rapid volley, but I have no idea where they came from. They seemed to be all around me. I vaguely remember being on my hands and knees on the ground, disoriented, with everything spinning. I also had the sensation of being moved or propelled. After that, I remember nothing.[34]

When June and I heard the beating on the door, I knew it was trouble. Probably the cops. When Huey spilled into the house, he was bleeding profusely. How he got to my house, I didn't know. I couldn't see the Volkswagen out front. Everyone freaked out and poured out of the house. Gene was saying something about the police. A couple of cops had been shot. We dragged Huey over to the couch. When I mentioned a doctor, taking him to the hospital, Huey protested. "Let me die right here. If you take me to the hospital, they're going to kill me. And if I go to jail, I'll go to the gas chamber." Or something like that. He was already weak. I was in a panic. I didn't know where Gene had disappeared to. When someone is shot, people tend to panic, run, and split.

I decided to load Huey into my car so that June and I could drive him to a doctor. The first hospital that popped into my mind was the Kaiser Oakland Medical Center. We drove the back streets, about five minutes away. When we left him at the emergency ward entrance, revving the engine and blasting the horn, after carrying Huey out of the car, I honestly thought that would be the final time I'd ever see him alive.

"I can vaguely remember going into the hospital because I can remember a platform," Huey testified later, according to *Free Huey* by Ed Keating. He continued:

The only thing in my mind was how was I going to get on top of this platform? It is an entrance, but it seemed that the steps had been removed. I went up to the platform as my left leg was going out, so I could hardly stand up on it, plus I was experiencing excruciating pain. I was sort of delirious at the time. I remember putting my hand up to this platform and kind of rolling onto the platform. Then I got up and walked inside the hospital.

The nurse on duty at the hospital's emergency room first heard our car speed off. Then she heard moaning and groaning, and someone saying, "I want to see a doctor."

A youngish black male staggered in and approached the white nurse's desk.

"I want to see a doctor right now."

The nurse, silent, barely looked up at Huey.

"As you can see," he stammered, "I'm bleeding to death."

The nurse said nothing.

Finally Huey shouted. "Goddamn it, get a doctor out here right now."

"Do you belong to Kaiser?"

"Yes, yes, what difference does that make? Get me a doctor out here, now."

"Well, do you have a Kaiser card?"

"Can't you see I'm hemorrhaging?"

The nurse peered over at Huey. "You aren't hemorrhaging at all. It's just a tiny opening. Have you been drinking? You don't look like someone who's in great pain, or you wouldn't be yelling and jumping around."

"You white bitch!" Huey screamed. "You want to stand there and watch a black man die, don't you?"

"Look here, I don't have to stand for anyone swearing at me. Now you just watch yourself."

Huey pulled off his jacket and threw it on the desk. "Can't you see all this blood?"

"There's very little blood here."

Huey began to get weaker, which finally concerned the Kaiser nurse. "Please, get a doctor," he begged.

"All right. Forget the papers. Come in and we will see you."

"No," Huey protested weakly, "Get a doctor out here. Or do you want to see me die?"

That's when the nurse called the cops. As she spoke on the phone, she kept a suspicious eye on Huey. Then she got up from behind her desk and led Huey back into the emergency room.

"I'll get a doctor right away," she said, leaving Huey lying on a gurney.

The clock struck 6:00 AM just as the cops burst into the Kaiser emergency ward.[35]

A cop who was part of the manhunt just two blocks from the Kaiser hospital in Oakland picked up the call on the radio. When he got to the emergency room, he nearly knocked over the nurse Huey had had the altercation with. When he saw him lying on the gurney, with one hand he jerked Huey's arm overhead and cuffed one wrist to the gurney. The cop officially arrested Huey and read him his rights. A minute later, three more cops stormed the ER, while a doctor examined the hole in his stomach. They grabbed Huey's hands, stretched them over his head, and cuffed him to the gurney. As the cops pulled his arms, Huey screamed in agony. The cuffs were eating into his flesh, and the cops began to beat him. Huey screamed, begging for help from the doctor, who simply looked on. A black nurse in the room became upset, but there was nothing she could do as the police hit Huey in the face, calling him names.

Cuffed and in agony, Huey remained defiant. "Some of the police spat on me, and I spat back, getting rid of some of the mucus and blood in my throat. Each time they came at me, I spat blood in their faces and over their uniforms. Finally, the doctor put a towel over my mouth, and the police continued their attacks. I was still screaming in pain when I passed out completely."[36]

According to the cops, it was Huey who did the shouting and the swearing. But Huey testified on the witness stand that the cops not only cursed him and beat him about the head, but also threatened his life: "You killed a policeman," said one officer, "maybe two, and you're gonna die for this. If you don't die in the gas chamber, then if you are sent to prison, we are going to have you killed in prison. And if you're acquitted, we'll kill you on the streets."[37]

Huey lost consciousness as the blood pounded in his head and waves of pain engulfed him. He lost all sense of time. The incident was a blur. He passed out in the Kaiser emergency room, and when he eventually came to, he was in a room at Highland Hospital, across town. His wounds had been treated, and tubes were running into his nose and abdominal area. The room was filled with police as machines extracted fluids and mucus. Whenever he'd fall asleep, the police would wake him. Huey lay hopelessly near death as he drifted in and out of a dreamlike consciousness.

> My fear was not of death itself, but of a death without meaning. I wanted my death to be something the people could relate to, a basis for further mobilization of the community.
>
> I remember a radio playing in the room and the announcer saying something about a song dedicated to the Minister of Defense. However, I was not sure I had really heard it. Perhaps it was my imagination. At that point, a nurse came into the room and, seeing I was awake, asked if I had heard a song dedicated to me. Then I knew my situation was not hopeless and that the people were relating to the incident, whatever it was. This gave me much comfort at the time, even though I was in the hands of my oppressors. I knew that the Establishment would do everything in its power to destroy me, but this small sign of community response helped me to begin to deal with the police in my room.[38]

Huey's feet were shackled and chains were connected to each ankle. As he awoke, he wondered if he was shackled in irons or if he was in the midst of a nightmare. It was no nightmare. He was shackled and guarded and constantly threatened. Considering he was shot in the stomach with a .357 magnum, his survival was a miracle.

The cops assigned to guarding Huey in his room engaged in cruel and sadistic mind games. Every time Huey dropped off, they'd kick the bed. One brandished a sawed-off shotgun in his face, warning him it might go off accidentally. Another pulled a razor, threatening to cut off the breathing tubes and let Huey suffocate. One predicted that Huey would commit suicide by pulling the tubes out of his nose. Sometimes they even removed the tubes themselves. "They repeated their threat that I would be gassed in the little green chamber at San Quentin; if I escaped, they said they would have me killed. They even took bets among themselves on whether I would get the gas chamber or life in prison. They made remarks like, 'the nigger's going to die. He's done for now; he's going to die in the gas chamber.'"[39]

Some of the nurses knowingly looked the other way. The police chased some of the others, especially the black nurses on duty, out of the room. Soon, Huey's mother and father could no longer take seeing their son being so abused. Though they could scarcely afford it, they hired nurses who would remain present in the room around the clock.

It would be nine long months before all of the details, evidence, testimony, drama, and the mysteries behind the killing of Officer John Frey and the shooting of Officer Herbert Heanes would be presented at trial and subject to unprecedented and intense public scrutiny. The district attorney's office would appoint their toughest and shrewdest assistant DA, Lowell Jensen, to prosecute the case. Huey and the Black Panthers would have to stage their own dramatic defense. It would be the trial of the century. Meanwhile we began organizing Huey's defense.

CHAPTER 9

FREE HUEY?

Even while lying in a hospital bed guarded by a squad of Oakland cops, as he was bound and chained to his bed and drifting in and out of consciousness, Huey was well aware of the severity of his predicament. "As I lay recovering from my wounds," Huey wrote, "I tried to assess my position, to think of the immediate emergency and also its larger meaning and significance. No doubt about it, I was in serious trouble. I was fully under the control of my oppressors, and I was charged with a major crime that could carry the death penalty."[40]

To Huey, not only was prosecution imminent, but so was death. It was a foreboding that Huey readily accepted. Since the days of the formation of the party he was living "on borrowed time." Now, even death had a higher meaning.

> As a matter of fact, I expected to die. At no time before the trial did I expect to escape with my life. Yet being executed in the gas chamber did not necessarily mean defeat. It could be one more step to bring the community to a higher level of consciousness. I was not trying to be heroic, but I had been preparing myself for death over a long period of time.

When the Party first organized, I did not think I would live for more than one year after we began; I thought I would be blasted off the streets. But I had hoped for that one year to launch the Party, and any additional time was just a bonus. When I landed in Highland Hospital, I was already living on borrowed time.[41]

More had been accomplished in one year than Huey and Bobby had imagined when they drew up their ten-point program at the North Oakland Service Center.

A new militant spirit was born when Malcolm died. It was born of outrage and a unified Black consciousness, out of the sense of a task left undone. In light of this, I was able to stand back a little and consider my own death. The Black Panther Party had been formed in the spirit of Malcolm; we strove for the goals he had set for himself. When Black people saw Black Panthers being killed not only by the police but also by the judicial system, they would feel the circle closing around them and take another step forward. In this sense, my death would not be meaningless.[42]

But Huey did not die. In fact, he would heal fast. Once his condition stabilized, he was transported to the medical unit on death row in San Quentin State Prison. Officially, he was being housed there for protection. But as far as the police were concerned, his arrival was hopefully a precursor to his fate following his trial. After Huey's arrival through San Quentin's east gate by ambulance, he was wheeled into the death-row infirmary and gurneyed down the dank death-row hallways to the chorus of correctional officers calling out, "Dead man, dead man, dead man." "He was pleased to be on death row," recalled Huey's brother Melvin. "My father and I went to see him, and he said, 'Well, they don't bother me here.' "43

Two weeks later, Huey was deemed fit enough to leave San Quentin's medical facility. They had carried him in, but he walked out. From San Quentin he was taken to Alameda County Jail in downtown Oakland. He would end up spending eleven months there, before and during his trial.

Right about the time that Huey was transferred to the county jail, John Davis, a criminologist for the Alameda County grand jury, submitted evidence to the jury that had been collected at the scene. The list included the bullet taken from Patrolman Frey's back, the bullet taken from Patrolman Heanes's knee, Heanes's revolver, two nine-millimeter cartridge cases that had been found in the street, two matchboxes containing marijuana found under the seat of the Volkswagen, and a photocopy of the Kaiser hospital records of Huey's emergency treatment. Heanes's gun was the only weapon found at the scene; the nine-millimeter casings had not been fired from it.

Testimony before the grand jury was given by Heanes, a witness named Dell Ross, policemen who arrived at the scene after the shootings, the nurse who admitted Huey to Kaiser, and ballistics experts. Seven shots had been fired on the morning of October 28. Heanes received three wounds, and Frey had been shot twice, in the thigh and back. A flattened, possibly ricocheted, slug was dug out of the Volkswagen door. On the basis of the powder residue, it was believed that Frey was shot from a distance of approximately twelve inches. Huey's law book was also diagrammed as being found on Seventh Street as part of the crime scene.

On the basis of the preceding evidence and the testimony of witnesses, at 2:49 PM on Monday November 13, 1967, the Alameda County grand jury indicted Huey P. Newton on three felonies: the murder of Patrolman John Frey, the assault of

Patrolman Herbert Heanes with a deadly weapon, and the kidnapping of Dell Ross, forcing him to drive to another part of the city at gunpoint.

Even with his life on the line, Huey refused to allow the trial to stray away from what he saw as its central premise—not to save his own life, but to keep the momentum of the party and the movement moving forward. Huey did not want to deal with legalities, just political strategy. The ideological and political significance of the trial was of primary importance. Huey planned to use the trial as a political forum to prove that having to fight for his life was the logical and inevitable outcome of the Black Panther Party's efforts. The party's activities and programs, the patrolling of the police, and the resistance to their brutality had disturbed the power structure; now it was gathering its forces to crush our revolution forever. Public attention was assured. Why not use the courtroom and the media to educate our people?

Ideally, what Huey needed was a lawyer who possessed a strong legal mind combined with a progressive political consciousness, a lawyer with enough staff and resources who could navigate his way through a complicated murder trial while understanding the depth of Huey's allegiance to the ten-point Black Panther cause.

Charles R. Garabedian was the son of Armenian immigrants, and was born in Selma, California, just outside of Fresno. As a young man, he moved to San Francisco, changed his last name to Garry, and after working his way through law school, zeroed in on labor law. During his first years of practice, he represented sixteen unions at a time when labor unions were perceived as anarchists and Communists. As a result, Garry became politicized. At the time Charles Garry and Huey met, Charles had represented at least thirty capital cases and hadn't lost a single client to San Quentin's gas chamber.

Charles Garry's name came up through Beverly Axelrod, one of his protégés. They'd met while she was a parole officer, but after starting her own practice as an attorney, Garry brought cases her way. "We were in Charles Garry's office," recalled Melvin Newton, "Eldridge Cleaver, Kathleen Cleaver, my sister, and myself. We told him what we knew, and the question was cost and would he take the case? He said that this case would take at least three years, and that it would be a hundred thousand dollars. Kathleen Cleaver kind of laughed and we said, 'We don't have any money, but we'll raise the money. Will you take the case, Mr. Garry?' He said, 'Of course.' "[44]

"Charles Garry came to visit me," Huey recalled. "That first day, we did not discuss strategy. Garry said simply that he admired my stand and would be proud to represent me. I returned the compliment."[45]

Garry maintained from the start that had it not been for the political nature of Huey's case, not to mention the political climate of the times, it would have been quite easy to win Huey an acquittal.

Together with his senior partner Benjamin Dreyfus, Garry began Huey's defense by filing pretrial motions (primarily written by Dreyfus) attacking the makeup of and the selection processes of the Alameda County grand jury. Judges generally appointed members of the grand jury from a pool of close friends and political cronies, hardly the peer group of poor folks and blacks or of average citizens. Garry argued that Huey was denied equal protection under the law as guaranteed by the fourteenth amendment of the U.S. Constitution.

Garry also filed motions attacking all jury selections. Traditionally, jury members were pulled through a raw list culled by the Alameda County jury commissioner. Garry's pretrial briefs questioned the validity of its methodology. He challenged whether his client would receive a fair trial judged by a jury of his peers, since the current jury selection system excluded poor minorities who weren't registered to vote. Although such motions were ultimately struck down, the nine months spent on them helped turn Huey's murder trial into a political one.

While Huey spent months confined in Alameda County Jail, the time spent filing pretrial motions virtually gave birth to the "Free Huey" movement. Nine months represented an exceptionally long time between Huey's indictment and trial, but Huey felt that the delays, because of Garry's pretrial hearings, worked to his advantage. Huey became a celebrity through television and through the newspapers' hysterical accounts. Soon the streets began to fill up. Even *before* the Frey shooting, the Oakland streets had been filled with demonstrators and hot tempers as a crowd of four thousand people had showed up to protest police brutality in Oakland. Protestors and cops clashed violently.

After Huey was transferred to county jail, and just before the start of his trial, the Black Panther Party struck an alliance with the Peace and Freedom Party. The Peace and Freedom Party, founded in 1967 as a leftist organization opposed to the Vietnam War, was now an active alternative political party that placed slates of candidates onto local and statewide ballots. Later, as a Peace and Freedom candidate for president of the United States, Eldridge Cleaver garnered nearly thirty-seven thousand votes. Many people believed that Huey was in jail because of racism and police oppression and that he had been falsely accused of Frey's murder. Soon, the famous phrase "Free Huey" became a rallying cry for people who believed in his innocence.

Meanwhile, the party was recruiting new members in nearly every major city. Sanctioned and nonsanctioned chapters were sprouting up across the country. Police repression continued in Oakland. I was arrested for passing out leaflets regarding Huey's case. As anticipation for the trial heated up with the press, Garry waged his own public relations campaign for the trial by granting interviews and holding press conferences. While all this activity was going down on the outside, Huey was enduring hell inside a cramped county jail cell.

Despite his confinement, Huey sent out letters and tapes with his lawyers to stay in contact with party members and friends. The eleven months Huey spent inside Alameda County were tough. Prison routine was deadly. The food was bad. The guards were corrupt. Huey spent most of the time in solitary after staging a protest against the way prisoners were treated. His cell was four and half feet by six feet, no windows. Eventually they cut a small hole in the door, but even that was covered by thick wire. Huey's cell could become so sweltering, he'd remove his clothes. Poor ventilation made breathing difficult.

A strong grassroots movement flourished in the communities, working on Huey's behalf collecting money, speaking on college campuses, establishing forums, and organizing rallies. The Free Huey movement was now in full swing. Bobby, finally released from jail in December, joined in on the fight. On February 17, 1968, two rallies in Oakland and Los Angeles attracted black leaders like H. Rap Brown, James Forman of the Student Nonviolent Coordinating Committee (SNCC), and Stokely Carmichael, who visited Huey in jail.

"Our visit lasted just long enough for us to disagree," said Huey. "Stokely began by telling me what it would take to get me out of jail. The only thing that would do it, he said, was armed rebellion, culminating in a race war. I disagreed with him. He objected to the Black Panther alliance with the Peace and Freedom Party. Stokely warned that whites would destroy the movement, alienate Black people, and lessen our effectiveness in the community. Later, he [was] proved right in terms of what happened to the Party, although he was wrong in principle."[46]

Huey rejected Stokely's argument. He felt Stokely was "afraid of himself and his own weaknesses." This was a class struggle more than a racial one. However, in the months Huey spent in jail, as the leadership faltered, frictions developed between the Black Panthers and the white radicals.

Huey's trial began on a Monday morning, July 15, 1968, amid a hail of protest and solidarity. The Alameda County Courthouse, the same building that housed the county jail on the tenth floor, resembled a fortress. A boisterous throng of 5,000 demonstrators gathered outside the courtroom, chanting. A cadre of 450 Black Panthers joined busloads of Huey's supporters who had traveled miles for the first day.

"Free Huey!" a group of Black Panther sisters chanted in unison at the courthouse entrance.

"Set our Warrior free!" others joined in. "Off the pigs!"

On both sides of the courthouse doors a pair of party members held an azure Black Panther banner high. Emblazoned across it was the battle cry, the spirit and purpose of the movement condensed into two simple words—*Free Huey*. One hundred Black Panthers in black berets, leather jackets, black pants, and black shoes strode to the entrance of the esplanade of the courthouse and stood at parade rest, gazing like statues, eyes forward. Black Panther Party security patrols with squawking walkie-talkies ringed the courthouse. Armed Oakland police guards sealed off two of the three courthouse entrances. The rest of the police were equipped with guns, helmets, clubs, and mace. Police snipers with high-powered rifles and scopes occupied the rooftops. Rumors circulated that just outside the Oakland city limits, the National Guard were lying in wait.

Inside the courthouse, the atmosphere was one of siege and security. Fifty helmeted cops were stationed inside the main entrance on the ground floor. Plainclothesmen brazenly strapped with pistols prowled the hallways, as did radio-toting deputies. In front of the only elevator that led to the eighth-floor jury room stood a guard holding a shotgun. Stairway entrances and exits were locked up tight and guarded.

As Huey silently entered the courtroom, two extra deputies seated within three feet flanked him. In the courtroom gallery, there were a total of sixty spectator seats. Twenty-five seats were reserved for the world press, while two rows were reserved for Huey's family and other important supporters, including LaVerne Williams and Huey's spiritual advisor, the Reverend Earl Neil, an Episcopal priest. Although the remainder of the seats went to the general public, a few often went to obvious plainclothes policemen.

The trial would take place on the seventh floor. Presiding was Superior Court Judge Monroe Friedman, a seventy-two-year-old dour and humorless human being. Throughout the trial, the courtroom temperature was kept icy cold. The judge was condescending to black witnesses as if they had trouble understanding the issues. He constantly sided with the prosecution. Never for a moment did Huey consider him fair.

In prosecutor Lowell Jensen, Huey saw a sharp, bright, but overly ambitious adversary. A Huey P. Newton conviction would obviously carry Jensen's career to new heights.

The jury selection for Huey's trial exemplified Garry's objections. Although several blacks were called in from the city's rolls, so many were eliminated and thrown back into the general jury panels that while Huey's trial was in session, juries in other courts had as many as six blacks on them.

The final seven-male-and-five-female jury consisted of eleven whites and one lone black juror. That one black juror was

David Harper, described as looking like a "heavy Harry Belafonte." He was well dressed and held down a management position at the home office of Bank of America. It was anybody's guess where Harper actually stood on the subject of the black liberation movement. Huey studied Harper throughout the trial. Which way would he go? Huey knew where the judge and the prosecutor stood. The jurors were something else. But Huey watched every move Harper made. He wondered, did his bank job give him satisfaction? "I asked myself whether he was so blinded by the crumbs the system offered him that he would go along with the racists on the jury and a corrupt state apparatus to secure his future—or what he hoped might be his future."[47]

Just as a performer might occasionally pick out and work to one member of the audience, whenever Huey was on the stand, he focused on Harper. When Huey testified, he directed his words to him. Huey felt a bond develop. He felt a glimmer of hope, though he never placed much confidence in Harper's ability to sway the other jurors.

Behind the closed doors of the jury room, and to the surprise of none of the other jurors, David Harper was quickly elected jury foreman in ten minutes. The question still remained: in what direction would his leadership guide the jury when it came time for final deliberations?

In his opening statement to the jury, Jensen charged that Huey had murdered Frey with "full intent" and that he'd shot Heanes and kidnapped Dell Ross. He claimed that Huey gave Frey a false identification, which was untrue. Jensen also claimed that after Frey arrested Huey, on the walk back to the car Huey had produced a gun and began firing, shooting Frey five times and Heanes three times. Jensen theorized that Heanes shot Huey once. During Huey's escape, Jensen said, Huey had forced Dell Ross to take him to another part of town.

The prosecution's biggest challenge was establishing motivation for Huey's alleged actions. Jensen claimed there were three motives. The first was that since Huey had been convicted of a felony and was on probation, having a weapon would lead to another felony. The second motive was that if the officer had found the marijuana in the car, it would be another felony. The third motive was that giving a false ID would have been another violation. Jensen painted Huey as a desperate man, one who would kidnap a citizen like Ross.

The truth was that Frey did stop Huey. He knew full well who he had stopped, as did almost every member of the OPD force. After the arrest, he tried to execute Huey, who passed out. Garry and his team had investigated Frey's past. He had a long history of racism and harassing blacks. Bringing in Huey dead might win him a promotion.

In his book, *Free Huey!*, Edward Keating, a coattorney for the defense, cited through court records four separate and disturbing past incidents that took place between Officer Frey and black citizens on his Oakland beats that could be construed as racist incidents. These citizens included a former schoolteacher of Frey's in Concord who had been present when Frey addressed his class on the life of a police officer, and had heard the officer refer to blacks as niggers and troublemakers. One black Oakland citizen, an insurance agent for Prudential Life, after dealing with Frey ominously warned him, "You're gonna make trouble in this area acting like that."

A crucial part of the prosecution's case involved proving motive and determining Huey's legal status once he completed his probation. The prosecution insisted that Huey's status as a felon was the prime motivating factor for his allegedly desperate behavior, a fact Huey vigorously disputed. "As for being a felon with a gun," he wrote, "I, of course, was not carrying a weapon but had been out celebrating the end of my probation that night. There was no reason for me to have a gun and no reason to avoid arrest on this count. Nor did I consider myself a felon... When I was convicted of assaulting Odell Lee with a deadly weapon, I was sentenced to three years probation, a condition being that I serve six months in the county jail. This meant I was a misdemeanant."[48]

Huey's 1968 murder trial can best be summarized by the testimony of a handful of key witnesses that included Officer Heanes; Henry Grier, a bus driver who claimed he saw Huey shoot Officer Frey; Dell Ross, the driver who was allegedly carjacked by Huey and Gene McKinney; and McKinney himself, Huey's passenger in the Volkswagen. And then there was Huey's own testimony.

Heanes's original testimony to the grand jury recalled the early morning of October 28. He encountered two cars on Seventh Street, Huey's and Officer Frey's. Heanes parked his police car behind Frey's vehicle. Once he got out of his car, he approached Frey, who had just pulled Huey over.

In his testimony, Heanes said:

I maintained my position to the right rear of the Volkswagen, near the curb, for a minute or so when I saw Officer Frey return to the patrol car. I remained where I was for a brief time and then went around to the driver's side of Officer Frey's car. He was talking on police radio. I asked him what had happened up to that time. We had a brief conversation, after which I stepped up to the Volkswagen while Officer Frey remained in his car. As I approached the driver's side of the car [the Volkswagen], I observed two males, one in the driver's seat and one in the passenger's seat.[49]

As Heanes told it, at that moment Frey approached Heanes and informed Huey that he was under arrest. Huey got out of the car and, according to Heanes, walked toward the two parked patrol cars, with Frey following behind. Heanes followed and stopped at Frey's car, while Frey followed Huey toward the rear of the second parked police car, Heanes's. His testimony continued:

> At that point Newton turned around and started shooting. At the sound of the gunshot, I saw Officer Frey move toward Newton. I started to draw my weapon. I had it raised when I received a gunshot wound in my right arm. I grabbed my arm momentarily and shifted my weapon to my left hand. Out of the corner of my eye I noticed someone standing on the curb between the Volkswagen and the police car. I turned toward him and raised my revolver at him. He raised his hands, stating that he wasn't armed and that he had no intention of harming me.
>
> At this point I turned my attention back to Officer Frey and Newton. They were on the trunk lid of my patrol car, tussling. They seemed to be wrestling all over the trunk area. At this time I heard gunfire; it came from the area where Officer Frey and Newton were tussling on the rear part of my car.
>
> The next thing I recall, I was on my knees looking at them. I saw Newton, he was facing me, and Frey was more in the street. It seemed as though he was hanging onto Newton.
>
> I aimed my revolver at Newton's mid-section and fired.
>
> The next thing I recall is that I was lying in the police car. I picked up the radio and called in a 940B [back-up]. After the call, I picked myself up from the seat and looked out the rear window. I noticed two men running in a northwesterly direction, toward the corner of Seventh and Willow."[50]

Heanes recalled that McKinney had on a brown suit, a vest, white shirt, a tie, and no hat. Huey, Heanes recalled, was wearing dark pants, a white shirt, a tan or dark coat, and "possibly a black beret." "I don't recall," Heanes concluded, "seeing a gun in Newton's hand."

Under Garry's cross-examination, Heanes reiterated that he never saw a gun in Huey's hand, yet he had testified that Huey turned around and began shooting. He didn't know who shot him in the arm, and he was confused in his description of what Gene McKinney was wearing.

"Did you shoot and kill Officer Frey?" Garry boldly asked Heanes on the witness stand.

"No."

Damaging evidence came from the police department itself. A ballistics expert testified that the bullets that had hit both Frey and Heanes came from police revolvers. They were lead bullets— not copper-jacketed as were the two nine-millimeter casings found on the ground at the scene of the shooting. This damaged the prosecution's case, because Jensen had maintained from the beginning that Huey had shot Heanes and Frey with his own .38 pistol, whose bullets would have matched the nine-millimeter casings found on the ground. Of course, this mythical gun was never found.

Over the course of the trial, and during a second and third trial, Heanes's testimony would continue to erode and crumble until he finally admitted to having possibly seen a third party on the scene of the shooting.

Henry Grier was a bus driver for A-C Transit, part of Oakland's bus transportation service. As Grier drove by the shooting scene the first time in his bus, heading west, he witnessed the beginning of an incident involving two men stopped by the OPD. Once he resumed his route, driving eastward in the opposite direction back up Seventh, the incident was still going on. "As I approached from Willow, east on Seventh, and this is in the early part of the morning, the lights was on, I observed one police officer walking facing me with a man, and he appeared to have him sort of tucked under the arm, and the other police officer was about ten paces behind the two people that I first observed."[51]

Stopping his bus, Grier noticed suspicious activity.

"Would you tell us what you saw?" prosecutor Jensen asked.

"At the time the officer that was tussling with the man had passed the front door of the coach, and at this time I took my eyes off the officer that had been shot, and at this time I was doing two things. I'm talking to the Central Dispatch, telling them what was going on, to get help, and I turned, looked to my right, and at this time is when I saw the shots being fired into the officer which was falling in a position like this—"

Grier demonstrated a forward fall, facedown in the courtroom.

"After that the last shot was fired, which I could see the fire, sort of an orange-blue fire from around the muzzle of the gun, after that—he fired the last shot, he went diagonally across Seventh, and where he went, I don't know, sir."[52]

Asked by the judge to identify the gunman in the room, Grier left his chair on the witness stand, walked over to Huey, and dramatically laid a hand on his shoulder. Garry had learned about Grier's scheduled appearance only a few hours before the trial when his name appeared on the prosecutor's witness list. He would have to bring out several inconsistencies between Grier's testimony and the statement he gave to an Inspector McConnell at the station shortly after the shooting. Up to the day Grier testified, the prosecution had sequestered him, holing him up and hiding him in a downtown Oakland hotel, on leave from his job.

Jensen made a crucial mistake in thinking he could get away with the inconsistencies between Grier's statements made an hour and a half after the shooting and what Jensen had coached him to say on the stand. He had Grier tell the jury that he was less than ten *feet* away from the participants in the shooting, whereas in his sworn statement to McConnell, Grier had said he was thirty or forty *yards* away. He told the jury in the courtroom that Huey had reached into his *shirt* for his gun, but in his original statement, he had said Huey reached into the pocket of his *jacket* or *coat* to get it. Grier testified during the trial that Frey fell forward, facedown, although he had told McConnell that Frey fell on his back. On the stand Grier claimed that the bus lights were shining directly on the scene and he could see plainly, but he had told McConnell that he could not tell how old the gunman was, because he had his head down and he "couldn't get a good look." He told Jensen on the stand that Huey had fled toward the post office construction site, but when McConnell had asked him if that was where Huey was headed when he had last seen him, Grier said no, that Huey was running northwest, toward a gas station (in the opposite direction, across the street from the post office construction).

Subsequently, in the months that would follow, Grier's testimony was nullified and invalidated. "When it came time for the defense to present its case," Huey wrote later, "Garry was ready with a special surprise for the prosecution: he was going to disprove the entire testimony of Henry Grier. Our surprise had been carefully prepared during the first and second trials, and now we were ready to bring it out. *Henry Grier had never been at the scene of the October 28 shooting.*"[53]

It was during Garry's first cross-examination phase that Charles Garry was able to pounce on Grier and systemically dismantle his potentially damaging testimony. According to Grier's police report, the gunman was no taller than five feet, "sort of a pee-wee type, you might call him," while Huey stood five feet, ten inches, and weighed 165 pounds.

It took only about three and a half hours of cross-examination for Garry to demolish Grier's credibility. In his examination of him and in his final summation, Garry showed that there were at least fifteen crucial statements in which Grier's two sworn testimonies were in conflict. Yet the final blow for Garry had to do with the gun and the jacket worn by Huey that night.

Garry's most dramatic refutation of Grier's testimony—and the one that went to the heart of the matter—came during his final summary for the defense. He walked over to the table in the courtroom where all the evidence for the trial was on display and picked up the black leather jacket Huey had been wearing on October 28. Then he picked up Heanes's .38 revolver and walked over to the jury box. The gun that the prosecution claimed Huey had hidden, a .38 pistol, could not have been much smaller than Heanes's revolver, Garry said as he put the gun into the jacket pocket. It immediately fell out. He put it into the other pocket, and it fell out again. He tried putting the gun in the pocket several times, and each time it fell out; the pocket was too small to hold it.

Garry was sowing the seeds of reasonable doubt in front of the jury. Had Huey pulled a gun from his leather jacket pocket, or had he pulled it out "Napoleon-style" from his shirt? Would the leather jacket pocket even hold a revolver? Not according to Garry's courtroom demonstration. And was Huey wearing a leather jacket or a tan coat?

Dell Ross, whose car was commandeered after the shooting, took the stand and promptly took the fifth, even after being granted immunity by the judge and prosecution. In an effort to aid Ross's "faulty memory," the judge and the prosecution planned to read Ross's grand jury testimony into the record. Ultimately Ross's hesitant behavior and his cloudy and selective testimony tainted the prosecution's case further.

When the prosecution finally located Gene McKinney, his testimony presented problems that were similar to Ross's. After admitting that he'd been a passenger in the car with Huey, McKinney also pleaded the fifth. The judge and the prosecution were now in trouble. If they offered Gene immunity as they had done with Ross, the prosecution feared that such a move might result in Huey being exonerated if Gene chose to take the blame for the shootings under the legal umbrella of protective immunity.

Soon the Ross kidnapping charge was dropped. Now two charges remained, and as the prosecution case unraveled further, other inconsistencies came up, including Huey's law book. How could Huey have carried and opened a law book to read from while brandishing a firearm, both with his right hand? Also, the locations of the bullet casings were found twenty to twenty-five feet apart. How could Huey have been in two places at one time, especially after being shot in the stomach? Also, a number of people in the area were close enough to witness the incident. One woman told police she'd seen three men running away in a westerly direction toward the Union 76 gas station. Another witness told the police he saw two cars speeding away, north on Seventh. None of these witnesses were ever called on to testify.

Then there was Huey's testimony. In addition to telling his side of the incident, he was able to expound on a short history of the Black Panther Party. In a sense, the trial became a political education session for the jury, the trial audience, and particularly the world press. Huey's strategy of combining his trial with political testimony worked. The notoriety of the trial gave him his largest audience so far in order to run down the basics of the Black Panther liberation movement.

Garry led Huey through an exposition of what the Black Panther Party stood for and an explication of its ten-point program. Huey recited the ten points in the courtroom and explained them. He felt comfortable, almost at home, on the witness stand. Recapping the history of black social struggle made him momentarily forget about his own personal dilemma of being a step away from San Quentin's gas chamber. "Sometimes, while I was explaining Black history and the aims of the Black Panther Party to the court, I forgot that I was on trial for my life. The subjects were so real and important to me that I would get lost in what I was saying. There were moments when I even enjoyed myself, especially when I had a chance to score points against Judge Friedman and Jensen."54

While Huey and Garry conducted a virtual black history class, prosecutor Jensen attempted to show Huey's association with the Black Panthers in a different light, concentrating on the guns and portraying Huey as a threat and menace to society and the police.

As the jury deliberated, another dramatic development occurred. One day into deliberations, the jury requested a copy of a transcript of Grier's police statement. It was only by accident that Charles Garry discovered that the typist in the district attorney's office had incorrectly transcribed one word from the tape that Inspector McConnell had made with Grier. And yet this one word was so important that it called into doubt Grier's identification of Huey from the picture McConnell had showed him at police headquarters. To make matters worse, Garry discovered this error only after the trial proper was over and the jury had been out deliberating the verdict for a day.

According to *Free Huey!*, the section in question regarding Grier's identification originally read:

Q: About how old?

A: I couldn't say, because I only had my lights on. I couldn't—I
    DID get a clear picture, clear view of his face, but—because
    he had his head kind of down facing the headlights of the
    coach and I couldn't get a good look—

Over the word "did," someone had written the correct word,
"didn't," which changed the entire crux of Grier's statement. The
prosecution attempted to hide this discrepancy until Keating,
referring back to the original tape, played it over and over, and
then back to the judge, who rectified the situation by correcting
the faulty transcription. By the time an updated transcript was
handed over to the jury, they soon finished their deliberations,
never knowing they were possibly just a few letters away from
gathering a completely different conclusion from the transcripts.

As the jury deliberated over Huey's fate, San Quentin lurked
not twenty miles from the Alameda County Courthouse and
County Jail. "I contemplated the gas chamber," Huey recalled.
"Only two thoughts concerned me: how the last minute would be
and how it would affect my family. First of all, I resolved to face it
with dignity right to the end. Second, I worried about my family
having to live through yet another ordeal. The whole experience
had been terrible for them. Yet I knew that if necessary, I would
do it again, even though it meant more suffering for them."[55]

By the fourth day of deliberations, on September 8, 1968, late
in the evening, around ten o'clock, the jury reached a verdict:
"Verdict of the jury. We, the jury in the above entitled cause, find
the above named defendant, Huey P. Newton, *guilty* of a felony, to
wit, *voluntary manslaughter,* a violation of Section 192,
Subdivision 1 of the Penal Code of the State of California, a lesser
and included offense within the offense charged in the first
count of the Indictment."

Then the clerk continued: "The next verdict, we the jury find the above defendant not guilty of a felony, to wit, assault with a deadly weapon upon a police officer."

Then, according to Huey in *Revolutionary Suicide*, finally: "The following verdict, we, the jury find the charge of previous conviction as set forth in the Indictment as true. David B. Harper, Foreman."

Ultimately, the verdict pleased nobody. Not prosecutor Jensen. Not Charles Garry. Certainly not Huey, nor members of the black community, many of whom were angry, particularly at the black jury foreman, David Harper. Huey, in typically unpredictable fashion, defended Harper in *Revolutionary Suicide*. He saw Harper's situation as tenuous and the manslaughter sentence as a compromise to Harper's own possible feelings that Huey was innocent. Perhaps, Huey postulated, Harper felt that a manslaughter charge would be reduced closer to the time Huey had already served. He called for members of the black community to forgive Harper. Huey issued a statement after digesting the verdict, which read in part: "The question has been asked: What do I think of the verdict of the jury? I think the verdict reflected the racism that exists here in America, and that all Black people are subjected to. I am very sure that we will get a new trial not because of the kindness that the appellate courts will show us, but because of the political pressure that we have applied to the establishment, and we will do this by organizing the community so that they can display their will."

Further, Huey was also adamant, as he had been during the Detroit and Newark uprisings, in urging the black community to remain calm in the face of the manslaughter verdict: "At this time, I would like to admonish my revolutionary brothers to use restraint and that we would not show violent eruption at this time for the reason that the Establishment would like to see violence occur in the community in order to have an excuse to send in 2,000 or 8,000 troops."

Huey also used his statement to send a clear message to his Black Panther Party members to serve as examples, and to follow his lead by not falling into the hands of the police by hitting the streets and reacting violently: "It is up to the Vanguard Party to protect the community and teach the community to protect itself, and therefore at this time we should admonish the community to use restraint and not to open themselves for destruction."

Ultimately it was the police who reacted the most violently. Although the vast majority of the black community stayed cool, two drunken colleagues of Frey took matters into their own hands by firing a volley of bullets through the front window of the Black Panther Party headquarters on Grove Street late that night. The offices were empty, so no one was killed.

CHAPTER 10

THE COURAGE TO KILL: HUEY AND ELDRIDGE

"I cannot help to say that Huey P. Newton is the baddest motherfucker ever to set foot inside of history. Huey has a very special meaning to black people, because for four hundred years black people have been wanting to do exactly what Huey Newton did, that is, to stand up in front of the most deadly tentacle of the white racist power structure, and to defy that deadly tentacle, and to tell that tentacle that he will not accept the aggression and brutality, and that if he is moved against, he will retaliate in kind. Huey Newton is a classical revolutionary figure."

—Eldridge Cleaver, October 26, 1968

When the nascent Black Panther Party actively recruited new members in 1966 and 1967, their numbers included the young, high-school aged, and the unemployed. They were the lumpen proletariat. Then in 1969 and 1970, college students, working class, middle class, and all strata of society joined our liberation movement, including veterans like Stokely Carmichael, H. Rap Brown, James Forman, Fred Hampton, and women like Elaine Brown, Ericka Huggins,

Patricia Hilliard, Audrea Jones, Francis Carter Hilliard, and many others. Of the pantheon of individuals associated with the party, Eldridge Cleaver was perhaps the most controversial, brilliant, and charismatic—as well as the most problematic, egotistical, and inconsistent. In spite of these extreme positive and negative attributes, Eldridge's involvement with the Black Panthers represents a major footprint in our history whose importance cannot be denied or discounted.

The first time Huey met Eldridge Cleaver was in early February of 1967. "This guy named [Marvin] Jackmon came by with Bobby," Huey recalled, "and he said, 'I'm gonna take you all to the radio station now. Eldridge Cleaver's down there, and he was with another guy who had just got out of prison, and on a talk show.' "[56]

Cleaver had been released on parole from Soledad Prison (more properly known as Salinas Valley State Prison) in November of 1966, after serving nine years of an eleven-year sentence for assault with intent to murder. He had a long history of run-ins with the law that started when he was sixteen, and had spent fifteen years in and out of juvenile hall, then on to San Quentin, Folsom, and Soledad State prisons. While inside prison walls, Cleaver perfected his skills as a writer and a journalist.

Through his attorney, Beverley Axelrod, some of his prison writings were smuggled out of jail and passed along to famous authors like Norman Mailer and Thomas Merton. They all agreed that Cleaver displayed considerable talent on the page. The articles were published in the prestigious leftist journal *Ramparts*, and he was also on his way toward securing a book deal with a major publishing house.

Upon his release in 1966, Cleaver settled in San Francisco. He had secured himself a job as an editor and journalist for *Ramparts*, which hired him straight out of the penitentiary. But

Eldridge had nobler plans than just being a writer. He decided that he would become the heir apparent to carry on Malcolm X's message and revive the famous black leader's Organizations of Afro-American Unity (OAAU). At that point, Huey decided to seek Eldridge out. "I kept hearing about this guy Eldridge Cleaver," Huey recalled. "He was at the Black House and we had formed the Party then. Guys kept telling me, 'well, you should talk to Eldridge Cleaver.' Then someone in the conversation said, 'he just got out of prison.' So then I got interested. He can't be all bad; he just got out of prison."[57]

Huey admired Eldridge for the same traits he had admired in Malcolm X—his intelligence, his confidence, and his ability to stir audiences. More importantly, Malcolm, Cleaver, and Huey himself had all developed their political ideology directly from the street, and all three had done their time in the American correctional system and survived the rudiments of incarceration. While in jail, Cleaver had served as a Muslim minister and studied the teachings of Malcolm.

When the car pulled up to the radio station, Eldridge's interview was already being broadcast over the car radio. "I was listening," said Huey. "He was giving some history of what he was doing, giving black history and showing the treachery of the European and the American against the blacks, historically and currently... I went down there [to meet him], but the real reason I'm interested was because they said he was out of prison. I said, 'I'm gonna recruit this guy, because he's very articulate, we need him and he seems to like to talk to crowds. I don't, so we need more guys who can do that.' "[58]

After Cleaver was off the air, Huey and Eldridge sat down together. Huey viewed Eldridge as an important new spokesman for the black liberation movement, and tried to persuade Eldridge to join the party. Huey recalled their first meeting:

I started blowing it to him after he came out of the radio station. I told him about the 10-point program, how we are a Socialist group, and Revolutionary Socialist, and ran that whole thing down.[59]

Eldridge only listened. Every once in a while he would nod his head in agreement and say, "I know." But he did not ask any questions or comment one way or the other about the program. When I finished, he told me that he was obligated to Malcolm's widow, Sister Betty Shabazz, and that he had promised to work with her to carry out Malcolm's dream and make it a reality.

I was puzzled by this first meeting. Perhaps he had not understood anything I was saying, even though he seemed to by nods and phrases of agreement. I figured that if he really understood, he would have asked some questions or made a criticism or two. When a man is interested, he wants to know more. Eldridge had been as silent as a sphinx.[60]

At that point, Huey, unsure whether he had gotten through to Cleaver, figured he had done his best. "I left him and told Bobby I wish we could get him, but we'd have to educate him because he doesn't understand or else he wouldn't have just said 'yeah, yeah.' "

But Huey pressed on that night.

I was over at his pad. I'm still rapping to him, still trying to convert him because I was trying to give him the ideology, you see, because I was tired of the cultural nationalists, and I knew he had potential to be out of sight because he was a strong character. He had been in prison . . . been to "graduate school."

Finally he gave me this manuscript. I started looking through it and I read this chapter on local, domestic, and international security. The local security was the police, the domestic security was the National Guard, and the international security was the regular army. And then he talks about the little gray men who are in the smoke-filled room whom he calls "the deciders."

He says in order to deal with the deciders, you have to first deal with their strong-arm men. Well, this was the reason for the existence of the Party, because that's what the Party had concluded, that in order for any change to come about, you're going to have to deal with the strong-arm men.[61]

The two would meet again days later when Huey, Bobby, and a group of Black Panther comrades drove over to the Black House to gather with a handful of activists in San Francisco. Sitting around a table in a small storefront on Scott Street (in the heart of San Francisco's Fillmore neighborhood) was a black coalition that called itself the Bay Area Grassroots Organizations Planning Committee.

The purpose of the latest meeting was to finalize plans for a large memorial rally in San Francisco on February 21, 1967 to commemorate the fourth anniversary of the assassination of Malcolm X. Arrangements were made to involve the black community and stage a rally at the Bayview Community Center in the Hunters Point district, and to invite Malcolm's widow, Sister Betty, to be the guest of honor at the event.

One of the groups in attendance was an aggregation left over from the Revolutionary Action Movement that included Kenny Freeman from Huey's City College days. Freeman was now chairman of a party that ironically identified itself as "the Black Panther Party of Northern California." Huey called the group a bunch of armchair revolutionaries who were "good for nothing but running a mimeograph machine and fat-mouthing." Huey scorned the fact that they had stolen his party's name. In my own contempt toward Freeman's new group, I had offhandedly referred to them as "the Paper Panthers." It was a term that stuck with Huey and me.

The Paper Panthers, along with other black nationalist groups, convened at Black House, where Eldridge maintained an office in the Fillmore district. It was also where "non-Establishment" black academics, like author Imamu Amiri Baraka (known at the time as LeRoi Jones), spent time when they came to the San Francisco Bay Area for guest lectures and college residencies.

Cleaver sat in on the Black House meeting, and like his previous encounter with Huey, stayed silent and just listened. Having showed up at the last minute that night, Cleaver was reluctantly involved with the planning committee as part of his efforts to begin his strategy to revive the OAAU. With Sister Betty coming to town, it would be an opportune time for Cleaver to head up and launch the San Francisco chapter. Sitting next to Eldridge that night was one of the main organizers along with Freeman, a fellow named Roy Ballard, who, according to Eldridge, seemed intent on reducing the event from a three-day event into a one-day pageant.

As Eldridge sat bored and stultified through the steering meeting conducted by Ballard and Freeman, he heard the sound of the front door being unlocked and opened. With his back to the entryway, Eldridge scanned the different expressions of the people around the table responding to the four late-arriving visitors. When he noticed a sexy gleam in one woman's eyes at the sight of them, he knew something was up. Cleaver later recalled the moment as follows:

> I spun around in my seat and saw the most beautiful sight I had ever seen: four black men wearing berets, black trousers, shiny black shoes—and each with a gun! In front was Huey P.

Newton with a riot pump shotgun in his right hand, barrel pointed down to the floor. Beside him was Bobby Seale, the handle of a .45 caliber automatic showing from its holster on his right hip, just below the hem of his jacket. A few steps behind Seale was Bobby Hutton, the barrel of his shotgun at his feet. Next to him was Sherwin Forte, an M1 carbine with a banana clip cradled in his arms.[62]

Ballard jumped up and introduced Huey and his comrades to the folks in the room as the *Oakland* Black Panthers, to which Huey took exception. "We're not the Oakland Black Panthers," Huey said. "We may live in Oakland, but our name is the Black Panther Party."[63]

The Black Panthers, who sat against the wall, outside the circle, captivated every eye in the room. Ballard continued the meeting, breaking the program down into groups: politics, economics, self-defense, and black culture. After the introductions were exchanged, Ballard asked if Huey's group wished to make a speech at the memorial and if so, under what section. Bobby answered with an emphatic *yes*. "It doesn't matter what section we speak under," Huey recalled in *Revolutionary Suicide*. "Our message is one and the same. We're going to talk about black people arming themselves in a political fashion to exert organized force in the political arena to see to it that their desires and needs are met. Otherwise there will be a political consequence. And the only culture worth talking about is a revolutionary culture. So it doesn't matter what heading you put on it, we're going to talk about political power growing out of the barrel of a gun."

There was a lot of concern among those in the meeting that there might be assassins lurking for the chance to shoot Sister Betty down. The issue of security was discussed. Huey also volunteered his Black Panthers to help assist with guarding Sister Betty. Bobby jotted down details and notes in a small black book. Sister Betty herself had become a valuable symbol of the black struggle; it was important that she be kept safe at all times.

On February 21, the day of the rally, Huey and his cadre of Black Panthers arrived at the airport to accompany Sister Betty off the plane. Before they showed up, Huey had pulled his group aside and assured them that nobody would submit to any arrests by the San Francisco Police Department. He had heard what happened to Ron Karenga when his organization US served as guards for Sister Betty at a previous Los Angeles event. The LAPD had deftly swooped in and dispersed Karenga and his henchmen. As a result, Sister Betty was left alone and standing unattended out on the street. Huey adopted a hard line among his party members: this time Sister Betty would be guarded and protected at all costs. What happened in Los Angeles, Huey warned, would not happen in San Francisco with him and Bobby.

On the day of the rally, much to the shock of the San Francisco airport security officials, Huey and his bodyguard descended and marched to the arrival gate with guns intact. As Sister Betty and Hakim Jamal, Malcolm X's cousin by marriage, walked off the airplane, Huey and his comrades formed an immediate tight circle around the pair and quickly escorted them to a waiting car outside.

The motorcade carrying Sister Betty arrived in downtown San Francisco, where she was greeted at the *Ramparts* magazine offices on Beach Street. Cleaver was sitting in his office when a secretary burst in the room and announced breathlessly that an invasion was occurring outside. Twenty men with guns. To Eldridge, they were friends. He looked outside his office door and saw a commotion stirring and a big crowd. He then maneuvered himself through the jam-packed and narrow hallway, filled with anxious *Ramparts* employees. A regiment of Black Panthers, with guns pointed to the ceiling, calmly, confidently, and protectively surrounded Hakim Jamal and Sister Betty. Outside on Broadway, a huge traffic jam was brewing. Sirens were screaming. The cops were on their way.

With the police on their way, Eldridge conducted a short interview with Sister Betty. Weaving through the crowded hallway again to fetch a glass of water for Betty, he passed Bobby Seale and a few Black Panthers. Huey stood like a sentry by the window with his shotgun cradled in his arm, surveying the premises.

Then a horde of police showed up at the *Ramparts* building. Warren Hinckle, the magazine's executive editor, spoke with a police lieutenant.

"What's the trouble?" asked the SFPD officer, pointing over to a battalion of Black Panthers with firearms.

"No trouble. Everything is under control," Hinckle assured the worried policeman, who then stepped back outside with the other officers.

At that point, a television cameraman from the ABC-TV affiliate barged his way into the office. Two *Ramparts* staffers told him he was trespassing and ordered him to leave. When he refused, they pushed him and his camera out the front door.

After her interview, Betty, with her eyes obscured by dark sunglasses and seeming a little tense, told Huey that she did not wish to be photographed outside. Huey took control by sending five men outside, first to clear a walkway through the crowd outside the door, most of whom were cops. Then he dispatched Hakim Jamal and Sister Betty, clustered inside ten more Black Panthers, while Huey and Bobby brought up the rear.

Cleaver walked outside and stood on the steps of the building to watch Huey and the Black Panther bodyguards leave. The

TV cameraman who had been tossed out of *Ramparts* was filming the scene outside. Huey, spotting him, pulled an envelope out of his pocket and used it to block the lens of the camera. "Get out of the way," the man shouted to Huey. But Huey kept holding the envelope in front of the lens until the cameraman reached over and knocked Huey's hand away with his fist.

"Officer," Huey said in an even tone to a large squad of police standing nearby, "I want you to arrest this man for assault."

One of the cops stepped forward. "If I arrest anybody," he responded, "it'll be you."

Huey turned back around and kept the envelope in front of the camera lens. When the cameraman reached over and smacked Huey's hand away again, Huey reached over the camera, grabbed the guy by his collar, and slammed him up against the brick wall of the building. Huey threw a quick left hook. The astonished man whirled around to catch his balance and staggered down the sidewalk, juggling his camera.

Seale ran up to Huey and tugged on his jacket. "C'mon Huey, let's get out of here." The two headed up the sidewalk together toward a waiting car. Minutes before, most of the Black Panthers had already put Sister Betty and Jamal into their cars and had taken off. Huey, Bobby, and three other Black Panthers remained.

By that time, the cops stood on the scene poised as though waiting for a signal to open fire. Sensing something was up, Huey called out to Bobby and his three other comrades. "Don't turn your backs on these back-shooting dogs!"

One short, stout cop stepped forward and unsnapped the strap of his holster, ready to draw. He yelled out angrily at Huey. "Don't point that gun at me. Stop pointing that gun at me!" said the policeman as he reached for his pistol.

Huey stopped walking and eyeballed the cop. Seale was yelling to Huey, "Let's split, Huey! Let's split!"

Huey ignored Bobby. Instead, he turned around and approached the cop and stopped within a few feet of the agitated lawman.

"What's the matter?" Huey quizzed the cop. "You got an itchy finger?"

The policeman stood there mute.

"You want to draw your gun?" asked Huey.

The other policemen stationed nearby yelled out to their fellow officer.

"Take it easy. Cool it," they said.

The cop kept staring at Huey.

"Okay," said Huey. "You big, fat, racist pig. Draw your gun."

The cop just stood there.

"Draw it, you cowardly dog." Huey pumped a cartridge into the chamber of his shotgun.

"I'm waiting," Huey said, baiting the policeman to draw his pistol.

The line of police moved back out of any possible line of fire. Cleaver, witnessing the chain of events, took a few steps back, too. As he surveyed the tense standoff, Huey positioned bravely among a group of cops and urging one of them to pull his piece—Eldridge in awe could only surmise, "Goddamn, that nigger is c-r-a-z-y."

The standoff ended when the cop staring down Huey gave up, let out a deep sigh, and lowered his head. Huey burst out laughing in the cop's face, then turned around and took off up the street.

"Work out, soul brother," Eldridge said under his breath according to *Ramparts* magazine. "You're the baddest motherfucker to shit between two shoes." He then went back inside the

Ramparts office to join in the nervous but excited buzz of conversation among the staff who had witnessed the confrontation.

"Who was that?" one woman asked Cleaver.

"That was Huey P. Newton," said Eldridge proudly. "Minister of defense for the Black Panther Party."

"Boy, is he gutsy!" she said with a swoon in her voice.

"Yeah," replied Eldridge. "He's out of sight."

"Like others of its kind," Huey later wrote about the incident, "the scene is chiseled in my memory; I can still see every detail in this tense, brief confrontation. And then we backed away to our cars, guns still ready, and drove off. We had kept our promise to Sister Betty."[64]

A few hours after the incident, Huey, Bobby, and the Black Panthers relaxed back at Eldridge's Black House headquarters. Cleaver elected to drive to the rally with Huey. Inside the car, he asked Huey if he could join the party, confessing that he had made his decision to join the Black Panthers when Huey first showed up at the event-planning meeting. After what went down between Huey and the SFPD, Eldridge was emboldened by Huey's actions and needed no more convincing to join the Black Panther Party.

Later that night, at the Bayview Hunters Point Community Center, Sister Betty had requested a personal audience with Huey and the Black Panthers. Instead, Sister Betty was spirited away by the Paper Panther organizers and the other "more legitimate" black nationalist academics. Although Huey and Bobby were scheduled to speak at the rally, Freeman, who emceed the event, kept them both from appearing at the podium.

Cleaver was blown away by the incident at *Ramparts*. According to a later *Ramparts* article, his plans to see the OAAU reborn were derailed. "When I decided to join the Black Panther Party, the only hang-up I had was with its name," he later said. "I was still clinging to my conviction that we owed it to Malcolm to pick up where he left off. To me, this meant building the organization that he had started. Picking up where Malcolm left off, however, had different meanings for different people . . . For Huey, it meant implementing the program that Malcolm advocated. When that became clear to me, I knew what Huey P. Newton was all about."

Cleaver saw Huey as the highest personification of Malcolm and his ideas. He saw Huey as the heir and successor of Malcolm's ideology. If Malcolm predicted the coming of the gun to the black liberation movement, then it was Huey who picked up the gun and used it.

After Eldridge joined the party, because of his skills as a powerful orator, Huey assigned him to the post of minister of information. The two enjoyed a deep, unspoken ideological and harmonious connection. Author Frantz Fanon's 1952 book, *Black Skin, White Masks,* had intellectually influenced both men. Among other points, Fanon, who was also a psychiatrist, wrote how the colonial white world identified blackness with evil and sin, forcing Afro-American intellectuals to don "a white mask" and disassociate themselves from their blackness and adapt to a supposed universal culture that was actually quite unequal with regard to color.

With Eldridge on board with the party, by April 15, 1967, Huey and the Black Panthers participated with over sixty-five thousand protestors at a massive antiwar rally that started as a four-mile march through the streets of San Francisco and ended at Kezar Stadium outside Golden Gate Park. Eldridge addressed the throng and spoke about Point 6 from the Black Panther ten-point program: that black men living under an oppressive, racist government should be exempt from the draft or having to serve in the military.

Early on, Cleaver's membership in the party did not cause much of a ripple with his parole officers. At the time the party was still growing out of Oakland and had yet to proliferate nationally and internationally. But after his parole agents, R. L. Bilideau and Isaac Rivers, saw excerpts of Eldridge's antiwar speech on the television news, his dissent began to make waves with the California Department of Corrections, Governor Reagan, and the Sacramento power structure.

Still, Cleaver savored his alliance with Huey. "In trying to express what I see to be the essential quality in Huey, the thing that is key to his character, I called it 'the courage to kill,'" Eldridge said in the summer of 1969. He went on to say:

I've never known anyone like Huey. I've known all kinds of people. I've known soldiers who have gone to war; I've known robbers who have placed their lives on the line to commit robberies; I've known people who were subsequently killed in political activities and also in crimes. I've known people who were tough guys, who didn't give a damn about dying, didn't care whether they lived or died. But that doesn't relate to Huey, because Huey loves life.

To my surprise I found that Huey plays the piano. He went to some type of conservatory, and he plays concert piano. I remember one time we had had a violent encounter with a rival political organization in San Francisco. Afterwards, we were all in this house. There had to have been some shooting, and we thought perhaps someone was dead. It turned out that there was no one injured or shot, and nothing came of it. But during the time when we did not know what had happened, there was a piano in this house, and Huey sat down and started playing it, and there was concert music. There was a wistful look in his eye that I had never seen before.[65]

During Cleaver's early association with the party, he walked a dangerous thin line between espousing his political beliefs and being seen as a convicted felon fraternizing with gun-toting Black Panthers. Especially after speaking at Kezar Stadium, he was now in danger of violating the terms of his parole. His saving grace was that since he held press credentials as an employee of *Ramparts* magazine, he was able to circumvent the possibility that his Black Panther associations would land him back in prison.

But as Cleaver began to get more and more publicly active with the Black Panthers, he also stepped into the crossfire of law enforcement repression when the police started raiding the homes of Black Panther leaders. On January 15, 1968, Cleaver and his wife, Kathleen, and Emory Douglass stood in astonishment as police armed with shotguns burst through the door. The officers trained their weapons on the three as they searched the house for weapons.

On March 1, 1968, Eldridge Cleaver's public image and personal stock as a writer and social critic soared. *Soul on Ice,* a declarative mix of autobiography and essays written while he was locked up in Folsom State Prison, was published by McGraw-Hill and became a hot best seller. As a convicted-felon-turned-black-revolutionary, Cleaver's commentary was highly controversial for its time, especially in its references to rape as an "insurrectionary" act against the white man's law. His voice on the page was clear and vital, and it leapt out at the reader like a panther. He discussed the black man's stake in Vietnam, the prison experience, patriotism, revolution, and the reemergence of the black male patriarch. In one chapter, Cleaver cast negative aspersions toward author James Baldwin's open homosexuality.

As a published best-selling author, Cleaver gave the Black Panthers another exciting attraction to help spread their message to the college campuses and the media. When he was invited to speak on the Berkeley campus at the University of California, then-Governor Ronald Reagan responded with total disdain. "If Eldridge Cleaver is allowed to teach our children," Reagan fumed, "they may come home one night and slit our throats."

With Cleaver still reporting to parole officers four times a month and having to check in whenever he left the San Francisco area, Reagan and those who despised the Black Panthers knew they had Eldridge on a short leash. All they needed was one infraction and he would be back on the yard at Folsom. He met with CDC agents, who became even more repressive toward him. He was ordered not to appear on TV, criticize any politician in public, or give speeches. He was forbidden to journey beyond San Francisco—even to Oakland, just 12 miles across the Bay Bridge. Eldridge dispatched his attorneys to fight the ruling.

As a result of his book and his stature with the Black Panthers, Cleaver was invited to appear on numerous radio and television interview shows. Standing over six feet tall, Cleaver cut an extremely forceful image with his black turtleneck, dark shades, and full goatee. The Left reacted in awe to Cleaver's unmistakably militant and radical silhouette. When he appeared on a highbrow national political discussion program in New York City called the *David Susskind Show,* he more than held his ground. Still, ironically, being a CDC "special study case," after taping the show he was admonished by his parole officer for not properly phoning in his request to leave the state. In Cleaver's logic, he had left jail and become a successful writer and had given up his criminal ways. Now he was back in the crosshairs of the CDC and could imminently be violated at any time. To him, the situation was grossly unfair.

Throughout 1967, with Cleaver active in the party and Huey subsequently imprisoned for the shooting of Officer Frey, there were no political or philosophical obstacles between the two men. During their early relationship, Huey and Eldridge each had a positive attribute that the other admired. In Huey's eyes, Cleaver was a prolific writer and was electrifying in front of crowds. To Eldridge, Huey was an unflinching and courageous revolutionary who stood up to police brutality.

Huey sensed that Cleaver was a shrewd self-promoter. Eldridge chose not to interact with the younger members of the party, nor did he wish to offer them any mentoring advice. That became a major difference between the two: Eldridge seemed to hoard the knowledge he gained and came off as self-centered to some members; Huey, on the other hand, loved to share facts and opinions, and often engaged them in ideological struggle. Eldridge did not volunteer to teach the political education classes that were required for all new members. Instead, he became involved with the San Francisco Haight-Ashbury and Berkeley Telegraph Avenue set. To Huey's ire, Cleaver courted the hippie/Yippie, white drug counterculture, and organizations like the Weather Underground at what Huey later saw as the expense of alienating the black community.

Being an accomplished editor and journalist, Cleaver was put in charge of overseeing some of the editorial tasks of the *Black Panther* newspaper.

As Huey, and later Bobby, sat in jail facing lengthy trials and hard prison time, the party, under Cleaver's influence, continued to engage the police and challenge powerful law enforcement adversaries, ranging from Oakland police chief Charles Gain all the way up to J. Edgar Hoover, the head of the FBI.

To Eldridge's credit, in the first half of 1968 he risked his very freedom to rally publicly for Huey's release. After his and Bobby's homes were raided, Cleaver was convinced the cat-and-mouse game would end up with his being back in prison and waiting out two years behind bars for his lawyers to get him

released again. Although in 1967 Eldridge initially cut back on
public appearances and became low-keyed, by 1968, in a devil-
may-care stand to help free Huey, he stepped up the speeches
and interviews. He railed publicly against the arrests of Huey, in
the Frey case, and Bobby, who was serving six months following
the Sacramento incident. Eldridge was our most effective public
speaker during a time when we needed to mobilize support for
Huey's defense, and he dedicated himself to helping keep Huey
out of San Quentin's gas chamber. By November 1967 he hit the
press trail harder, giving Huey's side of the story to TV, radio,
newspapers, and magazines.

In February 1968, before devoting the month of March to
travel and promote *Soul on Ice*, Cleaver helped organize a Free
Huey rally held at the Oakland Auditorium, a few blocks away
from the Alameda County Jail, where Huey was imprisoned. The
theme on the flyer and posters for the gathering was "Come See
About Huey." The public meeting was a success. Over five thousand people showed up. In addition to Cleaver speaking at the
microphone, H. Rap Brown (now known as Jamil Abdullah Al-
Amin) flew in for the cause. Stokely Carmichael (later known as
Kwame Ture), who had just finished touring Africa, Cuba, and
other Third World nations, also spoke on Huey's behalf.

During his stay in prison in 1968, Huey began to seriously
reassess and rethink the priorities of the party in terms of how the
Black Panthers were perceived by their own community. He worried out loud that although the militaristic stance of 1966 and
1967 made an enormous impression in terms of his self-defense
position on the average black person on the street, he believed the
Black Panthers' image was being manipulated by the government
and law enforcement circles, which portrayed them as trigger-
happy, gun-toting thugs who were more interested in gunplay
than substantive social change. "We soon discovered that

weapons and uniforms set us apart from the community. We were looked upon as an ad hoc military group," wrote Huey. "Perhaps we placed too much attention on military emphasis. We saw ourselves as the revolutionary 'vanguard' and did not fully understand then that only *the people* can create revolution."[66]

Huey later became convinced that Eldridge's affiliation with the party was an extension of his own manhood and macho. After all, when Eldridge saw Huey stand up to the police in front of the *Ramparts* office, his admiration for Huey was as a shotgun-toting icon. To Huey, it wasn't a coincidence that Eldridge joined the party after the *Ramparts* confrontation. Huey saw that the force, firepower, and intensity of armed confrontation was, to Eldridge, the revolution. "Eldridge's ideology was based on the rhetoric of violence; his speeches abounded in either/or absolutes, like 'You are either part of the problem or part of the solution.' "[67] "Revolution is not an action, it is a process," Huey continually stressed in our conversations.

As Huey began to retool the Black Panthers' overall image and strategy through his directives and manifestos from his prison cell, he informed his leadership that it was now time to move beyond the notion of guns as the only tool for political and economic power. He longed for fewer radical slogans and more community outreach, or as he called it, establishing "survival programs" to help the black community simply survive on a day-to-day basis.

Huey and Eldridge soon developed disparate opinions about evoking revolutionary change. Huey believed that the party's armed stance alienated it from the community. Philosophically, Cleaver could not accept seeing the Black Panthers become, in his words, "a reformist political party." He perceived the group primarily as an organization dedicated to self-defense. If they deemphasized armed struggle, they would be abandoning the original revolutionary principles upon which the party was founded. Eldridge preferred the guns to the breakfast programs, which he dismissed as "reformist." And he would not support the party's survival programs, which Huey felt were a necessary part of the revolutionary process in that they brought the people closer to a transformation of society. Eldridge believed that such a transformation could only come about through violence, by picking up the gun. As Huey saw it, "By refusing to abandon the position of destruction and despair, he underestimated the enemy and took on the role of the reactionary suicide."[68]

The swelling debate between Huey and Eldridge came to a head between April 3 and April 6, 1968, which also turned out to be four of the most incendiary days in the history of the Black Panther Party and the black liberation movement.

On April 3, a group of Oakland police raided a Black Panther meeting that took place at St. Augustine's Episcopal Church on Twenty-seventh and West Street. Suddenly the door burst open and a dozen cops, led by a captain, arrived with shotguns. I was the main officer running the meeting. Oddly, the officers had brought with them both a black preacher and a white monsignor from the Anglican clergy to diffuse any trouble. Father Neil protested the intrusion, but the cops didn't care. They pushed him aside and walked straight for the sanctuary, shotguns at the ready. Already in the sanctuary, I faced the guns and, with Father Neil by my side, blocked their way. The very next day, Father Neil called a press conference to denounce the behavior of the Oakland police, likening them to Nazi storm troopers. But Father Neil's press conference wouldn't receive much press. He would be tragically eclipsed by grimmer circumstances.

On the same day as the press conference, April 4, Martin Luther King Jr. was assassinated in Memphis. Like the past uprisings that occurred in Watts and Detroit, many United States cities were enraged and inflamed by King's murder. With the threats of violence hanging over Oakland, the OPD canceled all of its officers' vacation requests and tightened their grip by doubling the patrols of our black neighborhoods.

Well in advance of King's murder, the Black Panthers had planned a barbeque to be held in DeFremery Park on April 7. The party had invested three hundred dollars to stage the fundraising event. They put up posters around town and hired a sound truck to drive around and advertise the upcoming food fest. Originally the barbeque was designed to benefit the Black Panther Campaign Fund in support of the Peace and Freedom Party candidacies of Huey P. Newton for Congress and Bobby Seale and Kathleen Cleaver for the two California assembly seats in the East Bay. Eldridge was the Peace and Freedom Party candidate for president.

In the form of a directive from Huey in prison, and in light of the extreme volatility of the King assassination three days earlier, the barbeque and rally in DeFremery Park was to now serve as a forum for Huey to explain to the community through a statement how they should respond to the possibility of violence surrounding Dr. King's death. Huey planned to make a public plea to the people to refrain from street violence in their own neighborhoods. (After 1970, Huey later preferred the term "transformation of society" to "revolution." In his view, the people now had an "incorrect understanding" of revolution as merely meaning guns as opposed to an ongoing process.)

In marked contrast to Huey's approach, on April 5, Stokely Carmichael, a member of the Black Panther Party and the Student Nonviolent Coordinating Committee, appeared at a press conference in New Jersey and delivered a statement etched in anger and exasperation. "When [America] killed Dr. King," said Carmichael, "she killed all reasonable hope. When White

America killed Dr. King last night, she declared war on us. There will be no crying, there will be no funerals. The rebellion that has been occurring around the cities is just light stuff to what is about to happen. We have to retaliate for the death of our leaders. The execution of those debts will not be in the courtrooms. They're going to be in the streets of the United States of America. Black people know that they have to get guns."[69]

Cleaver unequivocally agreed with Stokely's position, whereas Huey and I, as the party's chief of staff, vehemently disagreed. We became opposed to inciting violence on the streets of Oakland, brandishing our guns, and burning down our own neighborhoods.

Around dusk on April 6, there was a flurry of activity going on around my house. Party members were preparing for the barbeque picnic by shuttling food back and forth between the Black Panther offices on Grove Street and the soul food restaurant located next door, over to my house on Thirty-fourth Street and Magnolia.

As he normally did, Eldridge had driven over to Oakland to the party headquarters from his office in San Francisco to conduct party business. This time, however, he had with him a caravan of almost a dozen automobiles filled with armed youngsters, many of whom I did not recognize. One kid was driving an Austin Healey sports car. Eldridge was fuming about the party's position regarding Dr. King's assassination. Sensing a confrontation, I suggested to Eldridge that he and this group drive away from my house so we could meet behind the California Hotel.

With the stepped-up patrols, it was obvious that there were police all over the vicinity of my house and the Black Panther office. Secondly, with all the nearby factories, this wasn't a good place for Eldridge to be moving weapons around, especially with all these carloads of people he had brought with him.

Outside the California Hotel, Eldridge and I had it out. "I'm launching a counteroffensive against the pigs," he said. "We need to respond to Dr. King's murder."

"You can't do that, Eldridge," I responded. "You'll be going against Huey's orders. And besides," I added, pointing to the carloads of people he had with him, "Who are these people? I don't even know them."

"Don't worry about them," replied Eldridge. "They're here to get down."

Some of those passengers could be police informants, I suspected.

"Look, David," said Eldridge, "We're the central headquarters of the Black Panther Party. We need to do what DC, Los Angeles, and Newark are doing. We must set an example."

It was difficult standing up to Eldridge, because he was my leader. He outranked me. I looked up to him, sometimes to the point where Huey criticized me that I was acting too much like him. "Be your own person. Be David, not Eldridge," Huey used to say to me. Now, here I was, standing on the street facing Eldridge, who had gone too far by disobeying Huey's clear directive.

"Look, Eldridge, I'm appealing to you," I said, cognizant of the patrols and the cops who were flooding our streets. "This is my community. You don't know what's happening in Oakland. I do. This is bad, both tactically and strategically. It's absolutely crazy."

"That's your opinion," Eldridge responded, "I'm in leadership, and we're going to put it to a vote, here and now."

The crowd on hand supported Eldridge's violent stance. The remaining members also voted alongside "Papa Rage," as we often referred to Eldridge.

Because of party rules, we never acted out alone or as a minority. At the time, Bobby had been pulled out of circulation, for security reasons. This was a matter that needed to be resolved now, without him. Since the vote was unanimous, I went from the sole minority to having to join Eldridge and the majority.

"It's time to intensify the struggle," Eldridge declared. "We gotta do the dog in Babylon."

I reluctantly climbed inside the car with Eldridge as the long caravan headed back past my house, taking the back streets toward DeFremery Park. I wanted to avoid the cops, even though it seemed impossible to be inconspicuous while riding at the head of a ten- to twelve-car caravan with Eldridge Cleaver. How I wished that Huey had been there with me and was not locked up in prison. Only he could have put a stop to the horrific chain of events that was just about to go down around the next corner.

CHAPTER 11

ELDRIDGE CLEAVER: HIDDEN TRAITOR AND INFANTILE LEFTIST

"With the defection of Eldridge Cleaver, we can move again to a full-scale development of our original vision, and come out of the twilight zone which the Party has been in during the recent past."
—Huey P. Newton, April 17, 1971

Eldridge drove and I sat inside the lead car of the caravan. We motored our way down Union Street in my West Oakland neighborhood. It was nighttime, April 6, 1968. The world was still reeling from the news of Dr. King's murder. The streets were tense as I directed Eldridge's growing convoy past my house on Magnolia Street. We took a right on Thirtieth Street, then a quick left onto Union. Union was a less-traveled back street, and I was hoping that by taking this route we would slip past the Oakland police, who had already begun aggressively patrolling the city.

We continued down Union toward DeFremery Park, where our barbeque and rally was scheduled to take place the next day. Suddenly Eldridge stopped the car on the corner of Union and

Twenty-eighth Street. The caravan jerked to a halt as Eldridge stepped outside into the night air to answer nature's call and take a pee.

The whole situation seemed peculiar. I felt uneasy. Some of the cars were loaded with food and barbeque to take down to the park site early, a half-mile down Union. When the party had first promoted the picnic, the cops, as usual, complicated things. We had obtained permission to hold the event (and advertised it on the radio on KDIA and KSOL), but then the police complained. Although the city permitted us to go ahead with the picnic, we were surprised to learn that we were forbidden to put up a sound system and deliver speeches or any direct messages from Huey inside prison instructing the community and the party to remain peaceful! Everybody in the party fully expected the police to use the event as an excuse to arrest more members and bleed the Black Panther treasury of more bail money.

There were four male Black Panthers in the car, a donated '61 Ford with Florida plates—Eldridge, Wendell Wade, Bobby Hutton, and me. There were two other cars behind us on Union Street, an old 1954 Ford and an orange Austin Healey sports car. We had an agreement within our ranks that well-known party members should not travel alone. If any of us were to be killed, we would at least have the benefit of valid witnesses. But this night, Cleaver brought along a veritable army to West Oakland to defend ourselves.

Then a vehicle approached Eldridge, no ordinary sedan. Two Oakland police officers, Nolan Darnell and Richard Jensen, had stopped next to the 1954 Ford and diagonally behind the 1961 white Ford. The cops ordered Eldridge to put his hands up and walk out into the middle of Union Street. According to Eldridge's published recollections, as he approached the officers and crossed the headlights of the white Ford, the cop on the passenger side of his car started shooting, and then the other cop started firing as well.

During the skirmish, we all jumped out of the white Ford and took off in all directions. In the confusion, I crossed the street on Union and jumped through a low window just off the sidewalk into a bathroom. Luckily, I had vaulted into the house of a Mrs. Bertha Mae Allen, who happened to be the godmother of one of my children. Hearing the gunshots outside and thinking her husband had just come home, then seeing me standing in her house, she became hysterical. I quickly tried to calm her down while she attempted to hide me from the police, who were pounding on her door, shouting, "Open the door, you black bitch!"

The people in the other cars behind the white Ford were yelling at the police. They honked their horns and soon bolted out of their automobiles, looking for safe haven. The neighborhood in West Oakland was primarily residential. I lived only five blocks away. A few factory sites stood nearby: ABCO Waterproofing (where I had worked briefly) on Filbert Street, a sausage factory, and the Chiodo Candy Company over on Adeline Street.

— After police headquarters received the call, Union Street was transformed into a war zone. They also called out for a "mutual aid pact" to enlist backup reinforcements from neighboring police departments. Then they sealed off the area over a several-block radius. Within minutes a helicopter was flying overhead, shining a bright beam down onto the street and the roofs of the nearby houses, including Mrs. Allen's.

Eldridge stayed down behind his car as he heard the windshield of the Ford shatter above his head. Then another police car pulled up to the opposite end of Union and Twenty-eighth and began firing several rounds in Eldridge's direction. We were surrounded.

The seemingly endless barrage of ammunition winged a comrade named Warren Wells. He let out an agonized scream as he crumpled to the ground. On the run, Eldridge nearly caught a few rounds himself as he dove onto the pavement in the middle of Union Street. He could hear the bullets ricocheting off the asphalt, a few nearly missing his head.

A cop firing off blasts from his shotgun was chasing Eldridge. Then Eldridge spied two Black Panthers running between two houses on Twenty-eighth Street. I was still hunkered down in the house on the corner of Union and Twenty-eighth. Eldridge and Li'l Bobby Hutton took off to a house next door, and Li'l Bobby scaled a fence as Eldridge followed right behind him.

Li'l Bobby fired back a couple of shots from a rifle he was carrying, causing the police to scatter for cover. A short pause had bought enough time for him and Eldridge to storm into the house on Twenty-eighth. A few seconds later, another relentless stream of gunfire rained where they had once stood. It was hardly a safe haven. The cops had trapped the two Black Panther comrades down into the cellar. Li'l Bobby and Eldridge were hopelessly boxed in.

Outside, the cops kept up a relentless volley of firepower. Ordinarily a shootout of this magnitude might last only a few minutes, but in this case the siege went on for an hour and a half as the clock ticked past midnight. Fresh police reinforcements rushed in, including some from the nearby town of Emeryville. The California Highway Patrol also joined in. More than fifty armed policemen converged on Union and Twenty-eighth, convinced that the Black Panthers had ambushed Officers Darnell and Jensen. Eldridge and Li'l Bobby didn't stand much of a chance emerging from the house alive.

A few minutes later, the little house at 1228 Twenty-eighth Street was being bombarded with tear-gas containers. The force of one canister's trajectory knocked Eldridge to the floor, nearly knocking him out cold. Li'l Bobby was wheezing and coughing from the wafting clouds that permeated the basement. Choking back the thick fumes, Bobby helped Eldridge strip off his clothes in a frantic effort to locate any open wounds. In the darkness, Eldridge searched his body for bullet holes or signs of rampant bleeding. After the onslaught of tear gas, multiple waves of gunfire started up again.

In a last-ditch attempt to flush Li'l Bobby and Eldridge out of the house, the police launched fire bombs inside the cellar. With their lungs raw from inhaling tear gas, Eldridge and Li'l Bobby were sure to die if they stayed inside the smoky, sweltering structure. Eldridge, still unclothed after being shot and hit with the flying canister, called out. The two men were coming out. Police sharpshooters stationed on the rooftop of the house next door on Twenty-eighth aimed their rifles into the cellar of 1228.

"Throw out your guns and come out," the police commanded Eldridge and Bobby.

Eldridge, lying on his back underneath a window, threw Li'l Bobby's rifle out of the house. Li'l Bobby then helped the bleeding older man to his feet and the two hobbled out together. Eldridge's eyes were nearly swollen shut. Exhausted and in tremendous pain, the pair collapsed on the driveway.

"Don't move! Keep your hands raised," the police shouted as they ran up to the two men from the street.

Eldridge was still butt naked; Li'l Bobby was shirtless. The cop in charge ordered the two men to stand up. Hutton helped Cleaver to his feet. They held on to each other tightly, neither one barely able to stand on his own. A squad car was parked out in the middle of the street. The cop in command pointed over at the police car and yelled to the two captured Black Panthers. "Run to the car!" he ordered them.

"I can't run, I've been shot," shouted Eldridge, grabbing his bloody leg.

Then another group of policemen snatched Li'l Bobby from Eldridge's grip. The commanding officer repeated his order. "Run to the car!"

Li'l Bobby was still coughing and spewing from the tear gas that lined his lungs. As he got up, he stumbled, regained his balance, and with his hands held high up in the air, as instructed, he began running toward the police vehicle. He had gone only a couple of dozen feet when a volley of police gunfire cut him down. With Li'l Bobby shot, his lifeless body sprawled near the house, a group of onlookers, black folks from the neighborhood, yelled out again to the police. "Murderers! Pigs!"

A captain with steely blue eyes approached Eldridge, still lying on the driveway. "Where are you wounded?" he asked.

Eldridge pointed to his leg. The captain stomped on the wound with his boot. Cleaver screamed out in pain. "Get him out of here," the captain sneered.

There was at least one eyewitness to the entire event. Charles Perry, an Oakland construction worker, was in the neighborhood visiting his cousin. Here are excerpts of Perry's actual words in an interview conducted by Charles R. Garry on a Sunday morning (accompanied by one of Bobby Hutton's brothers), May 5, 1968, on the corner where the shootout took place.

Q: You were present on April the sixth.
CP: April 6, 1968.
Q: You stopped your car at Twenty-eighth Street—
CP: And Magnolia.
Q: You were facing your automobile towards Union Street on Twenty-eighth Street.
CP: Right.

Q: Tell me in your own words what you actually saw.

CP: What I saw is when the police stopped the guys in front of
     this house at twelve-twenty-eight Twenty-eighth Street, and
     begin to question somebody in their car, the next thing I
     heard was a couple of shots fired. Then I backed my car up
     off of Twenty-eighth Street 'round on Magnolia Street, and
     got out of my car and walked to the southeast corner of
     Magnolia Street, and stood on the corner. And I seen two
     guys get out of the car, and a couple of girls, and go into the
     house at twelve-twenty-eight, where they went downstairs,
     upstairs, that I couldn't definitely say, because the step next
     door to the twelve-twenty-eight blinded me from seeing
     whether they went upstairs or went downstairs. Meanwhile,
     when they went in the house, I heard someone hollering
     about "Come out of there, come out of there, come out of
     there." So it was two ladies hollering that they was afraid to
     come out, because they were afraid they might get killed.

Q: Hold it a minute. Let's go over to twelve-twenty-eight. We're
     now walking over to twelve-twenty-eight. We were standing
     near Magnolia Street and Twenty-eighth Street when Mr.
     Perry was pointing the direction.

CP: Whether they went down this basement here or up the steps,
     I couldn't definitely say. I couldn't definitely say, but any-
     way, when they went up into the house, I heard officers
     make a statement from their car to "Come out of there, and if
     you don't come out of there, we're gonna blow the house up,
     or set it on fire, or put tear gas."

Q: Now when the shooting started, Mr. Perry, you went across
     the street where the firebox is, and you were in direct line of
     seeing two men come out from the side. And they fell down,
     and the officers, you couldn't see what the officers were
     doing with them. And you thought the man who was naked

[Cleaver] was detained there. And you heard someone say to the other man, the younger man, the smaller man [Bobby Hutton], to go forward.

CP: Yeah. Yeah.

Q: And when he went forward, would you tell me whether he had his hands up in the air or not?

CP: Well, the officer didn't tell him to go forward, the officer told him to run to the squad car.

Q: You heard that?

CP: I heard that. Run forward to the squad car.

Q: Where was the squad car in relation to the man that he was telling him to do that?

CP: The squad car was a parked object across the street from the house where he was shot at.

Q: And when he shot Bobby Hutton with his hands up in the air, where did the shooting take place?

CP: The shooting took place in the alleyway between the two houses.

Q: And it was right near the steps.

CP: Right near the front steps that come out of the house of twelve-eighteen. Now which way the man fell, on which side of the lawn, that I couldn't definitely say.

Q: The distance between where he [Hutton] started from and where he fell would be how far in your opinion?

CP: In my opinion, I would say it would be about twenty-five feet.

Q: That far.

CP: A possible twenty-five feet.

Q: Mr. Perry, would you tell me whether you have ever made any statements to anyone else.

CP: No, I haven't.

Q: Have you talked to any lawyers prior to this?

CP: No, I haven't.

Q: How were you found to be an eyewitness to this incident?

CP: I was on my way to Union Street to my cousin's house. I was trying to decide, should I go to Dr. Martin Luther King's funeral on Tuesday, and my cousin told me that if I decided to leave, to come by her house on Union Street and let her know, she'd go down with me. That's exactly why I was on my way until I seen the police trailing this particular car with these Negroes in it, and I slowed down my car behind the police car and followed them up to twelve-eighteen Twenty-eighth Street, where the trouble started.

Q: Were the people who the police were following, were they doing anything unusual?

CP: I didn't ... in my own opinion, I didn't see them doing anything unusual, just driving their car down Twenty-eighth Street. Now what they were doing prior to me seeing them, that I can't say. The time I saw them, they weren't doing anything but driving their car down Twenty-eighth Street.

Q: Who did you say did the shooting first when the police stopped over here near the car?

CP: After these fellows stopped their car in front of 1212 and 1218 Twenty-eighth Street, the police pulled alongside them and asked them a couple of questions. I believe he couldn't have asked them no more than about three or four questions at the most, and immediately they started to shooting. It was not the fellows in the car, it was the police, the police officer.[70]

I was one of those immediately arrested and charged with attempted murder. The Alameda County grand jury indicted eight Black Panthers who were apprehended near the premises of the gun battle. The grand jury investigated the slaying of Li'l Bobby and ruled that his death was justified.

Huey, in prison, was deeply hurt by the death of Li'l Bobby Hutton. Even at seventeen he was one of the most disciplined Black Panthers. He liked to describe himself as a "black liberation soldier." At the time of his death he was reading *Black Reconstruction in America,* by W. E. B. DuBois, and a self-improvement book called *Word Power Made Easy.* "Li'l Bobby," Huey wrote, "was the beginning—the very first member of the Black Panther Party. He gave not only his finances; he gave himself. He placed himself in the service of his people and asked nothing in return, not even a needle or a piece of thread. He asked neither security nor high office, but he demanded those things that are the birthright of all men—dignity and freedom. He demanded this for himself and for his people."[71]

After the shooting, when it became obvious that Eldridge's bail would surely be revoked and he would be returned to the penitentiary, he fled to Cuba, then later to Algiers, where he resided in exile with other Black Panther Party members who were fleeing prosecution from the state. He would never serve a single day in prison as a result of what went down on April 6, 1968. When the case involving the shootout finally came to trial, the presiding judge removed me from the list of the accused, citing a lack of proper evidence. However, in 1970 I was retried on new charges and convicted by an all-white jury of California statute 245PC, felonious assault on a police officer. I was imprisoned and served four years in the California State penitentiary system.

As for Huey and Eldridge, the contradictions would become antagonistic. When Huey got out of prison in August 1970, he felt the party was in a shambles. Both he and Bobby had been off the streets for a long time. It was impossible to handle the day-to-day details from a prison cell. By this time, law enforcement and government agents and agencies were constantly harassing the party. Many of our members were targeted, hunted down, and imprisoned. "But there was a far more serious reason for the Party's difficulties," wrote Huey, "one that threatened its very *raison d'etre:* the Party was heading down the road to reactionary suicide. Under the influence of Eldridge Cleaver, it had lost sight of its initial purpose and become caught up in irrelevant causes. Estranged from Black people who could not relate to it, the Black Panther Party had defected from the community."[72]

As Huey saw it, it was time to retool and adjust the direction the party was taking, especially considering how the Black Panthers were perceived not only by the general public, but more important, by the black communities.

Huey saw the party in a constant state of transformation and noticed the impact and progress the party was making on the community. He was also increasingly aware of the press, the public, and the communities' misconceptions concerning the party, especially when it came to the guns. He began to see Eldridge's either/or philosophy as "infantile" Leftism. He realized that it was to the advantage of the FBI and the government to promote the party in the image of gun-toting criminals. Huey was now deemphasizing guns in favor of setting up more survival programs in an effort to capture the hearts and minds of the community.

"Revolution is not an action, it is a process," Huey continually reiterated. But he also realized that over time, tactics were subject to change. After all, guns ranked as Point 7 in the ten-point program. Before the guns, there was freedom, employment, education, and housing. Our community programs—now called survival programs—were of great importance from the beginning. Huey believed that in 1966 and 1967 the weapons had been a necessary phase but now realized that the guns and uniforms set the Black Panthers apart from the community. Huey didn't want to be looked at as an ad hoc military group operating outside the priorities and the realities of the black community.

"Perhaps our tactics at the time were extreme," Huey admitted, "perhaps we placed too much emphasis on military action. We were a young revolutionary group seeking answers and ways to alleviate racism."[73]

Huey realized that in the eyes of the federal government and law enforcement, the party's direction more toward reform programs and away from guns would make the Black Panthers an even more dangerous revolutionary organization. Starting in September of 1969, the FBI's headquarters began mobilizing their field offices to begin participating and sharing information, working together in an organized campaign aimed at attacking and smashing the Black Panther Party (BPP) on a nationwide level. The result was a series of COINTELPRO (Counter Intelligence Programs) operations aimed at specifically disrupting the relationships between high-ranking members of the party, especially Huey and Eldridge. At first, COINTELPRO utilized a targeted and precise FBI letter-writing campaign, with letters sent out from various FBI field offices using phony BPP stationery and forged signatures of its members and leaders, including mine. But it was Eldridge and Huey who became primary targets. "In March, 1970," Huey wrote in an unfinished manuscript, "the FBI zeroed in on Eldridge Cleaver, then in exile in Algiers after he had been told to leave Cuba, when the Bureau learned that the high-strung Cleaver had 'accepted as bonafide' a fictitious letter 'stating that BPP leaders in California were seeking to undercut his influence.' "[74]

For the next twelve months, Eldridge would receive a flow of messages containing bogus information about various BPP leaders and activities. The messages especially centered on Huey after his release from prison, after the efforts of Charles Garry resulted in his sentence being overturned in August 1970. Those letters capitalized on the already tenuous relationship between Huey and Eldridge stemming from the death of Li'l Bobby Hutton. For instance, after Eldridge spearheaded a BPP-sponsored delegation to North Korea and North Vietnam, the Los Angeles FBI field office sent out an anonymous letter to Eldridge criticizing Huey for not aggressively promoting to the press the Black Panther Party's sponsorship of the trip.

By December of 1970 the FBI turned up the heat, concentrating their efforts to further undermine Huey and Eldridge's faltering relationship. As a result and according to FBI files included in Huey's private papers, "the Bureau issued instructions 'to write numerous letters to Cleaver criticizing Newton for his lack of leadership. It is felt that, if Cleaver received a sufficient number of complaints regarding Newton, it might . . . create dissension that later could be more fully exploited.' "

One phony letter to Eldridge, supposedly written by Connie Matthews, Huey's personal secretary, relied not only on the growing rift between Huey and Eldridge, but played on Eldridge's ego, alluding to the condition of the *Black Panther* newspaper and the foreign BPP chapters, programs that were of special interest to him. The letter's tone set out to undermine Huey's authority. It read in part:

> I know you have not been told what has been happening lately . . . Things around headquarters are dreadfully disorganized with the comrade commander not making proper decisions. The newspaper is in a shambles. No one knows who is in charge. The foreign department gets no support. Brothers and sisters are accused of all sorts of things . . . I am disturbed because I, myself, do not know which way to turn . . . If only you were here to inject some strength into the movement, or to give some advice. One of two steps must be taken soon and both are drastic. We must either get rid of the supreme com-

mander or get rid of the disloyal members ... Huey is really all we have right now and we can't let him down, regardless of how poorly he is acting, unless you feel otherwise.[75]

Other FBI letters, one supposedly from "Algonquin J. Fuller, Youth Against War and Fascism, New York, New York," one of Eldridge's white admirers, was written under the guise of trying to keep Eldridge informed of the party's domestic goings-on while he remained in exile in Algiers:

> Let me tell you what has happened to our brothers in the Party since you left and that "Pretty Nigger Newton" in his funky clothes has been running things ...
>
> Brother Eldridge, to me as an outsider but one who believes in the revolution, it seems that the Panthers need a leader in Amerika [sic] who will bring the Party back to the people.
>
> Brother Newton has failed you and the Party. The Panthers do not need a "daytime revolutionary, a nighttime partygoer, and African fashion model" as a leader. They need the leadership which only you can supply.[76]

As the FBI field offices followed their orders from central headquarters, disruptive letters were mailed to Black Panther chapters all over the world. Another letter to Eldridge in Algiers was mailed from the New York FBI office, supposedly penned by the "New York Panther 21," Eldridge's core group of East Coast supporters:

> As you are aware, we of the Panther 21 have always been loyal to the Party and continue to feel a close allegiance to you and the ideology of the Party which has been developed mainly through your efforts ...

We know that you have never let us down and have always inspired us through your participation in the vanguard party. As the leading theoretician of the party's philosophy and as brother among brother, we urge you to make your influence felt. We think that The Rage [Cleaver] is the only person strong enough to pull this factionalized party back together . . .

You are our remaining hope in our struggle to fight oppression within and without the party.[77]

By January 1971 the FBI began to see the fruits of their campaign. Fortunately for the FBI, Eldridge was keeping information about the phony communiqués to himself. According to FBI files, he considered them "good information about the Party."

Based on their success with Eldridge, the FBI's mission to create chaos within the Black Panther Party became a top priority. By February 2, 1971, FBI central command solicited no less than twenty-nine field offices to submit even more proposals and ideas on how to best disrupt local BPP chapters, especially the party's national headquarters in Oakland. The bureau command believed its four-year-long war against Huey P. Newton and the Black Panther Party was nearing victory.

In response, for the next three weeks, the flow of anonymous letters from the field offices intensified and capitalized on Huey's penthouse, where he had taken up residence after he was released from prison, which was actually being subsidized not by party funds but by well-to-do supporters in the Hollywood movie community. The accusations, however, cleverly played on Eldridge's exile and relative isolation in Algiers.

The messages became more and more vicious. On February 24 an urgent Teletype message from the FBI director authorized the most daring step in the campaign—a falsified message to Cleaver from a member of the party's central committee. A letter with the forged signature of Elbert "Big Man" Howard, editor of the *Black Panther* newspaper, told Eldridge:

> John Seale told me Huey talked to you Friday and what he had to say. I am disgusted with things here and the fact that you are being ignored. I am loyal to the party and it makes me mad to learn that Huey now has to lie to you. I am referring to his fancy apartment, which he refers to as the throne. I think you should know that he picked the place out himself, not the central committee, and the high rent is from party funds and not paid by anyone else. Many of the others are upset about this waste of money. It is needed for other party work here and also in Algeria. It seems the least Huey could do is furnish you the money and live with the rest of us. Since Huey will lie to you about this, you can see how it is with him. You would be amazed at what is actually happening.
>
> I wish there was some way I could get in touch with you but in view of Huey's orders, it is not possible. You should really know what's happening and statements made about you. I can't risk a call, as it would mean certain expulsion. You should think a great deal before sending Kathleen. If I could talk to you I could tell you why I don't think you should. —Big Man[78]

Once again, Eldridge took the bait.

On February 28, 1971, in an attempt to show solidarity, Huey telephoned Eldridge in Algiers to ask him to participate in a long-distance telephone interview to be aired live on a San Francisco television talk show, *AM San Francisco*. Eldridge agreed. Three hours later, Huey appeared on camera as Eldridge's voice was broadcast over the television airwaves. The two had agreed in advance to discuss the upcoming Intercommunal Solidarity Day for Bobby Seale and Ericka Huggins, who were on trial in Connecticut, and would announce an invitation for the party to send a twenty-person delegation to China.

Fueled by the bogus FBI letters, in disagreement with Huey over the party's survival programs, and angered by the expulsion of Eldridge's faction—the New York 21—in New York (after publicly supporting the Weathermen Underground and criticizing central committee leadership) as well as the party's perceived lack of support for underground fugitive members like Elmer "Geronimo" Pratt (a Black Panther leader from Los Angeles), Eldridge began attacking me toward the end of the live television interview. Huey felt shocked and betrayed when Eldridge launched into party business and central committee decisions on the air, including the central committee's expulsion of Connie Matthews Tabor, Cetawayo Tabor, the New York 21, and Pratt. All of these Black Panthers were guilty of serious offenses—actions that had jeopardized other comrades and the party. The New York 21 had written an open letter to the Weathermen saying they believed that the leadership of the party had lost its revolutionary fervor and that the Weathermen were the true vanguard of the revolution. That was all right, but the central committee decided that with that statement, the New York 21 had resigned from the party. Expulsion was simply the party's recognition of that fact.

On KGO-TV Cleaver proclaimed:

I just want to comment on the present situation that exists within the Black Panther Party, specifically in reference to the purge of brother Geronimo, the expulsion of the New York 21, opposition over here, and we have three members of the central committee of the Black Panther Party over here, is that this action is regrettable, it should not have taken place, it took place without proper consultation with other members of the central committee, and we lay the responsibility at the feet of David Hilliard, and we demand that David Hilliard be dismissed or resign from the position of chief of staff of the Black Panther Party, so that we can go about the work of putting the Party back together again because ... as a result of the actions taken by David Hilliard over a long period of time, the Party has fallen apart at the seams.[79]

Eldridge's surprise public tirade against me was the last straw for Huey. Huey was mortified and livid, so angry that immediately following the *AM San Francisco* debacle, he placed a telephone call directly to Eldridge in Algeria. In Huey's eyes, Eldridge's attack was aimed at him, since he knew I was only carrying out his plans and direction for the party. What follows is a heretofore-unpublished transcription of their conversation:

EC: Hello?
HPN: Hello!
EC: Hey, man.
HPN: Eldridge. You dropped a bombshell this morning.
EC: Yeah.
HPN: Don't you think so?
EC: I hope so.
HPN: It was very embarrassing for me.
EC: It had to be dealt with, man.
HPN: Yeah, but I have to deal with it, too, because, I think ... when you bring things like that, it should be brought to the central committee and discussed only there, not outside, you know?
EC: The way that our stuff is going down, it hasn't been done that way, man.
HPN: Hello? You there?

EC: Yeah.

HPN: Your whole section is expelled!

EC: Right on, if that's what you want to do, brother. But look here.

HPN: What?

EC: I don't think you should take such action like that.

HPN: I'll take that, brother. You dropped a bombshell, it's all over the country now that there's a faction, so I want your faction to be put to work. Because I wish I had devastated it, if it exists, but I don't think it exists. As far as you're concerned, you can go to hell, brother. But you're expelled, all communication will be stopped, and that's the end of it.

EC: Hey Huey—

HPN: What? I'm going to write the Koreans, I'm going to write the Chinese, and the Algerians to kick you out of our embassy.

EC: Hey Huey—

HPN: Or to put you into jail, because you're a maniac, brother. You and Timothy Leary, I think you're full of acid this morning.

EC: Hey Huey—

HPN: What?

EC: I think, you should slow down, because that's not gonna work, you know?

HPN: Well, I think it will. We'll see.

EC: All right. Okay, we'll see.

HPN: I like a battle brother; we'll battle it out.

EC: Hey Huey?

HPN: What?

EC: That's not the best way to deal with that.

HPN: This is the way *I* want to deal with it.

EC: Well, I think that you're a mad man, too, brother.

HPN: Okay, we'll battle then, two mad men will lock horns.

EC: We'll see, okay?

HPN: I think I have the guns.

EC: I've got some guns, too, brother.

HPN: All right. You put yours to work, and then I'll put mine to work, but I'm not a coward like you, brother, because you run off to get Li'l Bobby Hutton killed. But I stay here to face the gas, you see? You're a coward because you attacked me this morning. You attacked the chief [of staff, David Hilliard], but you attacked him, but you wanted to say my name, you see? And you're a coward and you're a punk, you understand?

EC: Hey Huey?

HPN: (shouting) YOU'RE A PUNK!

EC: I think you've lost your ability to reason, brother.

HPN: Hey brother, you heard what I called you, that's what I feel about you now. You're a punk!

EC: I'm not going to call you that, you see?[80]

When the central committee expelled him from the Black Panther Party for his behavior, Eldridge announced that the "real" Black Panther Party would thereafter be directed from Algiers. "Like an ultra-left sorcerer's apprentice with a gift for verbal magic, Cleaver frenetically tried to coalesce his own followers with transatlantic exhortations for immediate guerrilla warfare."[81]

Thus officially began Eldridge's defection and expulsion from the BPP. He was now surrounded only by his core constituency in Algiers, stubbornly loyal to his dream of armed revolution and insurrection with militant groups like the Weather Underground, groups whose tactics and philosophy sharply contrasted with Huey's bolder visions to continue setting up neighborhood "survival programs" like the Black Panther Breakfast for Children programs, programs that Eldridge now openly criticized. In addition, and as a result of the contradictions between Huey and Eldridge, as it widened, and as the FBI's infiltration and COINTELPRO operations increased, there would soon be bloodshed within party ranks.

Meanwhile the FBI was still hard at work with their COINTELPRO. On April 17, Samuel Napier, longtime circulation manager for the *Black Panther* newspaper, was assassinated. The hit team was composed of COINTELPRO agent provocateurs and Cleaver loyalists. The killers surprised Napier in the New York *Black Panther* distribution office, bound him hand and foot, gagged him, and then shot him six times with a .357 Magnum. They then burned the newspaper distribution office to the ground. Police officials told the media that the Eldridge-Huey factionalism was responsible for Napier's death, and proceeded to arrest the party members who had undertaken the task of arranging for Napier's burial.

Huey's official response to the people was printed in the edition of the *Black Panther* newspaper dated April 17, 1971, the same day as Sam Napier's death and the last issue Napier was to officially distribute. Huey clearly saw Eldridge's personal and political aspirations as ideologically and dangerously intertwined: "Eldridge Cleaver influenced us to isolate ourselves from the Black community, so that it was war between the oppressor and the Black Panther Party, not war between the oppressor and the oppressed community."[82]

Ever the self-critical observer of the party, Huey not only saw Eldridge's actions as a defection from the party, but also pointed out the party's *own* defection from both the black and white communities. According to Huey, the Black Panther Party had defected from the community long before Eldridge defected from the party. In addition, Huey saw profanity, something he always refrained from since his youth, as part of what alienated the party far from such influential black institutions as the church and the older black working class. Rather than a free speech issue, Huey saw the profanity printed in the newspaper as a wedge between the party and the community. Although he felt Eldridge's influence had brought it about, he blamed those of us in the party for accepting it.

Ultimately, Huey saw the defection of Eldridge from the BPP as more of an opportunity than a setback: "So the Black Panther Party has reached a contradiction with Eldridge Cleaver, and he has defected from the Party because we would not order everyone into the streets tomorrow to make a revolution. This contradiction and conflict may seem unfortunate to some, but it is a part of the dialectical process. The resolution of this contradiction has freed us from incorrect analysis and emphasis."[83]

In a manuscript that Huey was preparing before his death, he warned that it would be a mistake to "leave the so-called Newton-Cleaver civil war as merely a construct of the FBI." He went on to say:

> To comprehend the sad saga of Eldridge Cleaver, it is necessary to look back to his celebrated prison years. Cleaver, the super-masculine rapist, fashioned himself a "short" or "punk-hunter" (homosexual baiter). His prison masterpiece, *Soul On Ice,* was a manifesto of its time, a book riddled with powerful insights and contradictions. Cleaver devoted lengthy, furious passages in *Soul On Ice* to a literary pummeling of James Baldwin, his writing, his politics, and most of all his sexuality.[84]
>
> Once Cleaver was thrown out of prison into the much more threatening world, his sublimations were in ruins. In 1967, when the masculine stud, Cleaver, was courting the Black Panther Party, he was invited to attend a special dinner in San

Francisco for James Baldwin, who had just returned from Turkey. Cleaver in turn invited Huey P. Newton to accompany him to the occasion.

When they arrived Cleaver and Baldwin walked head into each other, and the giant 6'3" Cleaver bent down and engaged in a long, passionate French kiss with Baldwin, who is barely five feet tall. Baldwin, who had neither written nor uttered a word in response to Cleaver's acid literary criticism, had finally spoken. Using non-verbal communication he dramatically exposed Cleaver's internal contradiction, his "tragic flaw." In effect, Baldwin had said: if a woman kissed Cleaver she would be kissing another woman; if a man kissed Cleaver he would be kissing another man. Newton, astounded by Cleaver's behavior since it so graphically contradicted his scathing attack on Baldwin's homosexuality in *Soul On Ice*, later expressed his surprise. Cleaver pleaded with the Black Panther leader not to relate the incident to anyone....

The fuel for Cleaver's furies was, and is, his own psycho-sexual panic; his own self hatred and sexual insecurity; his pitiful need for a clear love/hate dichotomy and a clear-cut male/female dichotomy; his need to be a super-hero.... [85]

Cleaver, sometimes, following his prison release, stopped at bus stops where lone women awaited the next bus, forced them into the back of his Volkswagen bus and ravished them. He once climbed the fire escape of his apartment house, entered a woman's room, raped her, and upon departure presented her with a gift of a manuscript—his then unpublished *Soul On Ice*. [86]

Eldridge's deviant behavior toward women carried over during his tenure with the Black Panther Party.

In 1968, a Black mother contacted the Party headquarters in Berkeley and angrily complained that Cleaver had raped her 14 year-old daughter. When charged by the central committee, Cleaver's only response was, "I only wish that she had been 12 years old."[87]

While in Paris in exile [after Algeria], Cleaver told an interviewer that he had made a study of how cramped the male genitalia looked encased, as it were, in the traditional male trousers. This is clearly a man in danger of acting out his repressed homoerotic impulses, a man near the breaking point, compelled to stare at men's crotches. At the same time, Cleaver was dealing in drugs and women for high French government officials. Eventually, this dealing and pimping became so compromising that French intelligence finally forced the government to expel the exile. It was then, and only then, that Cleaver decided to return to the United States as a born-again patriot and Christian.[88]

None of this abhorrent behavior would have been news to Black Panther Party field marshal George Jackson. Five years after Jackson was shot to death, on April 14, 1976, the *Black Panther* denounced Eldridge Cleaver as an "active and willing agent in the FBI's COINTELPRO plan to destroy Black organizations by creating internal dissension." The paper also charged him with responsibility for the murders of Li'l Bobby Hutton and Sam Napier. In a letter written in 1971, nine months before his death, Jackson, who served time with Eldridge inside the walls of San Quentin, wrote:

Those who have more regard for their own egos or self-interest than they have for building a united progressive left, and those who abandon community altogether in favor of petty interests, are in direct opposition to our real interests. They are attempting another form of escapism.

I sent a letter reminding him [Cleaver] that his behavior while in prison was far from exemplary . . . I finally asked him simply to show proof that he was not a compulsive disruptor or agent provocateur. A very very mild request, I felt. He returned with a very scurrilous and profane set of invectives—in short, a piece of vendetta.

"Tell him," George concluded, summing up Huey's feelings as well, "that seven thousand miles, the walls of prison, steel and barbed wire do not make him safe from my special brand of discipline. Tell him that the dragon is coming."[89]

If the dragon spared Eldridge's life, then it was the demons that finished him off. In 1975 Eldridge returned from exile to the United States, and after a long legal bout, his attempted murder charges stemming from the April 1968 shootout were dropped in exchange for a guilty plea of assault, for which he served a period of probation. In secret he testified before Congress in front of the McClellan Committee's investigation of left-wing activities. His testimony was never made public.

After turning himself in and coming out of hiding, Cleaver disavowed his leftist past. He later flirted with disparate ideologies, including neoconservatism, born-again Christianity, and the teachings of Reverend Sun Myung Moon and the Unification Church. His political legacy became that of a chameleon, a personality muddled in a mass of contradiction. "I have gone beyond civil rights and human rights to creation rights," Eldridge remarked cryptically.

When he died on May 1, 1998, of an apparent heart attack, former minister of information Leroy Eldridge Cleaver had battled severe drug abuse, cancer, and diabetes.

In 1978 Huey summed up his feelings about his former party comrade and "hidden traitor," speculating that maybe the so-called split had been based more in fear and insecurity on Eldridge's part than rivalry. "I did feel hurt by Eldridge, though. If I had received a letter accusing him of acting against the interests of the Party, I would have gone to him about it. That is what friendship is all about. I was aware that people were talking about a split, so I arranged to go on TV with a hookup of Eldridge in Algeria to squelch the rumor the government was circulating. But there was Eldridge denouncing me. Maybe he was never my friend."[90]

ABOVE *Young Huey on a pony.*
(Courtesy: The Huey P. Newton Foundation)

RIGHT *Adolescent Huey. (Courtesy:*
The Huey P. Newton Foundation)

ABOVE *David Hilliard and Huey.* (*Copyright Temple University Libraries*)

LEFT *Ericka Huggins, founding member of the Los Angeles Black Panther Party Chapter, circa 1969, when she was in prison with Bobby Seale in Connecticut.* (*Courtesy: The Huey P. Newton Foundation*)

ABOVE *Huey and his family in exile. Huey and (clockwise) Ronnie, Jessica, and Gwen.*
(Courtesy: The Huey P. Newton Foundation)

RIGHT *Huey with Betty Fountaine, Gwen's mother who aided in their escape to Cuba.*
(Courtesy: The Huey P. Newton Foundation)

ABOVE *Gwen Fountaine, Huey Newton, and Elaine Brown in Cuba.*
(Courtesy: The Huey P. Newton Foundation)

OPPOSITE, BOTTOM *Huey in Cuba at work at the cement factory. "I worked there about six months. It was required to work ten hours for five days, then five hours on Saturdays, but I worked ten hours a day, seven days a week voluntarily. I never worked on cars before, so I wasn't too good, but everybody was nice to me anyway." (Courtesy: The Huey P. Newton Foundation)*

ABOVE LEFT *Huey and Charles R. Garry at the Havana Riviera Hotel in Havana.* *(Courtesy: The Huey P. Newton Foundation)* ABOVE RIGHT *Huey and William Brent in Havana who became a Cuban citizen and taught at the University of Havana.* *(Courtesy: The Huey P. Newton Foundation)*

LEFT *Fredrika Slaughter at age 18, the year she and Huey first met.*
(Courtesy: The Huey P. Newton Foundation)

BELOW *Left to Right: Arlene, Huey, me, Percy "Slim" Slaughter, unidentified person. At the Slaughter home, December 1970.*
(Courtesy: The Huey P. Newton Foundation)

ABOVE *Huey and Fredrika's wedding at the Hearts of Reno wedding chapel, September 14, 1984. Left to right: Greta, Fredrika, Huey, and Bert Schneider. (Courtesy: The Huey P. Newton Foundation)*

RIGHT *Fredrika and Huey at a wedding reception hosted by Huey's close friend, Bert Schneider, 1984. (Courtesy: The Huey P. Newton Foundation)*

ABOVE *A childlike Huey clowning with Kieron Slaughter in 1985 at the house on Sayre Road.*
(Courtesy: The Huey P. Newton Foundation)

RIGHT *Six months before his death. Huey Newton, CDC# D46648, San Quentin State Prison, Valentine's Day, 1989.*
(Courtesy: The Huey P. Newton Foundation)

CHAPTER 12

INSIDE THE PENAL COLONY

After his voluntary manslaughter conviction for the shooting of OPD Officer John Frey, Huey spent almost three years locked up. During that time, the Black Panther Party exploded in influence and popularity. While Huey sat in jail, chapters opened in cities across the country and the party continued to attract worldwide press. By 1970 the *Black Panther* newspaper would reach a weekly circulation of 150,000. The seeds of the party's "survival programs" would begin to sprout in cities across the country. Breakfast for Children, political education academies, health clinics, and sickle cell testing, as well as prisoner and family services—all of these programs were at their earliest and most vital stages of development.

Meanwhile the upper echelons of the federal government weren't taking the party's progress lying down. Early in 1969, Attorney General John Mitchell and his deputy, Richard Kleindienst, formed a special intra-agency Black Panther task force working out of the Justice Department. A "Panther Squad" began traveling from city to city, supposedly to help bring criminal indictments against the Panthers, but its main task was to exhort local officials to cooperate with federal agencies in a campaign of raids against party offices, service centers, and homes.

In Chicago, Fred Hampton and Mark Clark were murdered in their sleep on December 9, 1969, by the Chicago Police Department in a violent raid organized by the FBI. In Los Angeles, Mayor Sam Yorty and Chief "Crazy" Ed Davis's SWAT team fired gunfire, tear gas, and explosives into the Black Panther headquarters for six full hours. The party's death toll was rising. By August 1970, a total of twenty-two Black Panther Party members had been slain.

In September 1968, following his manslaughter conviction, Huey was sent back to the Alameda County Jail to ponder his fate. He would either be released on bail, pending an appeal to a higher court, or begin serving a two-to-fifteen-year sentence for voluntary manslaughter. After bail was swiftly denied, it was apparent that Huey P. Newton would enter the California Department of Corrections system given the special classification of political prisoner. Huey held a curious power over the prison authorities, who were worried about his role as a political prisoner and whether his incarceration would demand special treatment.

Huey's first stop was Vacaville Medical Facility, less than an hour-long bus drive from Oakland, where he went through a standard series of physical and mental examinations. Before he was assigned to a cell, he was called in to see the Vacaville warden, who warned him not to organize inmates, or else he would end up in solitary confinement. Huey later recalled:

> It struck me as ironic that even as he spoke, an isolation cell stood waiting to receive me. Tactics like this add to the nightmarish unreality of prison. Then the warden began dangling the carrot: if I cooperated, I could be like any other prisoner, not locked up all the time. They were going to treat me tight at

first, he said, to educate and orient the other prisoners to my presence, but if all went well, they would let me out into the general prison population—the "main line," it's called.

I sat silent, listening; I would never taste that carrot.[91]

Three psychiatrists ran aptitude and I.Q. tests, the latter upon which Huey scored extremely low, at about the third- or fourth-grade level. Huey's response was, if they really wanted to know his I.Q., why not measure creative disciplines like music?

After twenty-five days in Vacaville, Huey was assigned to a facility where he would serve out his sentence. California Men's Colony, East Facility, in San Luis Obispo, is a prison situated halfway between Oakland and Los Angeles. Once he was processed, Huey would soon find that life inside the colony would be similar to his other experiences in jail. Just as he had done time in Alameda County Jail, Santa Rita, and Vacaville in isolation, Huey's time at the men's colony would also be spent in solitary. As soon as Huey arrived in San Luis Obispo, it became apparent why the state chose to house him there. When asked (as if his preferences actually mattered), Huey had requested to be sent to San Quentin, Folsom, or Soledad, in that order. The men's colony (which Huey referred to as the Penal Colony, after a short story by Franz Kafka) was a completely different style of lockup, a clever move on the part of the state to isolate Huey from having an influence on not only the other inmates, but on the entire California prison system as well.

Fewer than 10 percent of the inmates at the California Men's Colony are black or Chicano, even though those two groups make up more than 50 percent of the prison population in California. Since there have been no riots, the institution has a reputation as a model prison. The Penal Colony was divided into four self-contained quadrants, each with approximately six hundred inmates. Its layout and organization make it almost impossible for an inmate in one section to meet the three-quarters of the population in other quadrants. In addition, and very important, 80 percent of the prisoners at the time, according to Huey, were homosexual.

Once again, Huey was immediately taken to meet the warden. Along with a counselor, both proposed a "rehabilitation program" in anticipation of Huey's reentering society after serving a decade-plus sentence. His rehabilitation would first include working in the prison dining hall, then a more permanent assignment—either making shoes, stamping out license plates, or performing laundry services for a salary that ranged from three to ten cents an hour. Huey offered a counterproposal. He would work in any job to which they assigned him provided they paid him union wages. In return, he would pay the costs of room and board. Huey's proposal wasn't even considered.

As an alternative, Huey asked to attend school, which would grant him access to the prison library, where he could also study independently. The warden refused and placed Huey under lockdown. Although the other inmates were free to roam the yard—inmates even had keys to their own cells—Huey was permitted out of his cell only during meals, visits, or on official prison business, such as going before disciplinary boards and attending parole board meetings. Huey would have no education classes, no canteen privileges, no cigarettes, no soap, no deodorant, no toothpaste or mouthwash. He was issued a toothbrush and institutional tooth powder, and intermittently received the *San Francisco Chronicle*, one day late. At first the newspaper was his only reading material, until his attorneys obtained a court order for a typewriter and writing material (provided such material was related to his case). Huey exercised rigorously and practiced "control of my thoughts, which I had perfected by then."

Huey chose to look at lockdown not as punishment but as "liberation from servitude." Once a month he was called before a disciplinary board and asked if he was ready to cooperate and come off lockdown. Each month he refused.

Upon entering the California Men's Colony, Huey had already spent weeks and months inside Alameda County Jail and San Quentin State Prison, which gave him a perspective and a strategy as to how he would conduct his life inside, which certainly didn't include rehabilitation. He'd been from county to death row in thirty-three months. As a result, nothing about prison life shocked or surprised him. He steadfastly resisted the illusion of rehabilitation, which bewildered his captors. If necessary, Huey was resigned to serve his entire sentence locked down.

"Certainly spending three years in solitary confinement taught me the value of meditation," Huey told *Oui* magazine in a 1978 interview conducted nine years after his release. "I think nonaction is perfectly valid—if you're in solitary confinement. What I learned in solitary confinement, I use as I use all my experiences—as a piece of equipment in battle."

It was in early January 1969, during his incarceration at the men's colony, that two Los Angeles Black Panther comrades, John Jerome Huggins and Alprentice "Bunchy" Carter, were shot to death on the UCLA campus after a meeting of the UCLA Black Students Union. Huggins and Bunchy were murdered by members of Ron Karenga's Organization Us. When the news reached Huey, he realized that all Black Panthers were now marked men. With the murders of Li'l Bobby Hutton in Oakland and Fred Hampton and Mark Clark in Chicago, people throughout the country began to suspect a national police conspiracy to wipe the party out.

Huey took the fatalities hard. The loss of men like Hampton and famed Soledad Brother George Jackson represented a tragic setback not only for the party, but also for the black liberation movement in general. These were men who were potentially heir apparent to fallen leaders like Malcolm X and Che Guevara. "This homicidal campaign caused my spirits to sink," Huey wrote. "It is very difficult to take the loss of valuable comrades and personal friends, even though we recognize death as a price we have to pay in a revolutionary struggle. You never get used to it."[92]

Huey's unwillingness to enter the main line or the prison workforce constantly befuddled prison officials, especially the correctional officers assigned to the men's colony yard. In an article smuggled out and published in the *Black Panther* as "Prison Where Is Thy Victory," Huey "taunted the guards for thinking that because a man's body is in prison they have won a victory over the ideas that inspired his actions."

Compared to his first experiences in solitary inside the Alameda County Jail's "soul-breaker," the men's colony was less demanding. Most of the books he was confined to were old and juvenile—with characters such as Rin-Tin-Tin, Hopalong Cassidy, and the like—but Huey also got hold of the Bible, which he loved, and which he read through for the third time. More equipped than the soul-breaker, Huey's cell contained a bunk, toilet, washbasin, chair, and tin desk.

During the time he spent incarcerated inside the men's colony, Huey, like comrade George Jackson, viewed prison as being more than just a place designed for punishment and confinement. It was where ideas about revolution and liberation were really beginning to take hold. On the "inside" of prison, Huey felt a growing political consciousness and a revolutionary spirit, especially during heavy raps with inmates during chow. "The world must become a place in which poor and oppressed people can live in peace and dignity. If we still need prisons after that transformation, they must be true rehabilitation centers rather than concentration camps. In the new society, the centers would not be called prisons or penal institutions and they would not be ancient rock fortresses in inaccessible areas. They would be an important part of the community, in which people who are not well or who are unhappy would still be made to feel that they are part of humanity."[93]

In April of 1970 Huey went before the parole board for the first time. Instead of pleading for parole status, he used the session with the board members as an opportunity to debate the system. The board inquired about his refusal to work. What gave him the right to selectively obey the rules? Huey's response was that he was willing to obey rules so long as they didn't deny his dignity as a human being. After the meeting, the board ordered the guards to allow Huey to have basic toilet articles in his cell. ("A small but sweet victory.") After that, against the advice of his lawyers, Huey resolved never to go before a parole hearing again.

Despite being in solitary, during the first months of his incarceration at the men's colony Huey became quite popular with his fellow inmates. Many were rooting for him to win an appeal for a new trial. Meanwhile, Huey's defense team, which included attorneys Charles R. Garry, Fay Stender, and Alex Hoffman, was still hard at work on his case. By May of 1970 a decision on Huey's appeal was to be handed down shortly. Expectations inside Huey's defense camp ranged from Garry's guarded optimism to Fay Stender's caution. Huey himself had already lowered his expectations considerably. Still, before the decision was handed down there was a hopefulness that permeated even the prison walls.

Outside in the yard, Huey heard a commotion. In anticipation of good news regarding Huey's appeal, a group of inmates had gathered, defying the rules against congregating in groups, throwing rocks in the air and clapping their hands in celebration. Huey began to feel optimistic, too. When the guards approached, the inmates threw their ID cards into the dirt, standing their ground while the guards kept a cautious distance.

Then came the appellate court's decision: on May 29, 1970, the California Appellate Court reversed Huey P. Newton's conviction. But his release would be delayed until early August, when the appellate court decision would become final.

When the news finally dropped that the appellate court had overturned Huey's conviction, there was shock and jubilation not only on the yard, but also all across the country. Garry and his team had scored an important victory. The appellate court reversed Judge Friedman's conviction based on incomplete instructions to the jury. According to the judge's instructions, the jury could have convicted Huey either of murder in the first degree, second degree, manslaughter, or not guilty. Friedman, however, hadn't designated the manslaughter category separately, neither voluntary nor involuntary.

Voluntary manslaughter would mean the jury believed that Huey had acted in the heat of passion and after severe provocation, but that he had nevertheless killed the policeman. This was the verdict that the jury did return. There was also a possibility of involuntary manslaughter, which would mean that Huey had been unconscious at the time as a result of shock and loss of blood, but that he acted without being aware of what he was doing.

The involuntary option was one that Judge Friedman chose not to instruct the jury to consider. As a result of his appeal, Huey would stand trial again for manslaughter, though not for murder, charges for which he was acquitted. Even better, Huey could conceivably be released on bail while awaiting trial.

Two months after the end of May, the ruling became final and Huey was quietly released at 3:30 in the morning on August 5, 1970, having served twenty-two months at the men's colony. Carrying two boxes of legal material (while a guard carried his typewriter and another small box), he was ushered through the visiting room and out the front gates. He was then signed over to the Alameda County Sheriff's Department, who would transport him back to Oakland in an unmarked car. Although he was still chained and shackled, Huey nonetheless took a giant step closer toward being free. "It was like a scene from Kafka or Genet's *The Balcony*," he later recalled, "—normal and logical on the surface but nightmarish and phantasmagoric in essence. It had the quality of a symbolic ritual; no one was truly involved or affected. We simply went through the motions."[94]

After signing papers confirming that he had all his property, Huey was now in the custody of two plainclothes deputies from the Alameda County Sheriff's Department. They would drive him back to Oakland for a hearing to determine whether or not he would be granted bail, and if so, how much. If Huey were granted bail, he would be free, pending the outcome of a new manslaughter trial.

Huey and the two deputies rolled into Oakland at about 7:00 AM. The city streets were deserted. New buildings had popped up while Huey served his time. By 10:00 AM, two of his lawyers met to discuss bail. The lawyers expected the amount to be $100,000, though they were trying to get Huey released on his own recognizance. Bail was set at only $50,000, but still it would be a difficult sum for the party to scrape up. Huey wanted to remain in jail until $5,000 was raised. Yet members felt he should be released as soon as possible.

The DA had promised a "happy medium," which turned out to be the $50,000 bail. Who had that kind of money? Huey knew that raising such an amount would be a tremendous hardship. He wanted to stay "inside" until the full bail amount was raised. Huey had always discouraged the party from putting up 10 percent of the bail bond for everyone, not just himself. The money was better spent on survival programs. But the party and Huey's attorneys argued that it was more important for him to hit the street right away, that the movement would benefit.

Huey did not return to his county jail cell. Instead, he remained with his lawyers. Outside, a confrontation was heating up. A group of police in formation had left the county building with a box of clubs to meet a growing crowd that had gathered outside. The streets were blocked with thousands of shouting people.

Eventually the bail and release papers were signed. On the tenth floor, where the jail was, Huey walked out of the gate and toward the elevator. I was there with him, along with his brothers Walter Jr. and Melvin. Reporters and newspeople, all screaming questions, lined the hallway. Huey, his brothers, and I made it to the elevator, which made it only to the fourth floor before stopping. Then we headed down the stairs the rest of the way to the first floor. Huey later described how he felt about being outside and free once again:

> On the first floor we made our way out to the main entrance on Lake Merritt Park. It was a bright, blue-sky day, just the kind of day I had wanted. Looking ahead, I could see thousands of beautiful people and a sea of hands, all of them waving. When I gave them the power sign, the hands shot up in reply and everyone started to cheer. God, it was good. I felt this tremendous sense of release, of liberation, like taking off your shirt on a hot day and feeling free, unbound by anything. Later, I did take off my shirt. I had to fight back the tears. It was wonderful to be

out, but even more exhilarating to see the concern and emotion of the people.[95]

Huey's sisters, Leola, Doris, and Myrtle, met us. Newsmen besieged his lawyers. I was still by Huey's side with my wife, Pat, along with Walter Jr.; Melvin; Geronimo Pratt, deputy minister of defense; and Masai Hewitt, our minister of education. In the euphoria, Huey held on to his relatives, friends, and comrades and was dragged along, his feet hardly touching the ground as he made his way to a waiting Volkswagen. The field of people cheered as police armed with clubs, shields, and helmets watched Huey give the power sign standing on top of the roof of a Volkswagen.

Although it was a beautiful day, the euphoria was soon replaced with demands for Huey to appear before the media. Despite all the attention, he was eager to get back to work. He was under immense pressure to grant interviews, accept speaking engagements, and appear on talk shows and television programs. Huey chose, instead, to lay low for six months. One Hollywood talent agency sent him a brochure. "You're star quality," they wrote. Huey rejected his newfound celebrity. "Too many so-called leaders of the movement have been made into celebrities and their revolutionary fervor destroyed by mass media," he later said. "They become Hollywood objects and lose identification with the real issues. The task is to transform society; only the people can do that—not heroes, not celebrities, not stars. A star's place is in Hollywood; the revolutionary's place is in the community with the people. A studio is a place where fiction is made, but the Black Panther Party is out to create non-fiction. We are making revolution."[96]

CHAPTER 13

FROM THE PRISON
TO THE PENTHOUSE

As Huey made the difficult transition from prison to freedom on the street, he found the conversion vivid and
mind-blowing. During his first few days out of jail, he
wondered when the reality of it all would sink in. He had literally
forgotten how to live "outside." He was used to the familiar patters
of prison routine. Life seemed "jerky and out of synchronization,"
and he felt bombarded by the sheer presence of television, radio,
doorbells, ringing telephones, even normal conversation. Life now
seemed hectic, chaotic, and overwhelming. He now had to make
simple decisions, like when to eat or go to bed.

Huey hit the street, visiting people in the community, visiting bars where he had done a lot of recruiting. "Everywhere I got
the same reaction: people wondered why I had come back to
them. I explained that neither news reporters nor television cameras had got me out of prison; the people had freed me, and I had
come back to thank them and be with them."[97]

The Black Panther Party had grown in his absence. When
Huey left, sometimes it was just the two of us raising money,
driving around in an old Oldsmobile. By the time he was
released, however, we were an organization that was now forty-

seven states strong. What started out as a small regional political party had since erupted into a worldwide cultural and political phenomenon. Once Huey was released, there was barely
time for adjustment.

From day one of his release, Huey was thrown into the fire.
Black Panther lives, caught in the clutches of the American court
system, hung in the balance. Bobby Seale and Ericka Huggins,
widow of slain comrade John Huggins, and six other BPP comrades were in jail in Connecticut, awaiting trial on first-degree
murder charges. (Bobby and Ericka were eventually tried separately, both cases ending in a hung jury. The state of Connecticut
declined to try them again and dismissed the charges.) Comrades
George Jackson, Fleeta Drumgo, and John Cluchette—dubbed the
Soledad Brothers—were nearing trial on a charge of murdering a
prison guard. Los Siete de la Raza, a group of seven Chicanos
from San Francisco, were awaiting trial on charges of killing a
police officer. Plus, Huey had his own day in court looming, a
retrial of the Frey case. He was looking at possibly a dozen years
or more in prison.

"There was major stuff going on," recalled Audrea Jones-
Dunham, a Black Panther leader from the Boston chapter.

David had announced on Juneteenth [a June 19 celebration to
commemorate the end of slavery] 1970 that we were going to
have two constitutional conventions, with a planning session in
Philadelphia in September and the convention in Washington,
DC, in December. In the midst of that, Huey Newton was
released from prison, and he had to get into the groove of all
the stuff that was going on at the time. When he got out of jail,
Bobby and Ericka were in jail. There was the New York 21.
There were all kinds of things going on. There was already
momentum, and Huey had to become part of that momentum,

and then he had to assert the leadership that had been through other people.[98]

To Huey, his own pending case seemed insignificant com-pared with the pressures the government was bringing to bear on party members. "I was facing only thirteen more years in jail, but my comrades, every one of them, faced death."[99]

As events stacked up, the FBI was still heavily involved with COINTELPRO operations. Immediately after his release, Huey stepped into the crosshairs of a vicious psychological war. The FBI wasted no time releasing a memorandum to their field offices across the country instructing them to directly target Huey. "To demythicize [sic] Newton," the memorandum read, "to hold him up to ridicule, and to tarnish his image among BPP members can serve to weaken BPP solidarity and disrupt its revo-lutionary and violent aims. [COINTELPRO actions] should have the 3-pronged effect of creating divisiveness among BPP mem-bers concerning Newton, treat him in a flippant and irreverent manner, and insinuate that he has been cooperating with police to gain his release from prison."[100]

In immediate response, the New York FBI office fired off three phony letters aimed at discrediting Huey, as did the Philadelphia FBI office to the Philadelphia BPP office, attacking Huey and mak-ing up stories about food, clothing, and drugs stolen from survival programs. They fabricated a story that the national office had con-sidered closing the Philadelphia chapter. Two other directives were mailed concerning Angela Davis—one from the Chicago FBI office written in pseudo ghetto-speak to *Ebony* magazine ridiculing Huey, and a hand-scrawled letter to the *Village Voice* alleging that Angela Davis was "set up" by Huey, the "fingerman," portraying Huey as a federal snitch. Another letter, mailed by the San Francisco FBI field office to the New York BPP offices was even more salacious:

Brothers,

I am employed by the State of California and have been close to Huey Newton while he was in jail.

Let me warn you that this pretty nigger may very well be working for pig Reagon [sic]. I don't know why he was set free but I am suspicious. I got this idea because he was in jail like the trustees get. He had a lot of privacy most prisoners don't get. I don't think all his private meetings were for sex. I am suspicious of him.

Don't tell Newton too much if he starts asking you questions—it may go right back to the pigs. Power to the People.[101]

FBI headquarters commended the field agents for their resourcefulness ("positive results achieved"), yet urged them to "take precautions to ensure letters cannot be traced to [the] Bureau." The audacity of the FBI was limitless. Records of large bank accounts, withdrawals, and check stubs were sent to supporters. Huey was supposedly living high on the hog. The FBI sent out letters accusing Huey of being an informer.

For the first three months after his release, Huey lived at the Berkeley apartment of two of his supporters, attorney Alex Hoffman and KPFA Pacifica Radio personality Elsa Knight Thompson. Within days, several telephone company employees installed a white box on the telephone pole opposite the apartment. Another employee sat on the pole for several hours. In addition, Hoffman noted, there was a constant presence of the Berkeley Police Department stationed in front of the building next door, as marked and unmarked patrol cars brazenly tailed Hoffman and Huey around town.

Upon his release, Huey began instituting his own signature changes to the party. He set up the Ideological Institute in Oakland in order to train our more advanced comrades by introducing us to the dialectical materialist method of thinking, the guiding principle of which was that contradiction is the ruling principle of the universe. Party members from all chapters would attend classes to study intercommunalism, a higher level of consciousness and a further development of Marxist/Leninist theory.

Before his imprisonment, not many of our Black Panther comrades outside of Oakland knew or had even met Huey. To many, he was an icon, a symbol, a man on a poster, sitting in a wicker chair and clutching a rifle and a spear. So I toured with Huey, and as we traveled from city to city, he began to understand the depth of the movement that had blossomed while he had been incarcerated. The party was going through tumultuous change. Huey needed to meet his supporters face-to-face, and they needed to meet him.

"When he first came out of prison," Audrea Jones-Dunham recalled, "and he stepped into this incredible amount of activity, it was a real learning curve. But then, of course, as we know now what we didn't know at the time, at the same time he was being fed this information from the COINTELPRO folks. So while he's coming into contact with all these people, it had to be pretty difficult. I felt that he really trusted David. From my interactions with the two of them, it seemed he relied on what David was telling him."[102]

This was the period of the changing of the guard and totally turning the leadership of the organization over to Huey. Making that transformation was a difficult period. Huey felt totally overwhelmed, because he didn't know most of the members. He didn't have a clue as to what was happening in the Boston, New York, and Chicago chapters. All of a sudden Huey was inundated with the possibility of all these people in the party who had their own agendas, not to mention the informants. It was a difficult time for Huey to try to understand that stuff. In his travels, he observed the work of a dozen communities, evidence that the Black Panthers had built a strong network. But in Huey's eyes, much more needed to be done.

While out on the road in New Haven, Connecticut, working on behalf of Bobby and Ericka, Huey met with Erik Erikson, a renowned author and professor of developmental psychology at Harvard University. Erikson was a legend, an artist and teacher in the late 1920s, who had met Anna Freud. He is generally credited for widening psychoanalytic theory's interest in social change, racial tensions, changing sexual roles, and other social, environmental, and cultural factors. Erikson's son Kai, a sociologist and master at Yale University's Trumbull College and a fervent admirer of Huey, arranged an epochal meeting between the two world historical figures, Huey Newton and Erik Erikson. The meeting of the minds would take the form of a three-day seminar attended by two faculty members and fourteen Yale students, eight white and six black. The sit-down was held in the library of Yale University Press. Afterward, Erikson published a book, *In Search of Common Ground*, a transcription of Huey and Erikson's kinetic discussions.

"They saw eye to eye," remembered noted playwright and author Donald Freed. He went on to say:

> Erik Erikson had been a high school dropout, and then he had gone on to become Freud's greatest inheritor, the greatest psychologist in the world. So with his son, a well-known sociologist at Yale when I was at New Haven, we put together this dialogue. The hottest ticket that was ever put together was Huey Newton and Erik Erikson. When they would take a break, Huey and Erik would be standing all by themselves, the two dropouts, sipping a brandy and talking. The other intellectuals—the toughs of the tender Left, the guerillas with tenure, and the various students and professors—were all sort of looking [over] at them, as if they were creatures in the zoo.[103]

Huey recalled his meeting with the famous psychologist:

I liked Erikson very much, and we got along despite some trouble communicating during the first two days of the seminar. At first we repeatedly talked past each other, and the students talked such madness that they impeded our conversations. They had come to hear revolutionary slogans and violent rhetoric and were not satisfied with anything less than absolute solutions to the problems besetting society.

Then the talks centered on Black Panther ideology, and Erickson saw the validity of the Black Panther approach. He pointed out that two people can love each other only when both have dignity. If one person is without dignity, then the relationship is something else. He brought many insights to our talks, drawing on his early days as a student of Freud and his studies of Gandhi and Martin Luther. Although there were moments of frustration, I think we both learned much from each other.[104]

"These conversations," Erikson wrote, "took place at a time when the various participants could not step away from the historical currents in which they were immersed, and this had an important influence on the tone of the proceedings."[105]

Putting Huey on the road and introducing him to the Black Panther membership often meant shattering people's expectations of who Huey really was and what he had to say. "Everybody was so excited to hear Huey P. Newton speak at Boston College," Audrea Jones-Dunham recalled.

People saw him as the baddest in the world. Then you have this guy come up with this intellectual discussion. He actually spoke in Latin. We had a lot of folks from Roxbury who came out to

BC [Boston College] to hear this speech. We had a lot of damage control to deal with after, because it wasn't what everyone's expectation was.

That was an important shift in the organization. We had actually cut down on the rhetoric, anyway. We hadn't quite taken the leap to the more abstract, theoretical stuff. It was much easier to break down Mao Tse-Tung to someone than intercommunalism and dialectical materialism.[106]

Upon his return, the Black Panther Party's central committee decided that, once home, Huey needed seclusion and security. Black leaders, particularly Black Panthers, were being routinely gunned down or jailed. With the FBI still operating in high gear, the committee feared that unless the strictest security precautions were maintained, Huey would meet the same fate as the other important black leaders of the sixties—Malcolm X, Martin Luther King, and Fred Hampton. Many of the BPP's top public leadership had either been killed, jailed, or exiled while Huey was in prison. Finding safe conditions in which Huey could carry out party work was a priority.

In October of 1970 Huey moved into a two-bedroom apartment on the top of 1200 Lakeshore Boulevard, a high-rise apartment building in a middle-class Oakland neighborhood located on the outskirts of downtown Oakland. His new home overlooked the Lake Merritt parklands. Also in plain view was the Alameda County Courthouse, where Huey had been jailed and tried. His apartment, 25A, was located at the end of a row of units situated on the twenty-fifth floor. It was both secluded and centrally located, but most important, it had front-door lobby security. Huey would be safer and left alone, or so we thought.

Though it was dubbed "the throne," 1200 Lakeshore was no fancier than any two-bedroom hotel room. "The penthouse was nice, but it was sparse," recalled George Robinson, a former Oakland Black Panther. "There wasn't a lot of furniture. It wasn't fancy inside. In fact, it was cold. Huey didn't like a lot of heat. He perspired, so he had his shirt off a lot. It wasn't cluttered. You'd be surprised how little furniture he had. It was very simple, a table and chairs, a stereo. It was the first time I heard 'The Harder They Come' by Jimmy Cliff."[107]

Rent was set at $650 a month, and contrary to allegations by the FBI, press, and law enforcement, it wasn't paid from the party's treasury. Rather, a group of rich white friends, admirers, and sympathizers, some wishing to be of help to the movement, guaranteed the cash flow so that Huey would have a place to study, run the party, and write four books "away from the hubbub of party offices and houses." Among those who contributed were author Donald Freed, inventors Herbert and Shirley Magidson, economist Stanley Sheinbaum, and especially, one of Huey's closest friends and confidants, film producer Berton Schneider. Schneider was well known as the producer of the hit movie *Easy Rider*. He was also involved in projects ranging from the creation of the TV rock 'n' roll band the Monkees to Peter Bogdanovich's classic film *The Last Picture Show*. As Donald Freed recalled:

> Quite a few in the Hollywood community tried to get active after the [Watts] rebellions of 1965, Operation Bootstrap, and so forth. At that time, by coincidence, Shirley Douglas was the daughter of Tommy C. Douglas, the Canadian revolutionary and head of the New Democratic Party. Shirley was a complete political person, who had married actor Donald Sutherland. With Shirley, there were a lot of women involved, like Jane Fonda, Vanessa Redgrave, Jeanne Moreau, Jean Seberg, Mia Farrow, and Shirley MacLaine. Then through Sutherland, there was

Elliot Gould and Barbra Streisand. These people were open to talking with the Panthers, hearing about their free clinics, free breakfasts, free legal aid, free visits to the prisons, the safety improvements, and the protection of their community.[108]

Although Huey's association with Hollywood would last until his final days, seclusion and security at Apartment 25A, 1200 Lakeshore, certainly wouldn't. By March of 1971 the FBI had bugged thirteen Black Panther Party offices, including Oakland, San Francisco, the Bronx, New Haven, and Chicago, including Huey's new residence there. The order came from the very top. The bureau had a field day sabotaging Huey's new apartment.

On November 20, 1970, FBI director J. Edgar Hoover requested official authorization from attorney general John Mitchell for "a microphone surveillance and a telephone surveillance at apartment 25A, 1200 Lakeshore, Oakland." Hoover considered it "likely that high-level party-conferences would be held at this location," and he reminded Mitchell "that existing telephone surveillance on certain Black Panther offices, all of which have been authorized by you, have provided extremely valuable information on Black Panther Party involvement in foreign matters and plans for violent acts against top officials of this country and foreign diplomatic personnel." Hoover's request concluded with the observation that "trespass will be involved with respect to the microphone surveillance."[109]

After John Mitchell approved the operation, local San Francisco FBI agents acted by hiring 1200 Lakeshore's engineer to help them break into Huey's apartment in order to bug the premises. (Later, in 1977, the apartment manager revealed the engineer's role in the break-in to Black Panther Party attorneys. He had long resented the poor job done of replastering the apartment, all after the "bug" had been installed.) After the bug was planted, the FBI's next chore was to put together a thorough press campaign about Huey's "plush penthouse" lifestyle. When the *San Francisco Examiner* ran an FBI-sponsored story on the front page, the San Francisco FBI field office anonymously mailed copies of the story to BPP offices across the United States and to three BPP contacts in Europe, as well as to newspapers in communities where Black Panther activities were active.

The FBI's "plush penthouse" campaign wasn't anything new. They had attempted to discredit Martin Luther King Jr. much the same way with an FBI-planted article that accused King of patronizing "the plush Holiday Inn Motel, white owned, operated, and almost exclusively patronized" while organizing a boycott of white businesses by black citizens during the Memphis sanitation strike of 1968.

The FBI continued with another fictitious letter about money, supposedly from a national Black Panther Party officer, sent to party chapters in Baltimore, Boston, Chicago, Indianapolis, Los Angeles, New Haven, New York, Philadelphia, and Washington, DC. Mailed from Oakland, the message scurrilously attacked both Huey and me for supposedly misappropriating BPP funds, saying: "Comrades: Too many of your leaders have now turned this movement into something to line their own pockets and have little regard for the man on the street selling the *Black Panther*. Ask the members of your chapter coming to the national where the Comrade Commander and the Chief of Staff live. Huey Newton lives miles from another nigger and you'll never find him in National Headquarters. If you're lucky you can see him buying drinks for white freaks in Oakland supper clubs."[110]

Quite a few observers of the party, on both the left and the right, were taken in by the FBI's stories and accusations. They expressed outrage that Huey would indulge in such bourgeois comforts and amenities. Yet, most of the allegations didn't wash with the black community, nor did they carry much credence with party membership and insiders. After Huey's home address was published on nearly every front page of every major paper in America, many of his friends in Oakland urged him to leave the city for his own safety. Huey refused. The address "1200 Lakeshore, 25A" would soon become familiar to a variety of nut-cases, cops, and bounty hunters as the FBI stepped up their sur-veillance measures even further.

The FBI was not content to leave things solely to chance. Beginning April 1, 1971, and for months thereafter, the FBI paid $540 per month for the rental of the apartment adjacent to the one in which Huey was living. There the FBI placed an under-cover agent with instructions to keep Huey under surveillance, as well as monitoring electronic eavesdropping devices. Hardly a day passed when Huey was not followed or observed by a plain-clothes detective on all of his travels to and from the apartment.

On November 18, 1972, Huey's wife, Gwen Fountaine Newton, surprised a squad of undercover cops ransacking their apartment when she returned unexpectedly. "After leaving the apartment with Huey," Gwen recalled, "I returned with Huey's niece, Deborah, because I had forgotten something. I entered to find three men robbing the apartment. They held me at gun-point. Their pistols had silencers on them. Huey's documents and other papers were strewn about on the floor."[III]

Eventually the FBI's raids and tactics bordered on the bizarre. A few months later, on a Saturday morning in February 1973, during the wee hours of the morning, a squad of Oakland cops staged a raid and a shootout on the twenty-fifth floor out-side of Huey's apartment. The operation was unsuccessful. The police were hoping to draw Huey out of his apartment, where he could then be shot. Nevertheless, the press reported news of gunfire at the "swank apartment...next door to Black Panther leader Huey Newton."

Nineteen seventy-one was a turbulent year of highs and lows. The BPP's survival programs and Ideological Institute were finally in motion, pushing the guns and the violent rhetoric into the party's background. The party was moving forward under Huey's vision. At the end of May, the charges against Bobby and Ericka were dropped. After a brief delay of legal paper shuffling, both were returned to Oakland. Huey later wrote about his reunion with Bobby:

> Seeing Bobby again was a moving experience. We had not been together on the streets of Oakland since August 1967, in the early, uncertain days of the Black Panther Party. Now, almost four years later, we were once again on the block with our comrades. We had gone through a great deal of danger and pain during those years, but we had survived, stronger and more committed than ever. Everything we had suffered had been worth the price. And during that time the Party had grown from a local group to a network of branches and chapters in North America and abroad. Many of our noble warriors had been cut down, and other early members had shown themselves unable to withstand the pressures of a protracted revolutionary struggle, but we were happy to be together again.[112]

Then came the setbacks. While the district attorney of Alameda County moved closer to retrying Huey for the Frey shooting, I was convicted on charges stemming from the shootout that killed Li'l Bobby Hutton. The district attorney himself conducted his prosecution in front of an all-white jury. In July, just like Huey, I was processed in Vacaville and sent to Folsom Prison to serve more than four years. More sobering events would soon transpire. No sooner had I begun serving my term than we turned our attention to George Jackson's upcoming trial. George was falsely accused of killing a prison guard at San Quentin. Two days before his trial was to begin, he was shot and killed by his enemies as he attempted to save his brothers in a San Quentin cellblock from being massacred by guards.

George Jackson's death was a tragic setback, both on a personal and political level for Huey. Huey loved and admired George's courage. It was Huey's prison communications with George that not only brought George to the party, but also helped make prison and prison reform a cornerstone program of the party. Huey "met" George in prison in 1967. Not personally, but through his ideas and writings. He was in Soledad while Huey served his time at the California Men's Colony. George was a legend throughout the prison system. Huey got the word out through the prison grapevine that he wanted George to join the Black Panther Party. He was eventually made a member of the People's Revolutionary Army with the rank of general and field marshal. Huey put him in charge of prison recruiting. "He inspired prisoners, whom I later encountered, to put his ideas into practice and so his spirit became a living thing. Although George's body has fallen, his spirit goes on, because his ideas live. And we will see that these ideas stay alive, because they'll be manifested in our bodies and in these young Panthers' bodies, who are our children."[113]

For the last years of his life, including some of the eight years he spent in solitary confinement, the party helped sustain and support George Jackson in his struggle to raise the consciousness of black inmates as he studied the works of Marx, Lenin, and Mao. His legal troubles continued in January 1970, when a guard at Soledad State Prison shot three black inmates dead on the yard. After a grand jury ruled the killings were justifiable homicide, a white guard was found beaten to death. George Jackson and two other inmates, the Soledad Brothers, were charged. His articles appeared frequently in the *Black Panther* newspaper. Yet, according to Huey, "he knew his days were numbered and was prepared to die as a true believer in revolutionary suicide." George Jackson was shot under murky circumstances that supposedly involved an escape attempt, a defense attorney, and the smuggling of a gun inside a wig; the same gun was traced back to the FBI's very own COINTELPRO program.

In a letter to Huey, comrade George Jackson warned, "Try to memorize my handwriting, that is how all messages will come in the future (if we have a future)."

After the first Frey trial, Huey escaped the gas chamber by beating a murder rap in favor of a manslaughter conviction. But it was during his second Frey trial that the Alameda County prosecution's case continued to further unravel. Lowell Jensen, the first prosecutor in the case, had become district attorney, and an assistant DA named Donald Whyte now argued for the prosecution. Whyte deviated little from the strategy of the first trial.

But prosecuting Huey a second time around wouldn't prove to be so easy. During officer Herbert Heanes's testimony, it came out that the law book Huey had carried at the shooting scene was now evidence lost. Dell Ross, the driver who was supposedly kidnapped and carjacked, was put on the stand by the prosecution. Recanting his previous testimony of the first trial, and going back to his original and damaging grand jury testimony, Ross had been hidden and supported by the prosecution. His appearance was a complete surprise, throwing Charles Garry temporarily off his guard. However, Ross self-destructed on the stand when, during a bizarre moment under cross-examination, Ross asked the court, "Is there anybody here who believes in the truth? Would you raise your hand?" Ross's credibility was crushed as trial two ended in a hung jury, eleven to one favoring Huey's conviction.

Trial number three, under prosecutor Whyte, again featured the same stable of witnesses to face Garry in the courtroom. It was the same tired old show all over again—prosecutor Donald Whyte, Herbert Heanes, Henry Grier, Dell Ross, and their supporting cast.

First Heanes broke down, bringing up the possibility that there likely could have been a third man on the scene, a man who had on a light tan jacket and wasn't a passenger in the Volkswagen that Huey and Gene McKinney were riding in. Then came the *coup de grace:* although Grier had originally told the police and then testified that he was within ten feet of the incident, his supervisor had other evidence. According to transit records and the driver's own time schedule, it was impossible for Henry Grier to have been at his required route checkpoints *and* at the scene of the Frey shooting simultaneously.

Once again, Charles R. Garry had scored an impossible victory.

Garry was considered one of the lions of the Left. Muckraker and author Upton Sinclair was his hero. Garry had run for Congress in 1948 on the Progressive ticket. Although he claimed he was never a member of the Communist Party, he was a joiner of organizations and considered himself a Panther. Away from the courtroom Garry was an eccentric. His former law clerk, Pat Richartz, provided the following description of him:

> When I met him in 1968 he had on three shades of navy blue and a red tie. He was color-blind, but his favorite color was red. He could see red, and sometimes he'd wear red from head to toe—same thing with navy blue. Sometimes he'd wear an orange-red shirt with a pink-red tie. He mail-ordered his

clothes, God knows from where. I thought he was the most ridiculous-looking person I had ever seen in my life. He looked like a gangster. He would drive up in a huge Ford LTD. Whatever the biggest car was, Charles had it, and usually it was black and white, like a police car. He used to tool around, speeding everywhere and not paying any attention to anything.[114]

At the hearing on December 15, prosecutor Lowell Jensen appeared in court. Huey had not seen him since his bail hearing during the summer of 1970. After the judge opened the proceedings, Jensen rose to speak, saying he had never thought he would see the day when he would be in court asking for a dismissal of Huey's case. The judge looked at him.

"Are you asking for a dismissal in the interest of justice?" he asked, using the proper legal terminology.

According to Edward Keating, Jensen replied, "No, it's not in the interest of justice, because it's not just. I didn't think I would ever have to say these words, but I think the case should be dismissed."

In another sense, Jensen was right. Justice had not been served. Huey had spent nearly three years in prison. His family was ripped apart. The party spent thousands of dollars on defense—money and energy that would have been much better spent on the party's survival programs. At last Huey was back among his comrades on the streets among the people of Oakland, working to return the party to its original purpose of serving the people.

CHAPTER 14

THE HUEY I FIRST MET

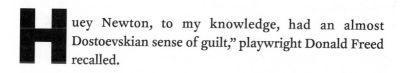uey Newton, to my knowledge, had an almost Dostoevskian sense of guilt," playwright Donald Freed recalled.

I remember once, after a long writing session, Huey was drinking. I didn't drink much, but he was drinking. Huey was not able to handle liquor, stimulants, or chemicals of any kind, in my opinion. He had a volatile temperament, a tremendously sensitive temperament. That's why, in prison, in some ways, he flourished. He worked out and he was reading books. He had a nervous system that the world impinged on with very great intensity. Some people are cursed and blessed with that. You know, artists and others have that kind of extra sensitivity. He started to tell me something. He said, "I'm a terrible person. You don't know." Part of his concept of a great leader was of a great sinner.[115]

With the FBI escalating their surveillance after the formation of a new super agency, the Drug Enforcement Agency (DEA), and with a drug-dealing FBI informant planted in the apartment next door, Huey attempted to maintain as normal a home life as anyone could expect under such circumstances. Out of prison, and now a permanent fixture on Richard Nixon's White House enemies list, Huey was now living with Gwen V. Fountaine.

According to her sister Demetra Gayle, Gwen "grew up some of the time in Berkeley, Southern California, Chicago, and in San Francisco's North Beach. We moved around." Fountaine married young, had two children, the first at age fifteen, and was divorced by age seventeen. After breaking up with her first husband in Southern California, she went to the Watts Skills Center, where she took up training as a legal secretary. Returning to Northern California, she settled into another relationship. But rather than start a new family and have more children, she joined the Black Panther Party in the winter of 1969, which triggered the end of her new relationship. I introduced Gwen to the party. During that time she was working for an attorney in Berkeley and had taken an avid interest in working with the *Black Panther* newspaper.

As soon as Huey came home from the California Men's Colony, I knew he needed a woman. Somebody strong. Melvin Newton and I immediately thought of Gwen and her commitment to the party and the movement. She was perfect for him— bright, intelligent, and beautiful. She was nineteen when she first met Huey. Obviously it worked, because Huey and Gwen were together for twelve years and shared many adventures.

Gwen kept Huey together. She was well organized and managed a nice home for the two of them. Living with Gwen, Huey was especially well dressed and coiffed. Later, she took an interest in interior design. She shopped and kept house immaculately. She could cook a gourmet meal. She organized Huey's life so that everything was easier for him. In a way, Gwen was Huey's bodyguard. She could be around important people and fit in, talk, and be gracious. But at times there was tension between Huey's and

Gwen's families. Because of disparate backgrounds, Huey's family, though supportive, tended to be more protective.

The tension between the two families was standard fare, as it is for any new couple that gets together. The only difference was that it involved a major figure in the human rights and black liberation movement.

George Robinson, a decorated Vietnam veteran and an Oakland Black Panther who would later sit on the party's central committee, remembers Huey's family: "Huey's mom was like my grandmother. She was sweet; she always wanted to make sure I was okay. She always asked about my grandmother and Louisiana, and when I was going back. We talked about the food, and she would cook some of the foods we talked about. I used to drive her to doctors' appointments and stuff like that. She was a nice person. She wasn't political. I would call Mr. Newton more political than she was. I think Huey got kindness from his mother and a toughness from his father."[116]

Under Huey's direction, the complexity of the BPP's survival programs and services soon began to expand. With the school and clinics in operation, the party was shifting and getting interesting in a different way. Huey was having people read different books and having discussion groups. People were starting to get healthier, starting to branch out in some new ways. They were doing unusual exercises at the school, like Thai Chi.

Ericka Huggins, by this time out of prison after her and Bobby's acquittal in Connecticut, was another of Huey's close comrades. Upon her return to Oakland, she took an avid interest in the BPP's Oakland Community School. "The Huey I first met," Ericka recalled, "was one of the most visionary and hopeful but pragmatic people when it came to faith in humanity."[117]

According to Huggins, the Black Panther Party was founded on the principle of humanity for all people, not just for blacks.

Huey's way of organizing the Black Panther Party was, in Huggins's words, "theatrical and creative." Huey didn't let city officials or black leaders tell him what to do or how to do it. Black Panthers were generally young, with a median age of eighteen to nineteen years old. For instance, when Huggins first heard about the Black Panther Party, she was barely eighteen years old, having left her junior year of college on the East Coast to move to California to become a part of Huey Newton's defense committee.

> We were all just doing it the best way we knew how—totally organic. It created itself as it went along until the Communists and the Socialists thought we were out of our minds. "What do you mean, you're going to feed people? What do you mean, you're patrolling the police? That makes no sense according to [our] ideological principles."
>
> But Huey didn't care. He was about creating a whole new world while the paradigm of the old world was still in place. So part of the story is that he was driven; part of the story is that he was driven crazy; and part of the story is that he was crazy and he was driven. The people closest to him knew it and tolerated it because what he was doing was so magnificent in the beginning.[118]

When Ericka was released from prison in 1971, she became a part of the writing team for the *Black Panther* newspaper, the Intercommunal News Service. The Oakland Community School had started in 1969 and was still in operation when she returned to Oakland. The schools started in two houses in North Oakland, eventually moving into another building, "like a huge house," Ericka recalled, "dormitory style, in East Oakland." By 1971 Huey created a corporation called the Educational Opportunities Corporation, from which he would fund the school.

The school was still operating in East Oakland, and Ericka was one of its teachers. When the director of the school left in 1973, Huey asked Ericka to take over. She became a director of the school and remained in that position until almost 1982. She was there until the end. "I can see now my own craziness in doing that, and my own idealism," she later said.[119]

The school eventually found a home on Sixty-first Avenue and East Fourteenth Street. Although it was geared for elementary students, there were also teen and senior programs set up that were interconnected.

According to Ericka, the school was Huey's design. Elaine Brown's mother went to Huey, complaining about the prospect of a poor education that her granddaughter, not yet school age, would be getting in public school. She assured Huey that many of the party's parents and grandparents held the same view.

Huey originally named the school the Intercommunal Youth Institute. As his vision for the school, based in the teachings of intercommunalism and dialectical materialism, began to unfold, he found instant support from the black community—not just from party members who staffed the school, but from families and teachers in the neighborhood communities as well. By 1973 many public school teachers in Oakland were willing to quit their public school jobs and work for a far lower salary. Soon, after applying for some grants, the school began to receive monies from the federal government and the California State Department of Education. In addition to providing an education, the Oakland Community School also fed hungry children. Huggins explains:

> We learned through the breakfast program, which prompted the United States government to do their own free breakfasts and lunch programs, that children sitting in a classroom who

wanted to learn couldn't learn if they weren't nourished. They had no fuel.

Over time, we had some of the best cooks and meals. We looked at what would be fuel and what would be junk. Every year we'd revamp the diet. We taught meditation and hatha yoga. We did all kinds of creative and innovative things that nobody else was doing, and many great souls came to that school.[120]

The school attracted scores of education administrators and curious visitors, including Cesar Chavez, Rosa Parks, James Baldwin, Richard Pryor, and Maya Angelou. Springing from Huey's approach to dialectical materialism and intercommunalism, the school's motto was "The world is your classroom." Visitors expecting a storefront school were surprised. Children from the first through the sixth grades were encouraged to question authority and the process. They were taught math, sciences, and arithmetic through pre-algebra. The students also studied political science, current events, dance, exercise, Spanish, art, music, and—rather than calling it English—composition and creative writing. The school made progress, as teens were taken off the street as a result of this new kind of alternative education. But running the school was demanding. Party members were included among the staff of thirty-five people. Sections A through E replaced grades. Students and classes were distributed by skill level rather than age. It was a student-centered education. Contrary to Huey's own past experiences as a schoolboy, the teachers at the Oakland Community School seemed secondary to the curriculum, which is why Huey loved it. "We never demeaned students, stuck them in corners, hit them, cussed or yelled at them," Ericka said. "If they were wrong, if they stole something, or got into a fight, we'd make them stand out in this open courtyard and do the hatha yoga tree pose, which required balance and focus in order to do it. They had to learn to breathe, and once they could do it, they would come back, ready to pay attention."[121]

The California State Department of Education sent representatives to the Oakland school to check things out. One visit was from one William Whiteneck, assistant superintendent of the Oakland Public Schools. Upon his arrival, a group of second graders approached him.

"Hello, what's your name?" one of the children asked.

"William Whiteneck."

"Is your neck white?"

"Well, I guess it is."

One little boy asked, "Can I give you a hug?"

Whiteneck, expecting a storefront radical, paramilitary school with guns, gave the school approval and recognition short of accreditation, satisfied that its curriculum was in keeping with what was required for an alternative education. Other school officials visited from all over the world, including Amsterdam, Switzerland, England, and throughout the United States, to size up Huey's new approach to education. The school was also invited to be part of the National Alternative School Association.

Ericka Huggins continued her fond recollections:

It was created from the blood, sweat, and tears of the members of the Black Panther Party. None of us got paid for it. We did it from a volunteer capacity. We were self-service oriented. No ideology, not the Democrats nor the Socialists nor the Communists, would have dreamed up that school. They weren't thinking about the whole human being. And Huey was.

Huey always had people around him who could carry out his ideas. He was more than a delegater. He intentionally had people around him who could see his vision and ground it. He couldn't ground it [himself]. Sometimes Huey would pace around a table. You had to be following the thread of what he was talking about to get what he was seeing. It was like he was seeing it full in his awareness.[122]

While I was still serving time in Folsom, the strains of pressure and self-doubt began to surface inside Huey. Inside his penthouse, or "the throne" as we called it, Huey was starting to feel like the walls of the world were closing in on him. Ericka recalled what he was like at the time:

When he would call me to his apartment, he wasn't loaded. That was the real Huey, the one in between the two extremes. Huey was depressed in his apartment. This wasn't when he was in his manic mode. This was [him] quiet, sitting on his bed, pondering what his life was about. I don't know how many people got to see him like this. I know that Gwen did. David wasn't around at that time. Huey couldn't talk to Bobby. Bobby annoyed the hell out of him, because Bobby couldn't keep up with him. It wasn't Bobby's fault. Very few people could follow his train of thought.

Huey pondered his doubts. What the hell had he done? He'd created an organization full of people depending on him. What was he supposed to do when things went wrong, or if the wrong direction was taken, or if people died?

"It was like being with a caged animal that didn't want out of the cage and didn't want anybody in the cage with him," Ericka said. "He had hyper vigilance for everybody in the room. He knew who was and wasn't clued in. You could get knocked over or slapped, depending upon the mood he was in. There were all these Hueys, and they all existed within one human being. I'm not saying that the Monday Huey was different from the Tuesday

Huey. It would just depend on which part was showing up. I got to know almost all of them."

Ericka's connection with Huey was spiritual. They talked about the school, meditation, or poetry. Here was someone who would merely listen, someone he could trust, and someone who wasn't going to report what he'd said to the six o'clock news.

As self-doubt settled in, Huey watched the world from the vantage point of his apartment. When you entered from the bottom floor, Huey saw you first on a TV monitor before you made it upstairs. Ericka recalled that seeing him look out the windows reminded her of a bird.

> Sometimes I would watch him stand at those big glass windows, and I had this feeling that he really wanted to take off. He felt caged, but he knew it was for his own good. Everybody and their brother wanted to kill him or get to him—the police, people who weren't well, and also curiosity seekers. But Huey was private, and, get this, a shy person. When a certain level of drugs was running, he wasn't shy at all. But there was a part of him, that when he would enter a room full of people he didn't know, he would want to hide. He was smart enough to have all different kinds of people around him who could meet all the different needs that he had. He'd have somebody like Elaine, who is gregarious, outgoing, who would engage him in conversation. It was like some kind of strange classroom. I didn't like it, because the energy felt so dangerous all the time. Life-threatening.[123]

When Huey visited the Oakland Community School, he couldn't get two steps into the building before the children surrounded him and hugged him. He spoke to each one. Inside the school, he felt safe. Among the presence of children, no one could harm him.

CHAPTER 15

"WILL YOU DIE
WITH ME TONIGHT?"

In between his second and third Frey appeal trials, Huey made a trip to the People's Republic of China in late September 1971. It preceded Richard Nixon's official visit by five months. Still out on bail, with no travel restrictions and using a valid passport, Huey flew from New York to Canada, then on to Tokyo before making it into China. Huey recalled:

> Police agents knew of my intentions, and they followed me all the way, right to the Chinese border. Two comrades, Elaine Brown and Robert Bay, went with me. I have no doubt that we were allowed to go only because the police believed we were not coming back. If they had known I intended to return, they probably would have done everything possible to prevent the trip. The Chinese government understood this, and while I was in China, they offered me political asylum, but I told them I had to return, that my struggle is in the United States of America.[124]

Huey and his bags were thoroughly searched in Canada, Tokyo, and Hong Kong. However, entry into China was another story. When he arrived at the free territory, where security was supposed to be tight and everyone suspect, "the comrades with the red stars on their hats" asked Huey and his comrades for their passports. After seeing that they were in order, customs officials simply bowed and asked if the luggage was theirs. When they said *yes*, the officials simply replied, "You have just passed customs." No bags were opened upon arrival or departure.

Huey and his delegation spent ten days in China. They traveled to various parts of the country, visited embassies, factories, schools, and communes. At every stop and airport, large groups waving signs and Mao's Little Red Books greeted them, the same red books the early Black Panthers Party members used to sell for a dollar on university and college campuses in order to raise funds. "While there, I achieved a psychological liberation I had never experienced before," Huey wrote. "It was not simply that I felt at home in China; the reaction was deeper than that. What I experienced was the sensation of freedom—as if a great weight had been lifted from my soul and I was able to be myself, without defense or pretense or the need for explanation. I felt absolutely free for the first time in my life—completely free among my fellow men."[125]

Although Huey had been promised an opportunity to meet Chairman Mao, since he was not a head of state, in place of meeting with Mao, there were two meetings with Premier Chou En-lai. With Premier Chou and Comrade Chiang Ch'ing, the wife of Chairman Mao, Huey discussed "world affairs, oppressed people in general, and Black people in particular." There were also meetings along the way with working people and factory workers.

Traveling throughout China, Huey felt a sense of déjà vu. "It was a strange yet exhilarating experience," Huey wrote later, "to have traveled thousands of miles, across continents, to hear their words. For this is what Bobby Seale and I had concluded in our own discussions five years earlier in Oakland, as we explored ways to survive the abuses of the capitalist system in the Black communities in America. Without fully realizing it then, we were following Mao's belief that 'if you want to know the theory and methods of revolution, you must take part in revolution. All genuine knowledge originates in direct experience.' "[126]

Besides overseeing the progress of the party, monitoring the school, traveling overseas, and writing, Huey began to espouse political beliefs that were far ahead of their time, especially in the black community. For instance, he began to teach party members to become more spiritual and to show more tolerance toward issues like the women's movement, as well as becoming an early advocate of gay rights.[127] Ericka Huggins remembered:

> It wasn't just that gays and lesbians are okay. To Huey, it didn't make sense to oppress them any more than it made sense to oppress black people. Huey was one of the first role models for me when it came to intersecting all of the "isms." Huey believed you couldn't unhinge racism and leave homophobia hanging out in your being. Or you can't say you loved children and hate teenagers. You can't say you loved humanity and be abusive to women. It was all connected and he knew it, and that was how he *wanted* to live. Whether he was *able* to live that way was another story.[128]

Huey liked being around powerful women in the party, and many women ran and controlled the movement, especially after the government killed and jailed so many of our male members. He saw in Greek mythology that all of the goddesses were female until man, through his own aggression, overthrew femininity. He cited the references to Mother Nature. He called his theory the Genesis According to Science. He believed that all life began in the womb as female. According to Ericka:

Huey's main way of acknowledging human beings was almost androgynous. He was very masculine, yet he really enjoyed things that you would think were feminine. He loved beautiful things and beautiful people. He loved people to braid his hair. He couldn't even comb his hair. He loved how women were with each other. He would tell us all the time, "I wish men were that way." That's a part of Huey that a lot of people don't know. He wrote a poem that starts something like this, "I'm not a man or a woman. I'm a plain born child." That's remarkable for a man who paced around the table, sad at night because he'd taken on too much. One time he whispered, "I'm not an idealist anymore, Ericka. What am I supposed to do?" It wasn't really a question he needed or wanted me to answer. He just wanted someone to know that he had the question, telling it to someone who wouldn't get all dramatic about him asking it.[129]

In order to keep the party solvent, the survival programs going, and the schools open, and to retain nationwide momentum, Huey needed help and especially funding. From the earliest days of the party, he believed that the movement should include not only those who were politically motivated and enlightened, but also those who made their livings on the street. Huey prided himself on being in touch intellectually with the party members across the country, as well as cognizant of what was going on locally in the streets. He wasn't afraid to reach out to the streets, a move that eventually became a dangerous proposition.

Huey liked having the social prominence of knowing the pimps and women who worked and survived outside the system. He referred to the pimps as "men of leisure." In the community, players were often looked up to as the people who had the most control over their own lives and futures. Since their support mechanisms dealt in drug dealing and other forms of beating the system, like check and credit card scams or other methods of survival, Huey saw the pimps and the players as "illegitimate capitalists." At the same time, however, these were men with no real political power. All they possessed was an outward show of wellbeing that included flashy cars, fine clothes, and a stable of women. Yet these were the original heroes of our community, and from our earliest days spent on the street corners together, Huey and I dreamed of someday tapping into the economic power these men had and somehow harnessing that power toward a movement that would be beneficial to the entire black community.

Huey continued to take increasingly courageous and dangerous stands. Once he was released from prison, he immediately met with the pimps, street hustlers, and even the mafia gangsters. I remember one meeting with the Ward Brothers and other pimps up at the penthouse. No other political group had ever approached them, unless they were trying to put them in jail. Huey called a meeting to talk about organizing the pimps and the prostitutes into a union. He also emphasized that everybody, including pimps, hustlers, and drug dealers, ultimately had an obligation to help and contribute to the black community. "You've got to recognize us," Huey used to emphasize, "and help transform the community. You can't stand outside. If you're going to work in the community, you've got to make contributions to our programs."

We were approaching them in a way to make them part and parcel of our movement, serving the community they lived in, so that they might no longer be looked on as outcasts or as a predatory group. Their trade was still a by-product of capitalism. A woman selling her body is still one of the world's oldest professions. But our thrust was to organize an illegitimate economic resource, connect it to our community programs, and put the money into our programs, with the end result being more respect for a segment of the community that had been historically criticized as a pariah. Historically, it was similar to when members of the American trade unions embraced organized crime figures to help further their cause of workers being enlisted and represented by union organizations like the Brotherhood of Teamsters and the AFL-CIO.

These meetings were yet another example of Huey's fearlessness, no different than when he stood up to the cops, shotgun jacked and ready. During these meetings, especially when negotiating his demands, Huey always operated in a certain way. First, he'd put it to you nicely, and at the same time, he gave you a way out. Huey never put people in a position where they didn't at least have a dignified way out of a discussion. Then if you didn't agree or meet his demands or terms, he would talk about your suffering the political consequences. There could be a mobilized boycott or something more extreme. Huey was rarely harsh. He seldom cursed, if ever. He didn't scream, nor would he get overly emotional. Instead, he spoke very deliberately, looking you in the eye, saying what he meant. That would be it. Either you agreed, got Huey's message, or you took the way out.

Meetings like these weren't limited to pimps and street hustlers. Huey also dealt the same way with our own black middle class as well as the white power structure. He believed that the black middle class was also obligated to pay homage and respect to the Black Panthers, since it was the party members who were taking all the blows while opening up avenues of opportunity. Never before in the history of Oakland had a black man challenged the 110-year vice grip rule the Republicans and families like the powerful Knowlands, who counted the *Oakland Tribune* as part of their vast holdings, held over the city of Oakland.

*

While Huey drank alcohol all of his life, starting as a kid in the neighborhood drinking wine on the corner and especially while living at 1200 Lakeshore, he developed his taste for scotch and Courvoisier, the cognac of Napoleon Bonaparte. Jimmie's Lamp Post became one of Huey's favorite hangouts. Over the course of living at 1200 Lakeshore, he became more and more nocturnal. Whether it was out of loneliness or fear that the police could kick down his door at any time, Huey spent most of the day sleeping. At night he would work or hit the streets. By nightfall he began to frequent the speakeasies and after-hours joints in and around Oakland and Berkeley. In a way, Huey frequented these places partly for pleasure, but also, recalling his early days recruiting the very first Black Panther Party members, it was partially for business.

People from the ghetto ran the speakeasies and after-hours clubs. These establishments frequently sold cocaine and marijuana. There was some gambling going on, but most of the Oakland speakeasies became havens for drinking and drug use. When Huey hit a speakeasy, his entrance was dramatic.

George Robinson was a BPP bodyguard who ran with Huey. He recalls:

> What Huey wanted was for everybody who ran an establishment to give part of their earnings to the breakfast program, the school, or the other programs we had going in the community. Huey demanded that, and of course, there was resistance there for a minute until they found out they were in the wrong league.
>
> I never trusted any of them. We went there, and it was always exciting for me, because I didn't know what was going to happen. The people in the speakeasies knew who Huey was, and some people genuinely liked and respected him, while others were afraid of him. It was as simple as that....

We would go in, and Huey might cut all the music off. We'd block the door and wouldn't let anybody leave. Huey would get up on the bar and make a speech. He'd simply tell them what he wanted them to do. Then things would go back to normal.

Huey could walk into a place and he had that charisma about him. As a matter of fact, he was good at meeting girls. He would meet a girl he never saw in his life, and he'd start reading her. He would tell her about her sister or her aunt or somebody, and they would be friends. In reality, he didn't know anything about them. Huey was a reader. He could sit down, and when he wanted to, or if he had the energy, he could be with a person he had never met and tell them what was in their bedroom, for example. I had never seen anything like it. He did say that anybody could do it, but that it takes a lot of energy and something about using all [the powers of] your brain.[130]

Dating back to his days at Merritt College, Huey was well versed in the Pavlovian theory of conditioning and used to talk about applying Pavlovian theory to hypnosis. He sometimes hypnotized people at parties during his college days. He had one guy crawling on the floor, barking like a dog.

Before we'd go out, he'd ask me, "Well, George, will you die with me tonight?" If you said *no*, fine. If you hesitated, then he's gone. But if you said *yes*, then you couldn't blame him. Anything could happen. If you wound up in jail, you were lucky, because at least you didn't die.

Huey would give you the shirt off his back. He could also be a very violent person. I'll put it this way. He's the only person I know where there could be ten guys outside who wanted to fight him. Normally a person would run out the back door when they had a chance. Huey wouldn't. He'd go right out there and fight all ten of them by himself. He was fearless, but he would often tell me, "George, I'm a scared fighter. I'll hurt you first because I'm scared you're going to hurt me."[131]

Under the aegis of a "war on drugs," super agencies evolved and were created and staffed by former FBI officials like William C. Sullivan. The plan was to "criminalize" our revolution by consigning it to a second front of the "war on drugs." In 1973 under Richard Nixon's watch, the Drug Enforcement Agency was formed, employing four thousand agents and analysts, including fifty-three former CIA agents and a dozen counterintelligence experts from the military and other intelligence agencies. Some of the key designers of the newfound "narcotics intelligence plan" became Watergate household names—guys like G. Gordon Liddy, E. Howard Hunt, and Egil Krogh. These were the men, along with William Sullivan, who ran a series of newly formed intelligence agencies before becoming permanently associated with the Watergate burglaries. The Black Panther Party was one of the first organizations they targeted. It was well known that the White House kept Huey's name at the top of its enemy list, and one of the DEA's most striking early accomplishments would be a leading role in the frame-up and subsequent exile of Huey P. Newton.

Pinning a narcotics rap on the Black Panther Party was no easy task. The party had always taken a strong stand against heroin and other narcotics, with one of its slogans being "Capitalism Plus Dope Equals Genocide." As part of its new political action campaign in Oakland, the Black Panther Party had begun a campaign to stop heroin dealing in the community. A special target of party propaganda was the network of ghetto after-hours joints, which police allowed the privilege of dealing heroin. Federal narcotics agents, in concert with the FBI, took advantage of this situation to begin a covert "narcotics counterintelligence" operation against Huey and the Black Panther Party.

In addition to the after-hours clubs, there was a strong drug trade operating out of the port of Oakland. Oakland had become a key port of entry for "Golden Triangle" heroin smuggled out of Southeast Asia during the Vietnam War. According to Huey, "while the port was controlled by the gangster-ridden unions, heroin flowed smoothly into Oakland by ship and plane, sometimes stashed inside the body bags of dead American service men, and then was transferred to trucks for cross-country transport."[132]

In a systematic effort, the FBI set out not only to criminalize Huey's plan to fight heroin dealing in the black community, but also to derail his idea to unite the Oakland street hustlers and prostitutes. The FBI sent out the following memo: "The Black Panther Party (BPP) is a thing of the past and . . . Newton is now attempting to create an organization type of movement in the area to control among many things, dope pushers, prostitutes, and private social clubs . . . Newton has, to date, been very successful in creating a 'family' type organization under which he rules."[133]

A counterintelligence proposal was drawn up by a special group of FBI agents known as Squad C-4. Their plan was to link Huey with the narcotics traffic at a certain after-hours club in Berkeley. However, the Berkeley Police Department declined the squad's proposal. Undaunted, on September 11, 1973, Squad C-4 presented the Oakland Police with a similar proposal. Three days later, attorney Charles Garry received a very strange telephone call from OPD chief Charles Gain.

"A couple of my investigators," Chief Gain began, "met with an informant on the twelfth. He related to them a meeting on the evening of September eleventh at a home in the Berkeley Hills attended by a black businessman and twenty-five pimps and narcotics dealers. At this meeting, it was stated by this black businessman that because of an alleged shakedown by the Black Panthers of prostitutes and after-hours establishments in Oakland and Berkeley, an offer of ten thousand dollars was made to the twenty-five pimps and narcotic dealers to set up and kill Huey Newton."

Gain paused, holding his breath.

"Now," Chief Gain continued, "also some other informants, at least one of whom has been reliable in the past, have said the same thing—that the murder of Newton might take place this night or this weekend. Obviously it was my obligation to call you."

Garry took Gain's phone number. "I'll call you back after I talk to Huey."

"I just talked to Huey," Garry told Chief Gain when he called back. "He said that he thanks you personally for the concern and that he wants to tell you that as far as the party is concerned, there is no such thing as this shakedown. He said that the party's position is absolute abhorrence and negativism toward any form of drugs, and that could be one of the reasons for the threat—because the party is opposing these things and talking about it in the paper, in terms of running the narcotics dealers out of the community."

Garry also passed on Huey's suggestion that a couple of Huey's associates might be allowed weapon permits in order to guarantee his safety. According to Huey's private papers recounting the story, Gain politely declined the request.

Within the month, Squad C-4 reported their progress of the DEA-initiated "contract." "The big time dope dealers in the Berkeley and Oakland area are out to get Huey Newton ... and are planning a robbery of some sort and expect to get $10,000 out of it ... source will report any information concerning the planned job."[134]

Squad C-4's plan was to get more agencies and police departments involved and on board with their investigation. Initially they met resistance. Only the Berkeley police furnished C-4 with a list of names, and most were interrogated in an attempt to recruit potential witnesses against Huey. The assistant U.S. attorney in San

Francisco turned Squad C-4 down, claiming there was "no basis for prosecution." Meanwhile the Department of Alcohol, Tobacco, and Firearms (ATF) had just begun a new "antiterrorist" operation, and Oakland was chosen as a pilot city. After a thorough investigation, the ATF came up empty. "No pertinent information or evidence had been developed indicating violations." Still, the ATF eagerly joined in with the FBI's Squad C-4, enlisting two black vice and narcotic undercover cops from the OPD.

By January 1974 the FBI became impatient with Squad C-4's lack of results. Heiress Patricia Hearst had been kidnapped, and the Symbionese Liberation Army (SLA), which had accosted her, was already tapping into the agency's budgets and manpower, not to mention capturing the general public's attention. Still, Squad C-4 was encouraged when the Los Angeles SWAT team incinerated a group of SLA fugitives live on prime-time television. Perhaps a similar scenario, Huey wrote in his unpublished papers, "could be used for a final assault on Huey P. Newton and the Black Panther Party. The DEA could provide most of the necessities—planted evidence, witnesses, pay-off money, while the FBI could manipulate its 'assets' for media approval. And the Oakland police and Federal Alcohol, Tobacco and Firearms agents could provide the necessary 'crime' cover."

More and more, Huey was beginning to feel the net—and the noose—tightening around both his neck and that of the Black Panther Party.

Huey had practically the entire alphabet of law enforcement after him. The DEA, ATF, FBI, IRS, and OPD all joined forces. The ten-thousand-dollar "contract" issued by the East Bay chiefs of the narcotics trade wasn't the only threat against him. Huey and the BPP had become enemies of extremist groups. He certainly wasn't making friends among the radical underground. The SLA had added him to *their* hit list after the BPP openly condemned the organization for ruthlessly assassinating Oakland school superintendent Marcus Foster. When the cops raided an SLA safe house in the nearby East Bay suburban bedroom community of Concord, they found a diagram of 1200 Lakeshore attached to another diagram of Huey's apartment. Ominously scrawled across the front page were the words, "Warning: deadly shot."

A month later, another underground army of black extremists circulated a communiqué that "sentenced" Huey to "neutralization." Whether or not these organizations were provided with information, informants, or diagrams by the DEA or the FBI was never revealed. Huey and the party weren't quite sure which organization was more infiltrated by government operatives—the narcotics trade or the extremist underground. Besides, by this time the Black Panther Party was using a more conventional means to gain power, namely the democratic system and the ballot box. During the 1973 elections, Black Panther candidates were making strong inroads, with Bobby Seale receiving forty-three thousand votes in an Oakland mayoral runoff. In addition, the party was using its influence in the community by throwing their support behind several different candidates in addition to running their own slate.

Across the nation, the FBI had its hands full. While Patricia Hearst and the SLA staged a daring daytime bank robbery in San Francisco's Sunset district, BPP chapters were being systematically raided. Even with Richard Nixon soon on his way out of office, his law enforcement machine was still hard at work. On April 16, 1974, the day after Patty Hearst and her gang knocked off the branch of the Hibernia Bank in San Francisco, during the wee hours of the morning more than twenty-five Oakland and Berkeley police, armed with M-14s and sniper rifles, kicked down the door of the BPP's election campaign headquarters in

Oakland. They arrested fourteen people, charging them with possession of illegal weapons, drugs, and conspiracy. The members were held for thirty hours on a total bail of three hundred thousand dollars until they were released for lack of evidence. Nevertheless, a photograph was staged and provided to the media. The arsenal that was pictured was apparently pulled out of storage at police headquarters for PR purposes. However, lists of BPP and volunteer precinct workers and other campaign records that were seized during the raid were never returned. Similar raids also went down in Chicago, Dallas, and Houston.

On July 30, 1974, two plainclothes Oakland cops who were tailing Huey and his party comrade Robert Heard drew their revolvers and detained the two men inside the Fox restaurant, a popular Oakland nightclub. At first only Heard was arrested. Later, the police came back with no less than twenty reinforcements and arrested Huey and six other members on charges of conspiracy, assault with a deadly weapon, and resisting arrest. After being handcuffed, he suffered a concussion after being hit by the cops and was taken to the hospital. He remained in custody for two days on "federal hold" until the charges were eventually dropped. Less than a month later, the Oakland police again broke down the door of 1200 Lakeshore, 25A, ransacking the apartment for ten hours. When they left, windows were broken and parts of the carpet and flooring were ripped out. The official property receipt showed that the police had seized two pistols and a shotgun, an armful of clothing, and odds and ends such as a cigarette butt and a matchbook. Not listed on the report was a missing tape cassette on which Huey had recorded an altercation between him and a man named Preston Callins. Also missing from the receipt were legal documents and party files. Shortly after tearing Huey's apartment apart, another squad of police armed with shotguns raided Jimmie's Lamp Post in downtown

Oakland, arresting four BPP members on charges of marijuana possession and outstanding traffic warrants. Soon, the district attorney's office made a dramatic announcement. A warrant was out for Huey's arrest. Huey later described the situation:

> The signal that all this police attention was not just petty harassment came in the early morning hours. About 1:00 AM, Newton learned about the raids and had his attorney, Charles R. Garry, call the Oakland police to find out what was happening. After some prodding, the watch captain admitted to Garry that there was an assault charge lodged against the Black Panther leader. So about 2:30 AM, Garry drove Newton down to the Seventh Street police headquarters to be booked and bailed out. But once they arrived, Newton was taken into custody and held, informed that an additional felony assault charge was being filed, pending $42,000 bail.[135]

Nine BPP houses were put up as collateral for Huey's bail.

The police announced the new charge to the news media on a Saturday morning. Huey, they said, had flown into a rage over a trivial remark and pistol-whipped Preston Callins. What's more, eleven days earlier (on August 6, 1974) the Black Panther Party commander had casually stepped out of his car, exchanged a few insults with a seventeen-year-old black prostitute, then drew out a pistol and shot her in the head. She was still in a coma, according to the police, and not expected to live.

The shooting incident came entirely out of the blue. When the police were asked why they hadn't pressed charges for the shooting sooner, they simply replied, "We knew he'd be around." The evidence against Huey, a tan sports shirt and a pair of Wallabee shoes, was seized during the raid on 1200 Lakeshore.

To those on the outside, it all added up to one thing: according to the government, the police, and the news media, Huey was obviously guilty. Besides, there was the ten-thousand-dollar price on Huey's head, and the extremists had already disowned him. The party was comprised of known criminals and cop haters. The FBI's recent year of investigation and infiltration had paid off.

Huey was virtually surrounded. On August 23, for the first time ever, he failed to show up for a court appearance, answering to assault charges lodged against him for the beating of Preston Callins and the shooting of a young prostitute. Huey was gone. For the first time in seven years, the FBI lost track of his whereabouts. According to FBI reports, although his disappearance was an embarrassment, it was also both good and bad news for the law enforcement agencies that had spent so much time and money pursuing him. Huey later recounted in his private papers after reviewing the FBI files that the bad news for the FBI was that they were clueless as to where Huey had run.

Next came the good news for the FBI: "Newton's disappearance has somewhat tainted any possible legitimate posture the BPP may have attained in the past with its community programs. The BPP appears to be in financial straits as evidenced by . . . a possible loss of several pieces of BPP real estate used as collateral . . . to raise $42,000 security bond for Newton which Newton forfeited at the time of his disappearance."[136]

Mission accomplished. It looked as if the backbone of the Black Panther Party had finally been broken.

The party was hit severely by the forfeiture of Huey's bail, which was no mystery. But a bigger mystery remained: where was Huey, and how could he have possibly managed to slip through the fingers of the FBI's intense surveillance?

CHAPTER 16

PATH TO THE LIGHTHOUSE: HUEY FLEES

The Oakland PD had arrested Huey and booked him on assault charges for the alleged beating of an Oakland tailor named Preston Callins. The legal walls closed in tighter when Huey was also named as the prime suspect in the murder of a seventeen-year-old Oakland street prostitute named Kathleen Smith. Instead of a single assault charge looming, OPD had added on a murder charge and on top of that, a tax evasion charge. If convicted, Huey was looking at a possible sentence of life in prison. A frustrated and exhausted Charles Garry scrambled to arrange bail. While waiting for his bail hearing, Huey thought long and hard about his predicament. He now had major felony charges pending. Out on the streets, there was also a ten-thousand-dollar contract on his life, put out by angry drug dealers and pimps who were unwilling to contribute to the party and its survival programs. "During my hours in jail on this charge," Huey wrote in his journal while in Cuba, "I thought of leaving the country because I felt my chances of acquittal at this time were slim."

Huey made his decision, and it was a tough one. A large chunk of the party's financial holdings were put up for his forty-two-thousand-dollar bail. Ten years of constant harassment and surveillance for his revolutionary political beliefs had reached an apex. Huey had reached his limit as well. With nearly every law enforcement agency breathing down his neck, Huey believed there was no way he could receive a fair trial. Plus, his safety could no longer be guaranteed on the Oakland streets. As with party comrade Eldridge Cleaver before him, it was time to leave the country. Huey's original plan was to go it alone. Once Garry got him out of lockup, he decided, he would jump bail and exile to Cuba. "I had always been sympathetic to the Cuban revolution, so I thought of trying to obtain refuge there. I also considered China and Tanzania, but Cuba would be closer to the U.S. and phone calls would be easier. And the language would be easy to learn." Huey told the *CoEvolution Quarterly*.

Our party had already struck up a familial political relationship with Fidel Castro's Cuba through its embassy in New York. When the Black Panthers came to New York City, they often visited the Cuban embassy. They also had an emissary in Cuba who regularly sent newspapers to the Black Panther offices, and in turn would arrange for Panther writers to contribute articles to several Cuban revolutionary periodicals and journals.

"When I was released on bail from the Oakland County Jail, I went to Gwen's mother's house in Berkeley, where I was to meet Gwen." Huey wrote in his journal. Huey peered through the curtains and saw a familiar sight: two plainclothes Oakland cops had followed him there and parked out front, set up for a round-the-clock stakeout. Huey phoned headquarters and arranged for a party member to drop by Gwen's mother's house and deliver some cash as quickly as possible. He then sat down with Gwen and her mother, Betty, and soberly explained his intentions to flee the country. It was an emotional and tense announcement, but not exactly a surprise to either.

"I'm leaving for Cuba," Huey said.

Gwen and Betty remained silent. Then he dropped the bomb. "Tonight."

Huey Newton's plans to abscond to Cuba were being worked out quickly and surreptitiously through contacts in Cuba (partly through their New York embassy), sources in Canada, and a few sympathetic acquaintances in the Hollywood film industry. "There wasn't time to say goodbye to the children," Huey wrote in his unpublished notes, "or to my family and we took nothing with us."

As Huey laid out his plans, Betty worried. She felt this proposed trip was a risky proposition for Huey, and of course for her own daughter. It would be a very difficult and dangerous adventure. It wasn't as if they could run to the airport and catch a direct flight to Havana. The FBI would be hot on their trail, and as fugitives on the run, this would be a grand opportunity for the feds to shoot and kill both of them.

Betty tried earnestly to convince her daughter to stay behind. She suggested that Gwen could perhaps meet up with Huey overseas at a later date, at least after things had cooled down. But Gwen made it clear: if Huey was on the run, then she would be, too. By the end of the discussion, Betty relented and gave the plan her blessings and unconditional support. She even offered to take care of Ronnie and Jessica, Gwen's two children, for as long as was necessary. Leaving her children behind, and not knowing if they would join her later, Gwen made an extremely painful decision.

Just as the requested money arrived, Gwen and Huey were packed and ready to leave. Convinced that Betty's phone was bugged, the three decided that she would leave the house and walk up the street to a nearby pay phone to finalize the arrangements for Huey and Gwen to be taken to a nearby Oakland airstrip. A private plane from Oakland to Southern California was arranged through friends and contacts in Southern California. Huey and Gwen would board the small plane that night and fly to Los Angeles. Once they landed, they would stay with friends who would assist them in crossing the Mexican border into Tijuana.

Betty returned from the pay phone after placing two calls—one confirming the plane trip, the other securing a ride to the airport. She told Huey and Gwen to grab their things. The plane would be leaving in an hour. Betty's sister was on her way over to drive them to the airfield. With the cops posted out in front, Betty had arranged for their ride to park around the corner and wait for Huey and Gwen.

"Back when Gwen and I picked Huey up at the courthouse," recalled Pat Richartz "the first thing he did when he got in the car was to stick out his leg and ask, 'How do you think I'll look as a woman?' Huey asked if I could bring him some clothes. I brought him one of my long hippie dresses and a cape that Judy Collins had given me. It was full length with a big hood. I also brought him a wig. That's what he wore when he left Oakland."

Betty led Gwen and Huey through her backyard, over her fence, and through another adjoining yard onto the side street where a car waited with the motor running. The two ran toward the car and jumped into the backseat. They lay on the floor of the backseat until the car pulled up to the darkened Oakland airstrip.

"We had already decided," Huey recalled in his unpublished notes, "on the names Betty and Peter Simon, and after paying, the pilot uttered not another word all the way to Los Angeles. I was very sad to be leaving Oakland as I watched it disappear beneath us." From the window of the small plane, Gwen and Huey watched as Oakland faded further into the distance.

For the first time in his life, Huey P. Newton had skipped bail. He was officially a fugitive in flight. Neither he nor Gwen possessed legal passports. The Oakland police had confiscated them the day before Huey was released from county jail, after officers ransacked their apartment. "Our clothing, files, personal items were thrown all over the place. Even Jessica's dollhouse had been broken by them. For some reason, one of the worst things about this to Gwen was the fact that the police had eaten our raisin and nut mixture that we kept in a jar in the kitchen. They had photographs of us lined up on a shelf in a row as though they were photographing them. It was an eerie sight." Huey wrote in his personal unpublished papers.

The day had been long and grueling. It began on a hard, cold bunk in a county jail cell, later being stuffed into the backseat of a car, then navigating a bumpy, two-and-a-half-hour, five-hundred mile, three-seater plane ride south. But the most difficult phase of Huey's escape, cited in his unpublished writings, was yet to come.

> I wasn't really outraged at having felt forced to leave my home, family, etc., probably because we had become so used to our situation by then. The phone tapes, being followed by agents and police, the killing of Party members, being stopped and harassed by the police so often over the previous six years or so. It was almost as if we'd learned to accept it all. After all, it had been my choice to be involved in a political life and I knew it would not be easy.
>
> Being Peter Simon was a great relief for a while. I had become tired of being recognized everywhere I went and it was nice to be anonymous and unbothered by people. But after a short time, I was very surprised to find that I missed myself—Huey—and the people who knew me, and it made me feel very strange. In the winter we long for the summer and in the summer we long for the wintertime.

After only a few hours of sleep, as they had done in Oakland the night before, Huey and Gwen dressed in disguises before the drive the next morning from Los Angeles to Mexico. Huey donned old clothes to look like a Berkeley "street type," while Gwen stuffed her dark, overflowing Afro into a light brown wig.

The car trip from LA to the Mexican border took only a few hours. The driver, a fellow who called himself Moses, talked non-stop all the way down about the personal problems he was having with his family. A preoccupied Huey let him blabber on. Besides, the man's nonstop gab distracted him from thinking about his own troubles and the long road that lay ahead of him and Gwen in their flight for political asylum.

After a long line waiting in traffic at the San Ysidro border crossing, the three passengers routinely presented their necessary IDs to unsuspecting American customs officials. Perceived as ordinary tourists, Moses, Huey, and Gwen were casually waved through. Once in Mexico, Moses drove the couple directly to the airport in Tijuana. From Tijuana, they boarded a flight to Puerto Vallarta, where they checked into a hotel. The second leg of Huey's escape was complete. The next would be more trying.

The following morning, Huey and Gwen boarded a small fishing boat and sailed to a tiny island off Puerto Vallarta called Yelapa. It was arranged that they would stay with a couple there who managed a hotel owned by a California businessman Huey knew. It was a time for Huey and Gwen to unwind a little and settle down while comrades in Mexico City finalized the details of their impending exile.

Years before Huey and Gwen's 1974 flight, in 1968, Eldridge Cleaver was one of the first Black Panthers to exile to Cuba by way of an underground network set up by supporters in Canada. Before that, those who escaped to Cuba did so through more desperate means—by hijacking American airliners at gun- or knifepoint directly to Havana. Seven Black Panthers before Huey had exiled to Cuba on skyjacked planes. The nightly news in America regularly covered stories about airliners being commandeered by American political leftists fleeing the clutches of the Nixon White House. Now, with Huey officially on the run, Cuba (and North Africa) became the Panthers' official haven for political refuge. The most prominent hijacker in the party was a member named William Lee Brent, who graduated from the University of Havana and to this day still lives in Cuba. He subsequently published a book, *Long Time Gone,* about his life as an expatriate.

For Huey, a few weeks on the lush, green island retreat of Yelapa was a welcome contrast to the endless legal wrangling and jail time he faced back in Oakland. With only about one hundred families living on the island, Huey and Gwen spent lost hours swimming, reading, horseback riding, or just walking on the beach. Plus, according to Huey's personal notes, there were environmental adjustments.

> It was very hard for us to learn to live with the insects and other creatures in Mexico. Gwen had a particular aversion to insects and suffered terribly, if in silence.
>
> One night, as we sat around talking in a thatched roof–type house, several bats suddenly flew in at us and we were so frightened, we could only sit there stiffly, which was probably the best thing to do. (Gwen was upset with me later for not coming to her aid and fighting them off, but I was really afraid of them and couldn't move.)
>
> Another night I happened to waken and saw a small animal sitting on Gwen's back as she lay next to me in bed. It scurried off when it sensed my movement and we never found out what it was. We learned to shake out our clothing and shoes

before we put anything on, but we never got used to living with these uninvited visitors."

Back in the United States, the FBI and the Oakland Police Department continued to scour the party headquarters and Oakland streets searching for Huey's whereabouts. Huey's family members were shadowed. The police dragnet intensified, using Huey's disappearance as an excuse to conduct round-the-clock, covert surveillance as more Black Panther Party members were rounded up and arrested. As the party's chief of staff, I was already in Folsom Prison. The OPD stormed business establishments and nightclubs like Jimmie's Lamp Post and the Fox restaurant, places Huey had previously patronized. On the Oakland streets, law enforcement officials kept the reins tight and the political climate hot.

"Most of the newspaper reports were unfavorable," Huey wrote in his personal notes, "except for one by David Harris, former husband of Joan Baez, who had written a very favorable piece. He interviewed people in the community—bus drivers, shopkeepers, etc., and most said they didn't blame me for fleeing because 'they had been trying to string me up for a long time.'"

Meanwhile, Huey's family had no idea where he was or what had happened to him. Following his disappearance, there were frequent "Huey sightings" all over the world. Some feared the worst. "When Huey didn't show up in court in Oakland, Charles Garry feared that he had been killed," recalled Pat Richartz.

During their stay on Yelapa, arrangements were being made for a boat to pick up Huey and Gwen in Mexico and whisk them off to Cuba. Unfortunately, on the way to the predetermined meeting point, the boat sank. Backup plans were then made for a plane to pick up Huey and Gwen and fly them from Mexico City to a secret checkpoint just outside of Havana. A pilot was enlisted and given a small down payment. However, he demanded more money and then disappeared, never to be heard from again.

A discouraged Huey and Gwen decided to backtrack. They headed back to Mexico City, where they were holed up in a hotel two blocks from the American embassy. According to his notes, Huey dared not to venture outside. Donning her wig, Gwen would occasionally duck out to buy American newspapers and food. Huey was a wanted man. "Though I felt something of a prisoner because of the way we had to live in Mexico," he wrote, "I also got a charge out of escaping the situation in the United States. The Mexicans would certainly have turned me over to the U.S. had they known I was in Mexico, so we had to keep a very low profile. Gwen had wanted to keep a journal, but it was too risky. We didn't want to involve people who were helping us, should [the situation] ever have fallen into the wrong hands."

Day by day, despite desperately missing her children, Gwen was surviving. To relieve the stress of being in exile, Gwen took to sewing and knitting as a diversion. "Gwen began making a dress in Mexico," Huey recalled in his diary notes, "In order to relieve stress, she sews and crochets, cooks and dances. She began gathering bits of lace and ribbon, fabrics, and buttons from the shops. It was white with about 75 buttons down the front and she had done all the buttonholes by hand and crocheted white designs on it. It was as though all that was being taken from her, she was giving back to herself with the dress. She would work on it in our room or in the car or bus whenever she could."

According to Huey's notes, living life as a fugitive in Mexico meant that Huey and Gwen adjusted to a different kind of relationship. "Gwen and I had been together about six years by August 1974, but during those six years we had spent very little time alone together. There was always an entourage wherever we went—on speaking engagements, Party meetings, working on books and articles. This was a time when we really got to know each other very well and we clung to each other and became very close. Though, as other couples, we had fought, I don't remember arguing or fighting [during] that time. Everything was too uncertain, I suppose, and we were like newlyweds, learning so many new things about each other."

Meanwhile, final preparations were made for a driver to leave Mexico City and take Gwen and Huey to a dock off the Yucatan Peninsula, where they would then sail on to Havana. It would take them six days to journey by car from Mexico City to a city called Progresso, where they would then connect with their boat. The driver in Mexico City brought his wife and child along for the trip. Disguised as a group of disheveled tourists, five people were crammed into one rented automobile.

> We stayed in many dreadful places as we traveled with this family. The restaurants we went into, and some of the rooms we stayed in for a night were so filthy we could not even bring ourselves to wash our hands in the bowls. To make it all even more unreal, at times we would stay in enormous, well-kept villas and mansions, arranged for us by our friends. One night it would be a filthy, horrible little hotel and a few nights later a villa with a swimming pool and servants and much good food."

The poverty we saw was very disturbing to Gwen and me. Entire families begging in the streets. Gwen would bring food out of restaurants to begging people and this would disturb me. Since I felt I was one of these people spiritually, and not a tourist, it didn't seem right. I felt guilty if we did give them money or food and guilty if we didn't. The horrible ghettos of Detroit and New York were not as terrible as what we saw in Mexico.

Although it was late autumn, the roads were very hot and humid as the five travelers stopped only for fresh water and sleep, usually eating at roadside cafes as Huey and Gwen tried to blend in and get along. As Huey tells in his unpublished story, *Escape to Cuba*, "They were very pleasant as we drove in the terrible heat in the old rented auto. We talked about Carlos Castenda's books, which I had read, and the man seemed to think of himself as a Yaqui Indian."

Late one afternoon they reached the town of Campeche. It was the final stop before Progresso. Gwen and the driver's wife and child went off to the store to buy provisions while Huey and the driver checked in to two separate rooms at a local motel. Huey and the driver shared a few drinks in Huey's room. As the booze flowed, the driver started to complain about money, possibly brought on by seeing some of the elaborate villas they had stayed in.

"Look," he said to Huey in broken English, "not enough money for the risky journey I'm on. What will happen to me if the *policia* find out who you really are?"

Huey didn't want to pursue the matter. "Listen," he said to the driver, "I had nothing to do with the financial arrangements for this trip. If you have a problem, I suggest you speak with the people who hired you. It's not my responsibility."

As the discussion became more heated, it turned into a full-blown argument. The driver grew more and more irritated at the financial arrangement.

"Well in that case, *señor*," he said to Huey, "we go no further until I'm given *más mucho dinero*."

Huey's stuck his hand out to the driver. "Well, in that case," he said, "just give me the car keys right now. We'll drive ourselves the rest of the way to Progresso. We don't need you or your family, so get out of my room."

Huey grabbed the drunken Mexican and opened the door. The driver stumbled out and staggered down the hall back to his own quarters. A few minutes later, there was a pounding on Huey's door. The inebriated driver was back, rapping loudly on Huey's motel-room door, yelling and screaming: "This is not Peter Simon, it is Huey Newton! Huey! Huey Newton! Open this door!"

Furious and seething, Huey opened the door and threw a punch. The angry exchange grew louder. A scuffle ensued after Huey grabbed the driver's car keys. The motel manager ran out to see what the commotion was about. By then the driver had returned to his room.

"Listen, just a *problema menor,*" Huey told the manager in his best Spanish. "*Mi esposa* and I will be checking out shortly when she gets back."

When Gwen turned up at the motel, Huey was already packed and ready for a quick departure. As he settled the bill, the enraged driver ran up to the motel manager, complaining loudly. "This man," he screamed at the manager, pointing at Huey, "has keys to my car he won't give back. It's a rented vehicle. Hired in my name."

A rapid-fire conversation in Spanish proved difficult to follow until Huey and Gwen heard the driver mention the name "Huey Newton" over and over again.

Huey's situation was rapidly deteriorating. He jumped between the two men and landed a few more solid punches on the bewildered driver. Then he and Gwen ran out of the motel, tossed the driver's car keys into the tall grass, and approached a taxi driver parked out front of the motel, waving a ten-dollar bill at the driver.

"Take me directly to *aeropuerto.* Quickly."

As Huey and Gwen climbed into the taxi, both the motel manager and the driver came running outside. "Stay where you are!" they warned the cab driver in Spanish. "Don't move. Do not take these Americans anywhere. The *policia* are on their way now!"

The taxi driver threw their baggage out of his car and swiftly drove off. Just then Huey spotted a rickety Mexican bus chugging down the main road. Gwen and Huey grabbed their bags and ran full-steam. They flagged down the bus and hopped inside. A breathless Huey pulled ten pesos out of his pocket and slapped the money into the bus driver's hand. "*Señor, señor,*" said Huey, gasping and puffing, "I need a ride. *Aeropuerto, por favor.* Can you take us? Now!"

The bus driver turned around to see the motel manager and Huey's ex-driver running after the bus, waving their arms and screaming for him to stop. "Mexicans," Huey recalled, "don't like the police very much. The bus driver laughed and all the passengers on the bus began to laugh and we drove off with everyone on the bus laughing and waving at the manager. It was really a scene out of a movie."

The bus driver abandoned his route, turned off the highway, and drove Huey and Gwen straight to the airport. Minutes later, the two boarded a plane back to Mexico City.

Back in Mexico City, Huey and Gwen were told that the boat in Progresso *still* had not arrived. Since they had no idea when the boat would finally dock in the Yucatan, Gwen and Huey rented a small apartment for the time being, kept a low profile, and waited.

The money was running out, and it would be another couple of weeks before more would be brought. Inside their small rented compound, Gwen sewed and crocheted her dress to kill more time. They would take late-night walks together. Huey would peruse books and magazines, while Gwen would occasionally slip out to buy food or do the laundry.

Huey read about Cuba, specifically the province of Santiago, a region where the earliest supporters of the Cuban revolution lived. Santiago had a predominantly Afro-Cuban population and was among the first to join Fidel Castro's struggle. In 1958, when Cuban citizens angrily boycotted the final elections set up by General Fulgencio Batista, over 98 percent of Santiago's voters stayed away from the polls. The black Cubans of Santiago were often seen as frontline heroes of the Cuban revolt, as the area was considered one of Cuba's more revolutionary provinces. That was another reason Huey chose to flee to Cuba; the island had a large mulatto, mixed Spanish and black, population. Once there, he decided, as a light-skinned black man, he could blend in better and be seen less as an outsider.

Still holed up in Mexico City, the couple could no longer stand being cooped up in their tiny apartment. They decided to break the monotony and visit a nightclub. Low on funds, they barely had enough money for the cover charge. The evening entertainment featured Flamenco dancers and traditional Spanish guitarists. Although it meant that meal money would be tight for the next week or so, it was well worth taking the night out.

> We felt we had to do it. Rather than spend a couple more days eating tortillas, we spent it all at once and had a good dinner and a good time. We then spent about two weeks with no food. We were getting pretty dejected with our situation when I heard that my father had died in Oakland. I had seen him in his hospital bed about a week before we left the United States and he was doing very poorly, so his death did not come as a shock.
>
> While visiting him in the hospital before I left, I was talking to him about how I needed to tell him I loved him. I never had. We were both crying. A nurse admonished me not to talk to him and upset him. I was outraged that she would interfere

with such a moment between my father and me, so I swore at her and ordered her out of the room. She responded by calling the police, who arrived to be in on yet *another* of my intimate moments.

Crushed, though not shocked at the news about his father, Huey immersed himself by studying his Spanish and constantly reading. Gwen worked on her dress. To occupy themselves, the two read and discussed Buckminster Fuller, Margaret Mead, E. L. Doctorow, Doris Lessing, Carlos Casteneda, and Anais Nin. Gwen also read cookbooks.

After four weeks in the Mexico City apartment, word reached Huey and Gwen that their getaway boat to Cuba had finally arrived. It was waiting to disembark from Cozumel, an island off the Yucatan in the Caribbean. Along with two friends, Huey and Gwen boarded a plane in Mexico City bound for Cozumel. A couple of days later, once they reached the island, they exchanged good-byes with their Mexican contacts and loaded one suitcase onto the "getaway" vessel, a sleek, forty-foot sailboat. The captain, Gwen, and Huey would be the only passengers on board. It would take just a few days to sail across the Gulf of Mexico to reach the shores of Havana.

On Thanksgiving Eve of 1974, months behind schedule, Huey and Gwen were finally on board the boat sailing east toward the big island of Cuba. The unplanned-for winter waters grew more and more turbulent. Through rain and shine, Huey and Gwen slept and ate on deck. As the rocky waves grew larger and more frequent, it became impossible and unbearable to sit down below in the cabin. Although the captain expertly navigated the tall breaking waves, Huey and Gwen were inexperienced on the open waters and felt the extreme effects of seasickness. "We barely ate anything but a few crackers and a little fish," Huey wrote in *Escape to Cuba*, "because Gwen and I were too ill. Our captain was sympathetic and sang Jamaican songs and played his guitar to us at night. He was a Scandinavian man who lived in Colombia who decided a few years earlier that all he wanted to do was sail around the world. Gwen thought he looked like a fish with his scaly parched skin and hairy body."

During the first two days of their voyage, time seemed to crawl, interrupted by moments observing threatening skies and sea life. "I remember a great school of flying fish one day as we sailed. I was amazed to see them fly about a yard over the water. There were hundreds of them—it was a beautiful sight."

On their third night at sea, Huey and Gwen spied land on the distant horizon. Their boat anchored fifteen miles off the mainland of Havana. Next came the most hazardous portion of Huey's great escape. The final leg of Huey's journey for asylum would be aboard a motorized rubber raft. The captain had brought along a small craft called a Zodiac, equipped with a tiny nine-horsepower outboard motor. The plan was for Huey and Gwen to motor their way through the last fifteen miles to Havana aboard the Zodiac. They would go it alone to avoid any problems the captain might experience should Cuban officials intercept his vessel while seeking safe harbor. The captain protested, volunteering to sail to shore. But Huey was adamant.

"I must tell you," the captain said to Huey and Gwen, "I believe this next part of your trip is far too risky. I don't know if you'll make it in such a small craft."

"We've come this far," Huey told the captain. "We have no choice. So far we've avoided any kind of surveillance. What would happen if you ended up in a Cuban jail cell?"

The captain shrugged as he helped Huey and Gwen load up the raft. He lowered down a five-gallon can of gasoline and a pair of wooden oars and bid them a dubious farewell. "When he realized I couldn't be dissuaded and that Gwen was going to go with me, he kissed her goodbye and shook my hand and said he would wait around to claim our bodies."

The raft trip was cursed from the start. The Zodiac was roughly five-feet-by-five-feet square. There was little room to maneuver once it was loaded up. With a sole gas can and a suitcase of Gwen's containing cosmetics and a letter in Spanish telling the Cubans who they were, the raft was filled to capacity. Immediately after Huey and Gwen piled onto the raft, one of the oars fell overboard. Worse, as they drifted from the sailboat, they realized, too late, that they had carelessly neglected to bring life preservers.

Huey and Gwen's Zodiac raft departed from the forty-foot clipper under the cover of darkness. The winter seas were rough and choppy. Their only landmark was a remote blinking lighthouse in the Havana distance. Huey figured that as long as he kept the raft on course, on path toward the lighthouse, they just might have a decent chance of reaching Cuba alive, and free.

After the first few hours, Huey struggled to keep the craft from capsizing. The weather worsened and the waves swelled to well over five feet high. The only way he could operate the motor was to turn his back to Havana, the direction in which they were headed, while Gwen faced forward and instructed and guided Huey around every large wave that came crashing toward them. Sudden impact with a gulf wave could easily flip the raft over. Yet they were still too far to make it ashore by swimming. If the waves didn't drown them, surely the sharks would devour them.

After eleven tense hours, the raft remained afloat. By morning it was time to gas up again. Unfortunately, Huey had forgotten to find out how to refill the gas tank. The shoreline was now totally visible. Deep, sharp volcanic rocks stretched across the

Havana shoreline. There were no calm beaches in sight. Finally, when there was no more fuel in the motor, as a last resort the exhausted fugitive sailors decided to paddle straight for the jagged coastline and take their chances.

Close to shore, a towering wave hit them broadside and flipped the Zodiac over. Huey and Gwen were tossed overboard into deep water. "When we were about a mile from the shore," Huey later wrote, "our boat turned over and threw us out. Gwen was caught underneath the raft for a while and we couldn't find each other. When finally we both freed ourselves from under the raft and got out from under the waves, we kept screaming at each other to keep moving, keep moving so the waves wouldn't dash us against the rocks. We did have quite a few cuts from broken glass and the rocks, but no broken bones or anything more serious," according to Huey's unpublished notes. Cut and gashed by the coral reef, but still alive and huddled together, Huey and Gwen scaled the tall rocks and found a protected spot where the waves wouldn't catch them and drag them back into the swirling currents.

As they pulled themselves out of the water and approached the beach, they looked up to see a group of Cuban locals dashing toward them, yelling anxiously. The men identified themselves as members of the Committee to Defend the Revolution. After the Cuban army was called in, Huey and Gwen were rushed off to the Cuban Immigration Department, where they were placed under house arrest and questioned until Cuban authorities verified their true identities. "The patrol who had picked us up," Huey wrote, "appeared not to know who we were or to be aware of our clearance to come into Cuba. But when we asked them if they didn't understand that we had been invited, they replied, 'Well, we didn't shoot you, did we?'"

Huey and Gwen were treated well. During the hours of intense interrogation, Huey convinced the Cubans that, yes, he was that famous revolutionary from California who had made it to Cuba.

"The next day the Cubans arrested our captain, who was waiting in the water, as he had said he would, to claim our bodies. Of course they didn't like people hanging around their waters, and not knowing that he'd been arrested, when they asked me if he had brought us, [at first] I said no, so they told me they were going to shoot him. It was then I assured them that he was not a spy and that he had brought us in, and when they were assured of this, the Cubans drank with him and sent him off waving good-bye."[137]

CHAPTER 17

CUBA LIBRE

W hen I went into Havana," Huey wrote, "it was at night and I was many miles out to sea, and I was told to look for this beacon light that flashes twice every 15 seconds."[138]

After Huey and Gwen had washed ashore onto the beach outside of Havana, it was a symbolic philosophical homecoming of sorts for Huey. Stemming from his early days at Merritt College, the Cuban revolution was his light, an original beacon, and an important ingredient from which he formulated his own political identity. From the very first sight of Cuban land at sea, Huey boldly followed the blinking light to shore. He was about to experience a lifelong dream of *living* the revolution firsthand. Once he and Gwen hit Cuban soil, members of the Committee to Defend the Revolution placed them under immediate house arrest, but only until Huey's identity could be verified. Then he was quickly assimilated into Cuban society. At first, though, he was a figure of curiosity among the Cuban leadership.

"My political status in Cuba was political asylum," Huey recalled. "I was a permanent resident and an honored guest of the government. That included special privileges, like I could always get a driver and a car. Transportation in Cuba is bad—the buses are like a sardine can and they have taxis, but they're not enough. And I could get reservations in restaurants on the weekends, when Cubans like to go out to eat. I had a delegation status, so I could get a table in any restaurant as the North American Delegate."[139]

Soon enough, however, after the newness of his arrival wore off, Huey began to melt into the ranks of Cuba's working-class society. His stay on the island lasted a total of nearly three years. For the first six months, he and Gwen lived inside the city limits of Havana. For the next six months, they moved to Santa Clara in the Los Villas province, where Gwen's children, Ronnie and Jessica, eventually joined them and attended school. According to Huey in the *CoEvolution Quarterly*, "Jessica's Spanish was so fluent, they thought she was Cuban most of the time."

After six months in the countryside, the couple moved back to Havana for another year, culminating their final six months in Alamar, a community just outside of the city, still within the province of Havana, where during the Cuban missile crisis, the waters were crowded with American navy destroyers as far as the eye could see. During Huey's stay, from 1974 to the summer of 1977, Cuba was in the midst of a campaign discouraging mass migration into the city of Havana, emphasizing more countryside and rural living.

The Havana that Huey and Gwen experienced in 1974 was a rundown city. Although the colonial exteriors of the houses shone in assorted pastel colors, many of the buildings were in need of paint jobs and repairs. There was a problem with litter and cockroaches. Yet even if Havana's appearance seemed on the shabby side, it also had a charming and lively side. The streets at night were filled with activity.

Since the United States' imposed economic embargo had begun in 1961, residents of Cuba experienced shortages of every kind, including everything from beer to milk to dry goods, raw materials, and manufactured products. Newer cars were especially difficult to come by. Parked along the streets or cruising the Havana boulevards were a fleet of American relics—vintage DeSotos, Packards, Hudsons, and Henry J. Kaisers, many with their hoods raised up, parked off the sidewalks, constantly being repaired, maintained, and carefully preserved. For Huey, living the collective lifestyle in Cuba was a far different cultural revolutionary experience than when he had visited China.

> China is such a breathtaking thing because it's so huge. And the Chinese way of going about things is much more efficient. Cuba is more of a laid-back thing. It's more relaxed. For instance, if a Cuban tells you you're going somewhere at eight o'clock, [and] if you actually come at eight and not ten, they'll think you're crazy. In China, if someone's going to pick you up at nine o'clock, at two minutes of nine, you can expect a knock at the door. The Chinese have a relaxed way of sitting down with a cup of tea like they're going to sit there for two hours, and then at straight-up-nine, everyone will just get up and start backing out the door while they're still talking. Of course I was in China only about twenty days, and Cuba three years. Cubans have more of a Black culture. I could feel more of a part of it. I was strictly an observer in China, and I felt integrated into Cuban society.[140]

During the first months in Havana, while Gwen worked as a teacher in a hospital, Huey jumped headfirst into the workforce, conforming to the Cuban ethic of productivity. Although Cuba at the time enjoyed near-full-employment, it was still a labor-intensive society with antiloafing laws. Adult workers earned just enough to provide for their families' basic physical needs. To get a taste of working-class society, Huey took the equivalent of an American blue-collar job repairing the trucks that were part of the cement factory motor pool. "When I first got there, they gave me a grand tour of the provinces, showed me all the schools and universities, construction sites, dams, coffee and sugar production. They offered me a job as a university teacher, but I preferred to work in a cement factory."[141]

"I worked there about six months. It was required to work ten hours for five days, then five hours on Saturdays, but I worked ten hours a day, seven days a week voluntarily. I never worked on cars before, so I wasn't too good, but everybody was nice to me anyway."[142]

Working at a full-time job was an enlightening and new experience for Huey. The social aspect of a work ethic was something Huey immediately cottoned to.

> [I took the job] primarily to enhance my own understanding of the people. It was essentially a very good experience. Hard labor in Cuba is a very different thing from hard labor in the United States. In Cuba, a job is not only a job; it also becomes the very center of communication. We ended up spending weekends at the beach with our co-workers, who were like a family. When our toilet broke down, for example, I immediately went into a panic. I asked my wife, "Who do we call? Where is the central agency? What do we do?" When we explained our problem to the people who shared our apartment building, they told us to report the problem to our fellow workers. I did, and some of the workers who knew about plumbing came out and repaired the toilet. I asked if I should pay. They said, "No, but when something breaks down in our home, we would like you to help us." I had undergone the collective experience.[143]

After living initially in one of Havana's tourist hotels, the Havana Libre, Huey and Gwen eventually settled permanently into one of the government apartment projects, where they encountered a more realistic and immediate sense of community among the Cuban people.

> There *was* a feeling that truly everybody is an extended family, and concern for everybody else's welfare. If you borrow some flour or some meal from someone, it's an insult to give them that back. If you get some extra beans or something, you'd give them that and then they would be happy because it's like a gift. You never have to worry about someone watching kids, because the whole building is glad to do it. Everyone's in the CDR (Committee to Defend the Revolution), and they meet once a week. Here [in the United States], it's a feeling of alienation, and there it's a collective. That's outside the political thing. They [the Cuban people] are interested in each other's life in a brotherly way.[144]

Although Huey missed his homeland, he didn't miss the constant surveillance that had become a permanently tense fixture in his life. "It was good for me. I didn't know how tired I was, I didn't know how much of a toll the constant surveillance had upon me until I didn't have that any more. For the last 11 years, I was obviously followed, even to the grocery store, pictures being taken. Everyone I contacted, they were eventually bugged and harassed by the FBI. In Cuba, I got a chance to do a lot of writing on Party history. And a lot of reading. I hadn't read a book in its entirety in years."[145]

When he wasn't working at the cement factory, Huey read voraciously, following up on his interests in science, society, and philosophy.

I read just about everything I got my hands on. I read [Alfred] Korzybsky, *Science and Sanity,* a book that I had for about six years. I finally read it and was as impressed as I thought I would be. I read a lot of Marx's works and Lenin. I read [Michael] Harrington, *The Twilight of Capitalism,* a very good book. I've always been interested in Existentialism. I read Sartre, *Being and Nothingness.* I read some books on Fanon. Of course I read *Roots.* A friend sent me *Five Rings;* it's a very small work, about this Buddhist samurai. It's a fascinating book. It seems it's all on combat, really it's on how to live.

I read some novels. Gore Vidal's *1876* and *Burr.* I read a lot of Saul Bellow, whom I like a lot. I hadn't read a novel in about ten years. I really entertained myself. I read about 400 books. It was really something to give the books away. I gave everything else away and I had read these books, but I found myself attached to them. I wanted to keep them, but people needed them there because it's hard to get some books.[146]

In addition to toiling in the cement factory and working on trucks, Huey also taught part-time at the University of Havana, instructing small student workshops on the history of social movements. "That was only a couple of hours a week. [University life in Cuba] was different because everybody there was interested in learning. That was different from schools I've been to and lectured at here [in the United States]. [In Cuba] they're really interested in their fields, and international politics. You get this singleness of purpose, from the university to the cane fields. You get the feeling you're a member of a collective, the whole country's a collective, and you're working to make life better."[147]

Huey's goal was to embrace and become a part of the Cuban culture. That included trying to get a job cutting sugar cane. "I had a cane-cutting machete, but I only used it to work on the yard. I asked to cut cane, but the Cubans don't feel North Americans can adjust to the heat. It's 110 degrees in the cane fields. Even the Venceremos Brigades, a sympathetic group of American youth, no longer cut cane. They only do construction work. But Cubans are tough. They can do it."[148]

For the second time in his life, Huey had a job earning a paycheck. The only other job he had ever had was a seasonal job as a young man at the Hunt's cannery in Emeryville.

> The lowest pay is 120 pesos a month, the highest is 400. Fidel gets 400. The average is roughly 250. I earned about 220.
>
> Each job provides a school; the worker can go to school for two hours, three days a week, and promote himself in his job area. There is some competition, obviously, but it's not like here [in the United States]. The framework of the competition [in Cuba] is friendlier. First of all, everyone is able to get his basic food. For a family of four, you spend about 27 pesos a month. Rationing limits the extent of competition.
>
> I liked Cuba. You don't have the developed sense of community here [in the United States]. It's hard to communicate the reasons why the Cuban people can feel so much joy in long hours of work with so little pay.
>
> If you create an environment where people are taught that they must supersede others in order to be happy, that will naturally breed mutual alienation. If you create an environment where people depend on each other, an environment where you promote cooperation rather than competition, then people will behave in a different way.[149]

In between the hard labor and teaching, Huey and Gwen found the time to marry. Gwen's wedding dress was the dress she had therapeutically stitched, crocheted, and decorated during their prolonged escape from the United States through Mexico. The two exiles were married in a wedding temple. A lawyer read the ceremony and also the family code, which says that by Cuban law, the male is required to take on half the responsibilities of childcare and housework as well as cooking. Huey found Cuban married life fair and adaptable. "I like to do dishes anyway, so I had no problem with that. And I think I can cook better than she can, some things. I did that long before the marriage. We'd been together four years before the marriage."[150]

For Huey, married life and the act of balancing a relationship with his dedication to the party wasn't as much of an adjustment as he had once thought, especially back in the days with Richard Thorne and the early tenets of sexual freedom. "If it was going to be a difference, I wouldn't have gotten married," Huey recalled in the *CoEvolution Quarterly*. "Maybe that's why I waited so long, because I had a certain amount of fear that things would be different. But I was pretty secure at the time, that we had a definition of the situation. I was calling her my second wife because the Party was my first, and I'm a bigamist. She accepts that."

Occasionally Huey and Gwen had visitors from the United States. Elaine Brown, the Black Panther Party chairperson who was running the party domestically in Huey's stead, made a visit in 1975. After the first nine months, Gwen's mother, Betty, came down with the children. Huey was also able to make occasional phone calls, especially when he was staying at the Havana Libre. Also while in Cuba, he was able to hook up with exiled comrade William Brent, who became a Cuban citizen and taught at the University of Havana. Brent had hijacked an airliner in 1969 and has been in Cuba ever since. He eventually graduated from the University of Havana and taught Spanish history and languages, specifically French and English. According to Huey, Brent was an exception when it came to hijackers adapting to life in Cuba.

"Just about all the other skyjackers—they have about 25—are in big trouble with the Cuban government for getting into black marketing and all sorts of things. They've gone to prison several times in fact, after they got out for invading the integrity of Cuban territory."[151]

Aside from the rationing and special times, Cuba during the late 1970s had made sociological advances. Illiteracy had been virtually eliminated. Free medical care was available on all parts of the island. Besides attaining full employment, women enjoyed the same legal rights as men. Food was sufficient, though not plentiful. The crime rate, while relatively low, was on the rise around the tourist hotels, though not in the countryside. There was scarcity and rationing, except for the tourist shops, where the Cubans weren't permitted to shop. Such shops served to bring in foreign currency in order to help the Cuban economy.

Replacing the billboards and advertisements around town were government slogans urging comrades to work hard and save money. There was no construction of individual housing, only functional cement-block housing projects, hospitals, and schools. There was little or no pornography, while at the same time Huey experienced the Cuban people as passionate and publicly affectionate. Families in Cuba remained very close and tightly knit. Every night at six, the government station would play rock 'n' roll while Cuban clothing mills produced inferior-quality blue jeans, bright polyester dresses, and tennis shoes. During his stay, Huey found Cuba effectively isolated from American popular culture. "It's all blacked out," he noted about Cuban television. "But every once in a while something would go wrong and you'd get 'Soul Train' for a few minutes."[152]

"Huey and Gwen were happy in Cuba," Gwen's sister Demetra Gayle recalls years later. "Huey looked like a Cuban. But my sister didn't like wringing chickens' necks to make chicken dinner. But short of that, she seemed really happy. She was teaching English to doctors and other professional Cubans. My niece [Jessica] still speaks Spanish."[153]

As Huey strolled by the Cuban capitol building in Havana, he couldn't help but notice that the architecture was "patterned after the Capitol in Washington." Living among the Cubans forever changed his view of what revolution truly could be, and grounded his personal expectations on how to revolutionize the North American people. "Generally speaking, too much of the time, the Left in the United States requires the people to make a big jump that they're not prepared for. The Cubans didn't even do that after a revolution. Fidel said in '59 that they 'won the right to make revolution.' They have to transform the man and the woman now. They only won the right to do that. So my whole attitude is changed as far as my approach to people no matter what their values are. I'll try to *slowly* stimulate their consciousness. That's one big change that I've noticed in myself."[154]

Life in Cuba taught Huey that one country's form of revolution isn't necessarily immediately adaptable to another's. His analysis back in 1977 is eerily prophetic, particularly in his grasp of the importance of technology in North America: "I think that Cuba is no blueprint for the United States. It's a whole different situation. It's a technological society. We would have to make our revolution based on our cultural history and the whole gestalt of our society. Some form of socialism will have to exist in the United States, but it won't be the Cuban form because the Cubans don't have the Soviet form or the Chinese form. They have a form of socialism consistent with their history."[155]

With Cuba and the United States separated only by ninety miles of water, Huey told a *Oui* magazine interviewer later, "Cuba was a good experience, but it was also difficult being in exile. This is my home."

Part of his decision to return to the United States was predicated by what he saw as a pronounced change of climate in the social-political landscape of the United States and California. With fervent support from the Oakland BPP chapter under Elaine Brown's leadership, the city of Oakland was no longer under the control of rich and powerful white Republican families like the Knowlands and the Houlihans. In 1977, the same year Huey returned from Cuba, the first black mayor of Oakland, a superior court judge named Lionel Wilson, was elected.

The only intangible factor surrounding Huey's homecoming was whether or not he could receive a fair trial, in facing the accusations of murder and assault, as well as the tax evasion charges drawn up by a staff of specially appointed IRS staffers who meticulously combed through the Black Panther Party's past financial records. Huey's return to face criminal charges was a gamble. Yet his decision to return was lined with optimism. "I don't think a fair trial is in the realm of possibility after having an eighty-thousand-dollar bail inflicted on me," he said. "But, yes, I do hope to be acquitted. I think that the United States has changed enough that people are at least somewhat aware that the police can commit crimes, that the FBI and CIA can spy on private individuals, and that the Armed Forces are a bastion of crazy people."[156]

The America that Huey returned to had just undergone a gradual deflating process of the post-Watergate era. For the first time in years, many American citizens were suspicious of their government's control over their everyday lives. Richard Nixon's "enemies list" included well-loved celebrities like Paul Newman and Carol "Hello Dolly" Channing. The collapse of the Nixon White House had added a layer of cynicism to people's confidence in politicians, the bureaucracy, and their elected officials.

By 1977 Huey was determined to take back the reins of the Black Panther Party, but it wasn't necessarily met with unanimous popularity among the party membership. There was some opposition to Huey reclaiming leadership within the organization's cadre. "Some of them opposed my coming back," Huey recalled, "and they couldn't stand another drain. Eighty thousand dollars in bail is a real financial drain [both] on the Party and on our whole standing in the community. Some people have left because they were tired, just fatigued after sacrificing so much of their personal lives."[157]

Huey's adamant shift of Panther revolutionary rhetoric after the Cleaver expulsion still rankled the Black Power movement. Huey told *Oui* magazine, "My posture in the Party while I was in prison was to eliminate the line of armed combat, and as a result many people left the Party then. Now I think that the conditions require that we take a different posture. Some people in the Party disagree with my coming back and going through the judicial process."

The BPP had indeed changed during the years of Huey's exile. For instance, cofounder Bobby Seale had left the party while Huey was in exile. The two had not spoken prior to Seale's exit. "He didn't talk to me about it beforehand—I guess the pressure was such that he didn't feel he could, and that was very sad to me. I wished we could have talked about it, but he felt otherwise."[158]

During his stay in Cuba, Huey was in daily contact with Elaine Brown, who was now running the party. As a result, he was able to keep up with the daily developments as well as transition and direction of the party.

At times, the thought of returning to America was a somber and challenging proposition for Huey. Returning meant coming home, but it also meant the return of constantly looking over his shoulder, stepping back into the crosshairs of the United States law enforcement agencies and the criminal justice system. Going home sparked a clash of contradictory feelings. He adopted a more pragmatic view of people around him. The camaraderie he experienced in Cuba was something he wanted to cultivate with his own party members back home in Oakland.

> A number of things have made me sad over the years. I guess I'm a very sad person, all in all. I'm much more aware of the contradictions, the conflicts of interests, the contradictions inside myself and the contradictions inside other people. It's taught me to be less harsh with others, to not regard them as lesser than myself. I understand now that people don't consciously work against their own interests. Many times, people work against their interests unconsciously. The primary problem is to lift consciousness. This doesn't necessarily preclude violence, but we try very hard to resolve problems in a different way. And when we have to hurt somebody, it's an act of tremendous sadness—you are damaging yourself, your extended self, a part of your own organism.
>
> Trust is hard to achieve. But if you stop having faith in the people you work with, you're just cutting yourself off. There's a very delicate balance between self-reliance and mutual dependence that you have to learn to maintain.[159]

Huey missed Oakland and his comrades enough to risk going to prison for life by returning via Toronto. Before Huey's departure from Cuba, his mother-in-law, Betty, had returned to collect the children. Then, after a brief tussle with Canadian authorities in Toronto, on Sunday, July 3, 1977, Huey made his dramatic and triumphant return to the Bay Area at the San Francisco International Airport. In front of fifteen hundred people assembled at the airport, flanked by his wife, Gwen, and

Black Panther comrades Elaine Brown and Larry Henson, Huey was poised to reestablish control over the Black Panther Party and fight the charges he had fled. Unlike Eldridge Cleaver and Stokely Carmichael before him, both of whom after visiting Cuba made negative and disparaging comments regarding the country's society, Huey was grateful to the Cuban people for giving him and his family refuge. Yet he was also defiant and confident in his desire to confront all the criminal charges leveled against him by the Alameda County district attorney's office.

After stepping off the plane, he addressed the throng assembled at the airport:

> I thank the people who helped me return. I express my love and appreciation to all of my friends. I also want to express my love and gratitude to the courageous people of Cuba, who helped me turn the obvious difficulties of exile into a positive and rewarding experience, who befriended me in a time of need.
>
> I'm happy to be home. I have returned to be freed of the false charges leveled against me. I want everyone to know I have not killed anyone. I am not guilty of any crime, including the claim of the so-called tailor, who in fact is a tailor of assassination, a government provocateur.
>
> When I left this country, I was aware of a conspiracy to murder me and to destroy the Black Panther Party. This conspiracy was planned by high-level government officials using petty criminals to carry out their plans.
>
> I have returned to continue my commitment to work for progressive change in our society. I will work for full employment and economic redistribution. I will continue my fight against a system that denies decent housing, clothing, and medical care to people, but spends billions on war and carrying out injustices against people. I intend to continue to fight against

the evil of heroin sales in our community, despite the contract put on my life by heroin dealers with the knowledge of law enforcement. I call upon the new mayor of Oakland to join us in this effort.

Now I am going to jail. I believe I will be acquitted, though it will be difficult to get a fair trial. However, I believe the people's consciousness has been raised. What they know and will learn will cause them to demand justice for me, for human beings.

As Huey looked out across the sea of faces at the airport, he made his closing remarks. "Stay with me, my friends," he shouted as he concluded his statement. "I look forward to being closer to you soon."[160]

CHAPTER 18

RETURN TO THE SCENE OF THE CRIME

"The trafficking of heroin is one of the greatest dissipating factors among the poor, not only Blacks but among Chicanos, Puerto Ricans, and other poor people. It is an evil that has to be driven out of our community. It is obvious that police forces have not seriously attempted to crush this growing evil, but have in many ways encouraged it, by either a lack-adaisical attitude or even, in some cases, participation in that trafficking. I have called upon the new mayor of this city to join us in this regard because I think that as the elected political leader of the city, it is his responsibility to begin to set the tone for change. It is just intolerable that heroin traffic exists. It can be cleared up and cleaned out of this city, and we certainly intend to put out every energy we have to do that. I believe good will triumph over evil—and I believe that the people themselves will run the dope dealers out of the community."

—Huey Newton, 1977

By July 3, 1977, Huey indeed found a new sociopolitical climate in the Bay Area. Back in Oakland, he fought off the charges of what he called "the murderous attacks that forced me to leave the United States in 1974." In many respects, the climate had changed since Huey's departure. Democratic administrations had replaced Republicans in Washington, Sacramento, and Oakland. Congressional investigations and Black Panther Party lawsuits had disclosed an unremitting pattern of provocation and conspiracy against the party by government agencies. And to a post-Watergate public, the idea that government agencies can engage in crime and cover-up was no longer unthinkable.

Huey's return overlapped with the mayoral inauguration of Judge Lionel Wilson, finally ending five decades of Republican control. Throughout the summer of 1977, as Huey reimmersed himself as the party leader, he and his attorneys prepared his defense for trial. By August they'd filed a 157-page discovery motion against not only the prosecution, headed by Thomas Orloff (now currently the district attorney of Alameda County), but also eighteen police and intelligence agencies who forced Huey into exile. Although the judge denied Huey's team access to state and federal government files, through their own investigations they learned that the prosecution's case was weak and porous. It was time for Huey to confront the charges that forced him into exile.

One incident involved a curious shooting in Richmond. According to press accounts, three heavily armed, masked men in blue jumpsuits engaged in a shootout with a fifty-five-year-old woman in the early morning hours of October 23, 1977. One person was killed—a former Panther, Louis Johnson. The shooting took place near the apartment of a key prosecution witness for the Newton case, Crystal Grey. The dead man, according to police, supposedly had been shot by one of the other men in a blue jumpsuit. A number of weapons were left behind. The encounter, law enforcement "sources" claimed, had been a bungled assassination attempt on Crystal Grey by a Black Panther "hit squad." Strangely, though the *Oakland Tribune* listed the names of current and former Black Panthers that it alleged were linked with the Richmond incident, the district attorney never filed any charges against anyone.[161]

The portion of the case accusing Huey of shooting seventeen-year-old prostitute Kathleen Smith on August 6, 1974, was wobbly. Huey seriously challenged the accuracy of Crystal Grey's account.

> Raphaelle Gary, a 32-year-old prostitute also known as "Crystal Grey" among numerous aliases, claimed to be the only eyewitness to the shooting that took place on a poorly-lit corner of 29th and San Pablo in Oakland by a man with slicked-back, "processed" hair. Gary testified that just before the shooting took place, someone said, "Hi, Leibo" to this man. Gary admitted that she did not identify Newton's picture the day after the incident when she was shown a photo lineup by the police, but identified the picture over a week later. She also emphatically swore to having seen the man she said shot Kathleen Smith in Oakland several weeks after Newton had already left the country.[162]

At the time, Oakland police routinely used a photo of Huey when presenting crime victims with photo lineups, even involving crimes that occurred during the time that he was in exile in Cuba. In a tape recording played in court, Gary was heard telling a journalist that before identifying Huey's photo from the lineup, the cops told her they wanted "to get" Huey, and that they had evidence to "put Newton away."

"Gary also said," Huey charged, "that she was promised no more prostitution arrests—and instead was offered money, a house, and a 'new life' in another city or country if she would testify against Newton. In court, Gary at first emphatically denied these conversations, but after huddling with prosecutor Orloff, she stated that she could 'neither deny or affirm' the taped statements. This was the prosecution's 'star witness.' "[163]

Then another witness discredited Ms. Grey's testimony even further. "Michelle Jenkins, 20, a seven-year veteran of the streets," Huey wrote, "testified that she and Kathleen Smith were the only two women 'working' the corner of 29th and San Pablo the night of the incident—flatly contradicting the previous testimony of Raphaelle Gary. Jenkins said the man who shot her partner had braided hair, a moustache, and was only 5'2" or 5'3" tall. She admitted that she didn't come forward with her alleged 'eyewitness' story until four days after the incident."[164]

A white Oakland police sergeant, during his preliminary hearing testimony, admitted that he received a telephone call from an Oakland undercover police officer providing information implicating Huey. The sergeant admitted that he offered "help" to Michelle Jenkins in exchange for her testimony against Huey. He also admitted not following up on leads provided by Kathleen Smith's mother and boyfriend, who specifically named individuals who might have done the shooting. Despite a weak showing on the prosecution's side and an admission by the police sergeant that the case was instigated by the Oakland police's "Panther Squad," Huey's case proceeded to superior court. The trial began in early February 1978.

After multiple trials, Huey emerged victorious. Once again, he was vindicated by twelve jurors and was acquitted of two murder charges after two juries were hopelessly deadlocked.

The case involving an alleged beating of Preston Callins was also on shaky ground when the alleged victim retracted his accusation. "Preston Callins," wrote Huey, "who three years earlier had claimed that Newton had pistol-whipped him, now could not recall the details of the incident and refused to identify Newton as his assailant."[165]

*

In 1978 Huey had decided to resume his academic activities by applying to a PhD program at UC Santa Cruz. Huey had bounced around the Bay Area educational arena for thirty years, first as a schoolboy in the Oakland and Berkeley school districts, later gaining an associate of arts degree at Merritt College in 1966. During 1972 and 1973 he had returned to his studies at Merritt before obtaining his bachelor's degree from UC Santa Cruz while associated with J. Herman Blake, a scholar who had assisted Huey in writing his autobiography, *Revolutionary Suicide,* originally published in 1973 by Harcourt Brace.

It was back at UC Santa Cruz that Huey met Professor Triloki N. Pandey. Throughout his career of research and teaching, Pandey's work centered on both Eastern and Western tribal cultures in India, Nepal, and the American Southwest among the Zuni, Hopi, and the Navajo as well as fieldwork in India and Nepal. Pandey told me about his experiences with Huey:

> I was his academic advisor. I was chairing the department during that period. Anthropology didn't have a PhD program, so Huey got his PhD from the History of Consciousness. It's one of the best departments in the world that started during the 1960s when the University of California–Santa Cruz started.
>
> First I heard that Huey was interested in history of consciousness from Herman Blake, who was the sociologist who had written with Huey. By that time, Huey and Herman were no longer on good terms. I don't know the details. Anyway, Huey applied to the program. There was a committee of six at that point. Huey had letters from the chairman of the board of regents and others. We asked him to come and see us. We interviewed him.[166]

With Huey's name back in the news, the College Board was curious about his desire to return to UC Santa Cruz.

> We asked him, "you are already a celebrity, why do you want to get the PhD?" He said, "I'm very much interested in doing educational work for my people. I think having a PhD will be very helpful." I said, "Fine, that's a legitimate response."
>
> The committee was quite impressed. Huey had a strong record and he was really an intellectual, a brilliant man. He was always thinking, so we admitted him along with nine or ten other students. Several of them have now become professors on various campuses and universities.
>
> Because of my temperament, I wanted to be his teacher. I did not socialize with him. I did not ask him about his life. When I was teaching at Columbia University, I would walk through Harlem. I have no fear of human beings. I knew Huey would not do any harm to me if I just did my job. I had no fear of him.[167]

There was one incident where the professor was concerned about Huey's behavior in the classroom.

> He took a course with me on science, codes, and myths, and there were about twelve students. One time, I thought Huey was aggressive. I used to take a break halfway between the three-hour evening seminars. I took an early break and I confronted him, and I said, "Look, the whole class knows who you are, and if you don't behave, then I'll just have to ask you to leave, because you are making a fool of yourself."
>
> I think in retrospect, I can see that maybe he had taken some drug and maybe he was not normal, he was not himself. But it was the only occasion when I saw him like that.

Unfortunately I had no clue that he was doing drugs. He was talking and talking, saying things that did not make any sense, which were not really part of what we were discussing. I could see that he was a little bit off, but I had no idea what was the reason for it. People were looking at me, and people were looking at him. What's going on here?[168]

Huey did show up for class at UC Santa Cruz with his bodyguards. "Two or three bodyguards were always sitting outside. They never came inside. Once I asked him, 'Huey, why do you bring all these people?' He said, 'As you know, the police are still not satisfied with what happened, so I have to have witnesses in case I get arrested or in case something happens to me.'"[169]

As part of the course's curriculum, each student was required to present a final project. When Huey's turn came, the situation on campus magnified. "We used to have a requirement in the program where you had to give a public demonstration of what your project was. So when Huey was going to have his public demonstration, some six hundred people showed up. It was held in the dining hall. We had to have security and all that."[170]

Huey presented a film and took questions from the crowd. "I was chairing the department, and we had a departmental meeting and people got upset. So it fell on me to tell them that we were not going to give him [Huey] a pass in this course. He had to redo his project."[171]

A minor academic standoff took place in Pandey's office. Huey made an appointment, but instead of coming alone, some of his faculty admirers showed up, about ten or twelve people. "Look, Huey," Pandey said, "as you know, you showed a film, fifty-five minutes. It was not a film you had made about the murder of Fred Hampton. The questions people asked were not really academic questions, and nor were your responses. So put yourself in my position and tell me how should we give you a pass?"

Huey's response was, "You bloody racist bastard! This is a racist university."

Pandey retorted. "You can't accuse me of racism, and whatever the institution is, you applied, you came. We had an agreement you were going to do the work, and we would treat you like any other student." So the department board had decided Huey had to do something extra.

> Huey was upset. I was disturbed. So Huey cooled down. He said, "No hard feelings." I had no hard feelings. I was just doing my job. Huey did the work, then he wrote a wonderful paper, *Science as a Western Myth,* but it was not written in proper academic fashion. There were no footnotes. He did not give us a list of the books he consulted. This was not acceptable. I wrote it on the paper. He was very disturbed. That's what I wanted him to be. He should be disturbed because he's capable of doing better quality work. The ideas were there, but this was not an academic paper. We discussed it, then he brought the paper in, fixed it, and it was fine.[172]

For his PhD thesis, Pandey felt that Huey could effectively document the history of repression in American society and conceptualize it with his own experiences. "And he did," Pandey said. "And it was wonderful work. We are very proud of the work he did." As for his own political persuasion, Pandey added, "I'm neither right-wing nor left-wing. I'm just an academic interested in these issues."[173]

Huey's graduation and appearance at the commencement ceremonies was front-page news in newspapers across the country, including the *New York Times.* According to Pandey:

I had telephone calls from all over the country, but the interesting thing was that the chair of the academic senate called me and asked, "Dr. Pandey, did he really deserve the degree? Are you guys just giving him a degree?" I told him I really resented his question. "How come you have not asked this question of anybody else? Why are you singling him out? His PhD thesis is in the library. Go and take a look at it."

Then I called the chancellor because I knew it would be discussed at the regents' meeting because I was very proud of him. I called him and asked, "Do you want me to brief you about Huey Newton and the work, since there may be a question in the regents' meeting?" "No, no," he said, "I checked out the thesis from the library, read it, and it's perfectly fine."[174]

Huey wrote several papers during his studies at UC Santa Cruz, including "The Historical Origins of Existentialism and the Common Denominators of Existential Philosophy," "The Roots of Existential Philosophy in Western Thought," and "Can Religion Survive?" Eventually, Huey's thesis was published under the title *War Against the Panthers: A Study in the Repression in America.*

Toward the end of his stay at UC Santa Cruz, Huey began to collaborate with the famed sociobiologist Robert Trivers. Trivers's scientific work and research concentrated on social theory. His theories on reciprocal altruism, parental investment, sexual selection, parent-offspring conflict, the sex ratio, and especially his most famous theories, on deceit and self-deception, have been cited more than seven thousand times in scientific literature. Trivers recalled his experiences with Huey:

I met Huey because he was a graduate student at UC Santa Cruz in 1978 when I moved from Harvard to there as a full professor of biology. He was one of the main attractions, actually, for my coming, because he was a good friend at the time with a man named Bernie LeBoeuf, a professor of biology and a famous student of elephant seals. He was telling me about Huey as a bargaining chip, knowing that I would be very interested in meeting and getting to know Huey. That was one thing he waved in front of me, that I would meet him through Bernie.

When I got there in the fall of 1978, Huey was in jail. I got a call. Would I give Huey a reading course while he was in jail? I said, yes, I would, but I wanted Huey to write a paragraph on what he wanted to read about. So before he could write that paragraph, he got out of jail and came down to Santa Cruz with Bill Moore, Mark Alexander, and Larry Henson. We met at Bernie LeBoeuf's home. . . .

We spent about two hours together. Huey was, in my opinion, almost trembling. If you picked up vibes, to me, he was just coming out of maybe two months of lock up. He had that kind of vibe of somebody coming out of that world.[175]

That night Trivers made a personal connection with Huey. "I remember asking him about being in solitary for three years . . . I asked him about whether there was a problem going crazy in prison. He said, yes, there was once when he felt like his whole mind was going to fly apart, and he described some scene of him holding himself together. I'm pretty sure we decided at that meeting to do a reading course on deceit and self-deception, which was a topic I was interested in developing."[176]

In his first meeting, Trivers perceived Huey as an extraordinary intellectual individual.

It soon became clear to me in talking with him that he was a natural-born genius of the sort of which I've met less than a

handful in my life. Tremendous mental powers. His forte was
logic, and what I would call aggressive logic. That is, running an
argument back at you that he could do with considerable force,
and work you into a position very quickly that you didn't want
to be in. That is, force you logically where you could choose at
each point to jump one way or another, and whichever way you
jumped, he already had a plan of how he was going to deal with
that and box you in further, if you will.

It soon became apparent, or at some point it occurred to
me, who was really the teacher and who was the student in this
seminar, because Huey was a master at propagating deception.
He was a master at seeing through deception. He was hell-on-
wheels on your self-deception. Like all the rest of us, he fell
down somewhat when it came to his self-deception. That was a
topic that was uniquely suited for him in a way, given his life
experiences, given his mental powers.[177]

Huey and Trivers produced almost thirty thousand words
for a book on deceit and self-deception, but the project collapsed
and died when the publishing company went out of business.
The pair assembled another book proposal, *Blues for Huey,* which
would tell ten or twelve stories from Huey's life, as both Huey
and Trivers had the same strange premonition that he might not
be around much longer to tell those stories. Trivers continued to
work with Huey on a reading course he had designed, coming to
Oakland from Santa Cruz for the second meeting of the course.

I went to his home for a very memorable five or six hours. I
later learned he had been up for two and a half days, or some
long stretch of time. His wife, Gwen, was concerned at the time
that he was going to screw this up, as apparently he had
screwed up some other opportunities that were important to

him. But he didn't. He put on a mesmerizing performance. Brilliant performance. I remember at the end of it, I was a little bit tired and I had to drive down the road to Santa Cruz. I asked to lie down. He immediately took me up to his master bedroom and insisted I lie down there, and covered me up. Forty-five minutes later, I got up from my nap and bade him good-bye.[178]

Trivers, like Pandey, soon noticed a shifting pattern of behavior that might have been drug related.

At his best, he was like a king, and therefore if you were a friend of his and in his presence, you were like a prince. It was a very heady experience. But he ranged the full gamut from a wonderful person to be with, brilliant, stimulating, very gentlemanly, almost courtly and old-fashioned in his manners when he was ready to be. On the other hand, he could be one of the more frightening creatures you would ever run into.

I had joined the party in 1979, but the party was over with in more ways than one. That is, Huey didn't want to run an organization anymore. A lot of people had left him. There were not that many people who were members. They ran the school over in East Oakland. I think the health clinic had dried up by then. I think Huey just didn't have any interest in it any more."

Trivers soon joined Huey in a few of his late night exploits around Oakland.

I can remember one memorable evening where we almost ended up in an armed robbery. I was out with him and George Robinson. George was, at the time, the second bodyguard. Huey would point out things to me. I was so naïve.

Later, I used to run in Oakland on my own, and that made Huey nervous. I used to go to some after-hours clubs that I had learned of through him. I'd get pissed off if they charged me a dollar or two-dollar entry fee and no one else was charged. Huey would say, "You don't know how dangerous some of these places are, and you don't know who you're dealing with. I don't want you going by yourself." The clubs didn't even have names, they were just locations. There was once when Huey did send me out with a member of the party as my sort of body-guard for the evening, and I sure didn't enjoy it.[179]

Trivers recalled one night when he and Huey visited a night-club in West Oakland.

I remember there was some guy in the men's room that offered Huey some blow, which he consumed on the spot. Huey told me the guy was homosexual, and the next thing he was going to do was offer him women. Within fifteen minutes, the guy came over and asked if he could bring over a woman or two to intro-duce to Huey. Anyway, he did, and we're sitting around joking. We ended up being about the only people there, and it was five minutes before two o'clock.

Huey asked the waitress for a drink. She said it was closing time and she couldn't serve a drink. Then Huey got up and walked over to the bar, with two men at the bar with the bar-tender. He asked him to serve him a drink. The bartender said he couldn't, it was closing time. Huey sent George to his post. He was at the door to the establishment, and George was at the door to the men's room. Then Huey said, "Okay, if you don't serve us a drink, I'm going to knock this place over," the sugges-tion being he was going to rob the place and everybody in it. At that statement, both bodyguards, who wore coats and ties, loosened their jackets, as if making them able to reach more quickly for a weapon, assuming they had one.

There was a pause, then this elderly African American man says, "Well, serve them a drink." It sounded so incredibly reasonable. The bartender hops on it. Huey comes back and sits down. They come over and bring Huey his drink. Huey gives the woman five dollars. She pushes it back and says, "No, it's on the house." Huey says, "No, it's on me." "No," she says, "it's on the house." Huey pays. "I insist." He puts down the five dollars, drinks the drink rather quickly. We got up and left.

While we were driving off in my car, Huey laughed and explained the details to me. If, for example, he did not pay for the drink, then it is robbery because he threatened robbery in order to get the drink. Technically speaking, he cited, you have robbed them of a drink. That's why he insisted on paying. As for leaving quickly, he said, "I believe in getting out before reinforcements arrive. After all, it's just the four of us, and who knows who they may have called, whether it was the police or someone else."[180]

Generally, according to Trivers, if Huey was armed, he'd say so.

Huey did not have a gun, and rarely did in my experience, unless he was hiding it from me. And yet, there were times when I would pick him up and he would say, "I'm dirty," and tell you right off the bat that he's either carrying a quarter ounce or he's carrying a gun. As an ex-felon, he's dirty.

Climbing through Oakland's crack bins at night could be scary. I didn't feel nervous in Huey's presence. It was only later when he threatened me that there was a period of a couple of months where I was nervous, because I didn't know the true intentions of the man. I knew I didn't have it in me to try to take him out if it came down to that. I doubt very much I could pull it off. Plus, I think he could read me real quickly.

Incidentally, Huey was a stickler for obeying driving laws, especially late at night. He would often get mad at me if I violated them. For example, I would make a U-turn down near Grove Street or downtown and he would berate me. "That's an illegal turn. You're in a business district." His father had been a stickler teaching him misdemeanor law, and had said that they used the misdemeanors to catch you in the felonies. You didn't want to be stopped by the cops or give them any excuse to interact with you, especially at three in the morning.

I came to dislike him on his drug of choice. I can think of a specific time when he got out of jail. I threw a party for him down in Santa Cruz, a coming-out party. It was a great party. I found some wonderfully attractive, nice undergraduates, and we rented out this room in this Chinese restaurant that we all liked. But he's got to find some blow, and it's a party for him, and it's Huey P., and so I had to find some. Then the whole tenor and tone of the evening changed from the moment that drug got into the evening, which I didn't find enjoyable.[181]

In addition to hanging out, Huey and Trivers continued their educational collaboration.

Huey decided to take a second reading course on evolutionary theory itself, or sociobiological evolutionary theory, which really was my field. Again, if he was straight and doing his work, then he was a very good student and a pleasure to talk to. But he believed that drugs could cut corners for him, which I don't think they can. For example, he used to say that all we need is one twenty-four-hour working period and we'll have this whole book down. Well, that's just complete nonsense. You don't end up after twenty-four hours of nonstop work writing with much of anything that's useful.

The evenings could go on forever. He would not let you go. I would be up with him all night. I have a wife and children at home in Santa Cruz. I still have an hour and fifteen minutes I have to drive [from Oakland]. He was Jekyll and Hyde on that drug. When he was at his best was during periods when he was drying out, where he had done the drugs so hard that he would go on six weeks where he would just drink tea and meditate. Then he was much more enjoyable to deal with.

Meanwhile, Trivers found himself under surveillance on the Santa Cruz campus as a result of his friendship with Huey.

I know they swept my office for guns once. It was the most absurd thing I'd seen. I happen to come in around eight-thirty one evening, shortly after an article appeared in the *Santa Cruz Sentinel* on Huey and my efforts to do this self-deception book. There had been some complaints to the university from husbands of women that worked up on the floor where I had my office.

My office was wall-to-wall books, with bookcases on four sides, everywhere except the doorway. I come in and find two men, strapping policemen types, pleasant-looking but muscular. One of them immediately said, "We're washing your walls." There were no walls to wash. They were up on a ladder holding some kind of device, which was, needless to say, not a scrubber. It was a metal detector going through all my books. I knew the university was a bit paranoid about Huey. I know he didn't feel he was respected too often by the professors there.[182]

Toward the end of Trivers's association with Huey in the early 1980s, Huey's unpredictable behavior persisted.

Once he burst into this room where I had laid down to sleep for the night, and his face was two inches from mine with his eyebrows raised up. He told me, "You did it again. You can sleep here, but as soon as you're ready, you go down the road." Naturally I recovered from my sleeplessness pretty quickly. That was when he excommunicated me and said it was for my own good. Then we were out of touch for seven or eight months in 1981.

He expelled me for my own good, which I also think was true. He said to stay out of "my territory."

I don't know how many people Huey threatened, but I know when he died, there were probably two thousand people in the San Francisco area that heaved a sigh of relief, in my opinion, because if he threatened you, it was scary. You knew he had the capacity, both in terms of internal motivation and the capacity to actually affect it.[183]

After Huey's graduation from UC Santa Cruz, as happy a moment as it was for Huey and his family, he began his downhill slide. The 1980s were a difficult decade for Huey. The Black Panther Party was finished. As his dependence on drugs and alcohol increased, by December 1982, Gwen could hold on no longer. Gwen's sister, Demetra Gayle, recalls how bad the situation was:

Huey ran the car off a hill with the kids in it. He was high and they almost died. He totaled the car. Gwen gathered up the kids to move to Chicago in the dead of winter. Huey wouldn't let her get any of her things, just a very few things. She lost a lot of her life. They had no winter coats, so it was a serious breakup. It was a vindictive thing.

My sister was exhausted. I never understood how she could do it. There's [Huey's] cocaine and the alcohol. When I see a bottle of Remy, I see Huey's face. She couldn't deal with her alcoholic addict husband. It was Huey P. Newton, alcoholic addict. When she left, she was exhausted.[184]

Huey wouldn't stay single long. Soon he would rekindle the flame with a woman, Fredrika Slaughter, who he'd been involved with for over fourteen years.

CHAPTER 19

SURVIVING HUEY: FREDRIKA'S WORDS

I t was 1970. I was going to school in Salem, Oregon.[185] Screwing up, not really focused. I was a kid, seventeen, when I went to Willamette University on a scholarship. They were recruiting black students to go up to Oregon, so they'd come to the community colleges and scoop people up. I felt really isolated up there. I was studying music, but I wasn't going to classes and I wasn't prepared for the academics. There were thirty-five black students in the whole school. Soon I was engaged to be married to a young law student in the school.

"How did I get into this," I asked myself, "and how could I spend the rest of my life in this depressing town?"

But I'd made a commitment and he was doing all the right things. Plus, it pleased my parents.

I came back home to Oakland to find that my mother, Arlene Slaughter, had been working with the Black Panther Party as a realtor. Our home was always filled with very interesting people. Tom Hayden lived next door. When I left for Oregon, I was wearing a dashiki that belonged to Eldridge that Tom had given me. Once, while my parents were gone for the weekend, Tom's partner, Ann Sheer, asked if I could house some Panthers who were underground, going out of the country.

At the time, there was a lot of hoopla and bad press about Huey living in a penthouse. I found out that my mother was instrumental in getting it for him. Then my mother said that day that Huey was going to be coming over for brunch. Up until then, my only experience with the Panthers was on Shattuck Avenue, where they had an office. Next door was AJ's Artistic Fingers, where all the pimps and hustlers used to get their hair done. So, between the Panthers and the pimps, I stayed on the other side of the street. I didn't want to be harassed by those pimps, and feared that the Panthers might harass me, too, because I wasn't wearing a big Afro and was apolitical.

I had mixed feelings about Huey Newton. I'd read about him in the paper. I didn't think he'd be very nice. That day, all the Panthers at my house intimidated me. I wasn't involved in any politics. I was the complete opposite of my mother. I wanted to wear makeup, and it wasn't politically correct to be interested in fashion, and that's all I was interested in.

When Huey came to the house, there were all these Black Panthers standing in the corners. John Seale, Bobby's brother, was there. David Hilliard was there. Huey was sitting at the head of the table, eating everything in sight. There were all these white students around, asking esoteric questions. But I wasn't interested. It soon became clear that everybody in the room had at least said something to Huey and I hadn't. Since I didn't have anything heavy, deep, or political to say, I just asked him what it was like in prison. Huey was gracious and kind. He didn't think it was a stupid question at all. He made eye contact. He told me that prison was a very lonely experience. Then I made my escape with my girlfriend to go out shopping.

Later that night, I was washing dishes at home when I got a call from Pat Hilliard, David's wife.

"This is Pat. Huey wants you to call him at this number."

Me? Huey wants me to call? He was at the Lamp Post. So I called my girlfriend.

"Huey Newton wants me to call him. You call him. Pretend you're me, and call me back and let me know what he says."

My girlfriend refused. "*You* call him and call *me* back."

I called and there was a mix-up. Huey wasn't there. Why did he want me? I'm certainly not joining any Panthers.

Then John Seale called.

"This is John Seale."

"John Steele?"

"John Seale. You know, the brother who was standing in the corner who you wouldn't talk to."

"I don't even know you."

"Did you make that call?"

"Yes, but nobody was there."

"I'll pick you up. I'll be there in twelve minutes."

"Huey wants me to come to his apartment," I told my mother. "It was ten o'clock at night and I'm a *very* young eighteen.

"It's a beautiful place," she said, "Let me know how you like it."

I was wearing purple tie-dyed pants and a tie-dyed shirt. We went to the high rise at 1200 Lakeshore. I'm blown away. We go upstairs to the penthouse. John knocks. Huey opens the door. He has no shirt on and it was freezing in the apartment. The windows were all open. Huey was holding this drink. I still remember the clinking of the ice and the drink. "I Stand Accused," by Isaac Hayes, was playing on the stereo. Then it was over. One look and I was gone and stayed gone for a long, long time.

What most intrigued me about Huey was the difference in how he was perceived publicly and how he was privately. At the apartment, he was really shy, making awkward kind of moves on me. He wasn't smooth at all.

"What's this here?" he'd dab my cheek. Then he'd lean over and try to kiss me. Real lame. He couldn't really kiss. But he won me over. I spent the night there and was scared because I had to sneak back into the house the next morning. I told my mother I had fallen asleep in front of the television.

The next day, Huey kept calling. He'd call me and threaten to jump off the balcony. "I'm going to fly like a bird. I'm so depressed, I'm going to kill myself. I need you to come see about me."

That's when I started taking care of Huey. Sneaking out the window at night. Going down to the Smokehouse burger joint nearby on Telegraph Avenue to catch a cab. I was going to Huey's to save his life. I'm just a kid, but he was in trouble. He was depressed and felt isolated from the organization. He felt like he didn't have a connection with the people. Most of the people who were party members—the rank and file—Huey didn't feel a connection to. So he'd escape from the penthouse and meet me and we'd do odd and normal things. Like when Huey would pump gas at a gas station for customers at a gas station at Alcatraz and Telegraph in Berkeley. A car would drive up, and Huey would pump their gas and wash their windows. One guy even did a double take, and then we'd have to run. The bodyguards didn't know where he was.

In 1970 I joined the party, thinking that's what he wanted. But it really wasn't. He didn't care. I thought he wanted me to be a revolutionary. He didn't. We never had conversations about the party. It eventually became burdensome to him. He never talked about the party wistfully. He was never nostalgic.

By then I had left school and I wasn't going back. So I started working at the Black Panther school as a teacher. I worked inside the party for a couple of years. I'd see Huey only when he wanted to see me. It was always on his terms. (It didn't become my terms until we got married. And then I stuck it to him.) I was angry for a lot of years having to live on his terms.

After a couple of years, I wanted out. We walked a picket line in front of Bill Boyette's liquor store on Grove Street from 6:00 AM until 2:00 AM daily. I'd see my friends heading for the freeway toward East Oakland, where all the parties were. They'd honk and here I was on this picket line. I wanted to hang out. I was twenty years old. I wanted to be with friends. One night I snuck out, me and my girlfriend and I went to a party in the Oakland Hills. I decided I wanted that life, and I was soon out of the [Black Panther] party. I wanted to go back to school and have fun. I told Huey I was leaving. It was okay with him. I didn't have to escape or lie. I was through. I stayed in town. I moved into an apartment over my mother's real estate office in Berkeley.

But once I was out of the party, I started seeing Huey again. I didn't like that Huey was seeing other women. I'm sure it wasn't just Gwen. Huey was the man. I would keep coming back, and I was always in his face. I stood up to him. Maybe that's why he was interested in me. I'd do things like pour his liquor down the sink or throw away his drugs while he lived in the apartment on Lakeshore. That made him angry. One time he was seething, so angry he was almost laughing. Shaking. "Don't *ever* do that again."

I saw his abuse go from drinking to the first time I ever saw cocaine. I had never seen cocaine before. I didn't drink. But we were good together.

Running the party, Huey spent a lot of time in bed and on the phone. Huey did a lot of his work in bed. He was compulsive about cleanliness. One of the reasons he kept 1200 Lakeshore so cold was because of his hot body temperature and his sweating. Another reason was germs. The place was stark. He was compulsive about keeping everything clean and in order. You couldn't make the bed. He had to make the bed. He had to make it just so. Everything had its place.

I remember the split with Eldridge. Huey was in the bed, screaming at Eldridge after the television show, almost crying he was so upset. One of the bedrooms was an office, and Gwen would be in there typing. One time we were looking down at the street through the telescope, and he saw a member named Calvin selling newspapers. Then he set the papers down and walked away. Huey saw him. Calvin got in trouble. Others, like David, would administer most of the day-to-day stuff for the party. You rarely saw Huey in the offices. I never remember him being that hands-on. He'd do a photo op on the picket line, but because of security, he rarely left the apartment.

We went out, maybe to the Lamp Post, or places where he was secure. Later, we went out to speakeasies. By 1973, the night before I went east to go back to college, we went to a couple of after-hours clubs. I was accepted to Wesleyan University in Connecticut, and I was going away, so this was my big night out.

These were illegal after-hours clubs where people used drugs and drank, completely underworld and smoky. There was music, a bar, cocaine, drinking, and sometimes dancing. Huey would frequent several after-hours places. One place was literally a hole in the wall—you actually had to climb through a hole to get to the backroom where the drugs were. In the back was another bar with cocaine. All of a sudden, Huey and his friends were beating this big man down, stomping him. I remember Huey, shouting, "Sugar Bear, Sugar Bear, Sugar Bear." A fight had started and we were ushered out fast. Then we went to another speakeasy. We rode in big long cars, while the guys wore long leather coats. Huey carried a swagger stick. Huey was a good fighter, but he always had a broken hand, usually in a cast. He wasn't a big guy, but his wrist was always broken fighting somebody.

The next day I got on a plane to Connecticut and made my way to Wesleyan University, where there were all these young students asking me if I wanted to study in their dorm rooms. Quite a contrast from the night before. I went back to college in Connecticut in 1973 and finished up in 1976 and came back to Oakland.

While I was still back in Connecticut, I had read in *Jet* magazine about Huey. There was a picture of him at the Hotel Havana Libre. So I called him there and billed the call to the university. Later someone from the FBI came and asked me about the call. Surprisingly enough, I got through and Huey answered the phone, but he sounded strange. He asked me about my family and the weather. He was real impersonal.

I had just come back to Oakland from Wesleyan in Connecticut when I was with my son's father, Andy. Santana was going to play at the Black Panthers' school in East Oakland. Andy wanted to see the show. My son was a baby then, about one year old, and my son's father and I were trying to make a go of it.

Andy and I were trying to make our relationship work, and he really wanted to see Santana. I asked him if he was sure, if he really wanted to go out there, because I'd read that Huey was back in town from Cuba. I hadn't seen him. After that last phone call, I'd dismissed him in the way he dismissed me. But Andy wanted to go.

So we went out to the school. There was a big crowd, and I remember seeing Huey from afar amid a couple of thousand people. I could see his eyes scanning the crowd. As he was slowly and methodically scanning the crowd, I was looking at him. Then our eyes locked, and that was it. He made his way around the crowd to come and see me. I hadn't seen him in years, because he'd been in Cuba and I was in school. I gave him my number. I don't remember him giving me his number.

Of course, Huey was married now. Later that day he called me. We met and talked. Where I was living there was a cottage behind the big house. We were on the deck of the house talking. (I have a picture of that day with my son.) There we were off and running again. Except it was different because Huey was married. He was now living in a home in the Oakland hills, where before he had lived in a stark apartment, the penthouse on 1200 Lakeshore. Now he had a home with a wife and her children. I knew things had changed, because he talked about having curtains. Huey never had curtains where he lived.

I started seeing him again. This was during the summer of 1977, right when he got back from Cuba. It was very painful and it was back and forth, back and forth. Eventually I couldn't handle it. I think one time he didn't call me for a couple of weeks, and I was so strung out on him that he told me—and I had only a vague recollection of this—that I went to his house, banging on the door, cursing him out: "Get the fuck out here, you're fucking with me. I'm tired of it. Things are different now. You have a wife." I was in a rage. I couldn't handle it on his terms anymore, where I always had for all those years.

Everything in my life revolved around Huey. Any man I was with had something to do with him. Either I was getting back at him or someone reminded me of him. There was always a link to Huey in any major relationship that I had. One night Huey was supposed to meet me at a nightclub for my twenty-eighth birthday. We were on and off again. During this period of time, we were on and he was supposed to meet me, although he was still married to Gwen. But she knew about me. They had an open relationship. Huey had many relationships outside of their relationship.

I was modeling at the time, in and out of the country, and I traveled so much, I didn't have an apartment, I was living with my mother. Anyway, Huey didn't show. Huey's brother-in-law, Mark, brought me flowers, telling me that Huey couldn't make it tonight. I always found Mark to be kind. When Huey and I would spend time together, Mark would be the driver. He was bright and sensitive. He tempered Huey in a really nice way. Mark and I started talking and developed a close relationship. We connected. I really liked him. Then he told Huey. What could Huey say? He was with Gwen. I remember Huey even calling me to counsel me about Mark. I saw Mark for five years. I was in love. I wasn't seeing Huey. If I were dating someone, I would bring them to the Lamp Post, Huey's club. I did that on more than one occasion.

I broke up with Mark in August 1984. Several months prior, I had run into Melvin, Huey's brother, and gave him my phone number. Out of the blue, Huey called me from his brother Melvin's house. He had seen my phone number on Melvin's refrigerator. It was September 7th when he called me. I hadn't seen nor spoken to Huey in almost five years.

"I'm calling you because I want to marry you."

"What?"

"I should have done this a long time ago. One of my biggest regrets is that we didn't marry, so I'd like to do it now."

At a Hollywood party, according to Huey, they always "asked the hard questions." Gwen was with him. The question was if you weren't with your spouse, who would you be with? Huey said he'd be with Fredrika. That was his regret, that we hadn't gotten married when I was young. Thank God we didn't. Although I wouldn't have had to share him with anybody anymore, I don't know if I would have been able to take it. Still, I would have gone to Cuba in a heartbeat. I know Gwen made some hard choices [in] leaving her children [and] going to Cuba. Could I have left my child? I like to think not.

I had read in the paper that Huey had gone into drug rehabilitation. Richard Pryor paid for his treatment. So I thought

Huey was clean, even though I'd heard all the stories about how Huey had gotten psychotic when he was drug-addicted.

"I'd like to meet with you," Huey suggested. "Let's get a hamburger."

"Okay, but I'm taking my son with me." That was my protection.

"Please bring him."

We met. It turns out Huey didn't even have money for a hamburger. He borrowed the money from a woman he had been seeing.

Afterward he took me up to his house in the hills. He really wanted to marry me. I was unsure, so I told him that he needed to talk to my father and my brother. I wanted him to ask them for my hand in marriage. And he did. Huey visited my father and asked for my hand in marriage. My father, a man of few words, agreed.

I went to my brother Mickey and told him I was getting married.

"To who? No, not Huey."

"Yes."

"Oh, no," he shook his head. "You're like a moth attracted to a flame."

We planned our wedding a few months down the line since Huey was facing a possible jail sentence for an old weapons charge. But Huey wanted to marry sooner in case he might have to go to jail. September 14, 1984, we were married. Huey's friend Bert Schneider, who was married to a woman named Greta, met us in Reno. Greta was my maid of honor and Bert was Huey's best man, and we got married at the Hearts of Reno wedding chapel, right across the street from city hall. Our picture is still up on their wall. I modeled at two fashion shows that day for Nordstrom's, so I was earning money and able to take care of my son and myself. After we got married, we went out to dinner. Huey laughed at me because I ordered milk with my dinner. It was funny. I wore a crummy, very provincial dress and there was a heart-shaped bed in the hotel we stayed in. Bert gave us a few thousand dollars to gamble with. I wanted to take the money home, but Huey gambled the money away. Here I was, a former single parent. Let's just gamble half.

On the plane ride home, Huey got drunk on the plane. Then he got really belligerent with the flight attendant because she wouldn't give him any more liquor.

"The pilot says no more drinks," she said.

"Well, let me go talk to the pilot," Huey demanded.

A little old lady was sitting next to Huey.

"Calm down, honey. Didn't you just get married? You have a new lovely bride. You don't want to get in trouble."

When we landed in Oakland, the police were there to usher us off the plane. By now I'm thinking, *what in the world had I gotten myself into?*

I didn't move into Huey's house for a couple of months. I needed a transition. Plus, I wondered what Huey did all day. The [Black Panther] party was over. He was working on a film project. So I would go out to the malls and hang out. I was working in the fashion industry as a model, so my time was flexible.

I couldn't be at home with him all day. His energy was too intense. I had never spent a lot of time with him, just nights. I never lived with him, and I had never been married before. His house didn't feel like a home, even though he told me to do whatever I wanted to his house so I would feel comfortable. "Make it your home."

When my son first came to the house, he thought we were rich. There was a maid. Brand-new phone answering machines. Finally I loaded all my stuff into a pickup truck and moved all my stuff up the hill into Huey's house. Huey was looking out the window, smiling, saying, "Here she comes."

I was apprehensive, but I was up for it. There seemed to be enough space in the house where I could be alone. I liked solitude. But up in the hills where this house was, I soon felt isolated. I was used to neighborhoods. I felt marooned. The lights would go out. My friends stopped coming around. It was lonely up there, though at first it was fun when we entertained a lot. Then things started to turn stranger.

After we got married, my friends were giving me a bridal shower at the house. The night before, Huey didn't come home. I was up all night, frantic, calling his brother Melvin. Should I call the police? We were having the shower that afternoon, and I'm a wreck because I'd been up all night long. As my friends were coming over to the house, my cousin took me aside and whispered to me: "Huey's downstairs."

I ran outside and there was Huey, hanging out of the car. He looked like death. His eyes were hollow. When he was using cocaine, his jaw would be off to one side. He was mumbling incoherently. We ushered him upstairs the back way so my friends couldn't see him. He looked terrible, all bent over. I had to keep checking up on him upstairs. He reeked of alcohol. He was filthy dirty. There was brown dirt underneath his fingernails.

"What is wrong with your fingernails, Huey?"

"I had to grab somebody in the ass," he slurred.

"That's ass under your fingernails? Huey, where's your underwear?"

"Where's my underwear? Hmmm. I know I didn't fuck anbody. Where's my underwear?"

It was pathetic. He was talking loud. He ordered oysters. Then a male stripper came, and Huey was upstairs looking down at the stripper. I was nervous he would come out and embarrass me in front of my friends. That was the first time he disappeared, but not the last.

After we got married, we planned a honeymoon. My dad had given us tickets to fly to Hawaii. I booked a hotel. The night before we were to leave, Huey didn't come home. I knew the police hadn't arrested him because I checked, so I called my girlfriend and told her to fly to Hawaii with me. While we were there having a good time, Huey called and finally flew over. I spent my honeymoon with Huey and my girlfriend, who got her own room.

That's when I knew I had *really* made a mistake, and that's when I started seeing a therapist.

"I have made a mistake. Huey is an alcoholic. He's not clean."

"Stick it out a little bit."

I felt like I was my therapist's source of entertainment. Plus, I didn't want to let my friends down. My girlfriends felt that after I married Huey, I'd made it for all of us. I was doing all right. I had moved to a fancy neighborhood. I didn't need to work. I had the glamorous life. Supposedly. So I didn't want to leave Huey. Unfortunately, it never got better.

On the other hand, because Huey was so childlike, he was wonderful to my son. They played together a lot. We had a lot of kids over. He played with them. It was like having another child. Huey had an interesting magnetism. I felt maternal toward him. I also had sensual feelings, but it was hard to also have maternal and sensual feelings toward a man at once. But we were a family. We had Thanksgiving at our house so I could meet Huey's family. His brothers and sisters were older, so we kept the closest contact with Melvin. We'd spend holidays there, and it was nice. We were trying to put together a family: Huey, my son, and me. We'd go to Disneyland or fly kites. Huey joined my church. I didn't push him.

Huey had one leg that was a couple of inches longer than the other. When he got nervous, he would limp. Plus, he was dyslexic. He couldn't make out a check and sign his name if someone was watching him. He'd get nervous at the grocery store, and rather than make out the check, he'd dash out. The day he joined the church, he hobbled up to the altar, nervous. Amidst all of this chaos, we'd do the things that happy families did.

One day it was my son's birthday, so Huey rented a limo and picked him and all his friends up at school. My son was in the sixth grade. Huey hired a chauffeur with gold teeth to ride the kids around town to the ice-cream parlor. It was Huey's idea. He and my son were close. We even went to Sears to get our family portrait taken. Huey was looking to live a normal life.

Huey was working on a film idea. I was not at all interested in that Hollywood scene. I went down once for our wedding reception, and I felt very intimidated by the movie stardom. I was more interested in family things, which goes back to earlier in our relationship, when he'd sneak away and pump gas and do these ordinary things that Huey couldn't do when he was isolated in that apartment tower.

Eventually the police raided our house up on the hill. Twice. It was scary. I was on the phone one night. Huey was cooking. He used to do all the cooking. He struggled with his weight. He'd cook chili, and then we'd go on diets and eat nothing but broiled chicken and salad.

"Don't open the door," Huey said, but my son didn't hear him and opened the door. In comes the SWAT team, about twenty-five policemen armed with rifles. They found parts of a rifle underneath the bed. Huey went to court for that, but we beat it. We were separated at the time, but the police found shoes under the bed. I told them they were my son's. We marched him [my son] into the courtroom one day. The prosecution objected. As I was ushering him out, we were riding the elevator down with the alternate juror, who looked down at my son's feet. The next day, that alternate got on the jury panel, and because my son had big feet, we dodged that bullet. That case hinged on those shoes.

Huey had chunks of time as far as sobriety. Toward the end of his life, he had the longest periods of sobriety since I'd been with him. But before that, he started to get paranoid and delusional with cocaine, and became abusive to my brother and family. Our times as a normal family were always on the brink of disintegration. The family life was built around the chaos. Since there was no more money, I went back to work as a nurse. Then we lost our house to a forced sale, because Huey lost an IRS judgment against the house. When I got married to him, they attached my wages immediately. Eventually we were homeless. My house was rented out, so I couldn't get rid of the tenants. So we took to the road.

The beginning of the end for Huey was when we lost his house. One day the real estate people were showing the house, and Huey had come back from a drunken binge. He would snore really loud, and you couldn't wake him up. He was upstairs, knocked out, on the bed asleep, spread-eagle, butt-naked. So I just covered him up. When the realtors came, they went upstairs, then left panic-stricken. Upstairs, Huey had kicked off the covers.

When the movers came in to take all the furniture out, the last thing they could take out was the bed, because Huey was just lying there on the bed, looking at the television. There was no other furniture in the house but this television, his remote, and a mattress with him on it. Clicking away, he stared at the television. It was really sad.

So we took to the road. We moved everything into storage and went to Santa Cruz and stayed in the St. George Hotel for a few weeks, just Huey and me. While we were homeless, it was kind of free not being encumbered. When we were on the road, we could make a left turn or a right. It didn't matter. It was our choice. We drifted around for about a month. We hung out with Bob Trivers; Lorna, his wife; and his beautiful kids, one of which was Huey's godchild.

Huey was demoralized when we were able to move into my house, but I was so happy to get away from his. I was back where it was familiar. But that wasn't Huey's dream. His dream was to take care of my son and me. It's something he always said he wanted to do. Finally, when everything collapsed, and I went back to work, he couldn't handle it. When he was with Gwen they had money. Bert was very supportive. Their relationship transcended politics. They used to call each other "brother." But Bert was tired of supporting Huey.

Huey would say, "I'm a disaster," broken when he lost his house in the hills. It was even shaped like an "H," so he felt like the house was built for him. He really loved that house. He called it his treehouse. While the move back to my house wasn't good for him, it was good for me. I was no longer isolated.

We were struggling financially a lot, and I couldn't live with him. After my son's father, Andy, died, and after I came back home from the funeral, the house was a wreck. Huey had turned it into a dope house while I was gone. Then he started stealing and selling things from the house.

He'd take the car and not pick me up from work. He'd be gone for four days, come back, and be in bed for days. When he'd come off a binge, he'd pay my son fifty cents an hour to stay inside with him to watch TV. "I'm lonely," he would cry. I'd hear him upstairs talking to the cat. "Come here, Tiger. I'll be nice." One time I was so sick of him, I pumped him full of Valium, hoping he'd just die. But Huey wouldn't die. Looking back, I should have had him committed, because he was so psychotic. It was drug-induced psychosis and he was out of his mind, and he needed help.

I'm convinced Huey was bipolar and could have benefited greatly from the meds that are now available. Yet people with that diagnosis are the most resistant to taking their meds, because they feel good during the manic phase, when they're most creative. I should have had Huey committed on a 51/50, a psychiatric hold where one is a danger to oneself and to others. Huey was certainly psychotic, delusional, and paranoid enough for me to have warranted it. But if he wasn't ready to stop using, there was nothing anybody could do. Huey liked to dance into that other life.

Finally, Huey said that he would go to a drug-treatment hospital. So I called and arranged for a bed. Then I went into the bathroom, where I took a bath, getting ready to go and take Huey to rehab. Suddenly Huey jumps into the bathtub with all his clothes on. From behind me, he puts a knife to my throat.

"I'm going to kill you right now."

He had never done anything like that. He slapped me once years before, but nothing like this.

I was in danger. I figured if I could look him in the eye, make some eye contact and talk to him, I could escape. So I turned around slow, trying to talk him down. "Huey, don't do this. You don't want to do this."

I slowly got out of the bathtub. "You don't want to kill me."

"I'm gonna cut your fucking throat."

While I'm talking, I'm slowly putting on my clothes. "You don't have to go if you don't want to."

Then I dashed out of the house, running down the street. Huey was running behind me. I was hoping the neighbors would see us and call the police, but they just looked on. I got in my car, started it up, and while I'm driving, Huey jumped up on the roof of the car. He's pounding on the windshield and I'm braking, trying to get him off the roof. What happened later, I don't recall. I guess I've blocked that memory out.

I must say, in 1989, during the last six months of his life, Huey was sober. When people talk about him being in West Oakland during his last couple of weeks, it's not true. Huey got really calm. He was easy to be around. He started giving his things away, especially his suits. He'd call his brother Lee, who he hardly talked to. His suits were beautifully monogrammed on the inside with his handwriting. So he gave a suit to Lee. Then he gave a signature suit to Sonny Man. He must have known something was about to happen. A couple of weeks before Huey died, he told me in the kitchen, "You better get some insurance out on me."

I knew he was sober, since it was no secret when he was using. All hell would break loose. Huey wasn't one to sneak drugs. You knew. But this time he wasn't. He was clean for our longest period of our time together. We still needed money, so we were going to sell Panther memorabilia that was stored in my basement. So we put an ad in a newspaper. We were going to have the sale on a Saturday, August 22, 1989. It was the day he was killed.

During those final days, I had foster kids in the house. Because he was a felon, he wasn't supposed to be in the house with the children. But Huey was calm and helpful with the children. Plus, we were waiting for his film biography to go through. Then Huey got the phone call. The deal didn't go through. We'd been waiting on this deal. It was our ticket out. It was supposed to happen. It was just a matter of when. When the phone call came that the deal was axed, Huey was devastated. I had already quit my job at the hospital as an RN.

Huey came into the kitchen, where I had four kids, all less than five years old. The social worker was on her way to pay a visit. I couldn't talk to Huey about his film deal. He was supposed to pick up my son at day camp, and then we would talk later, after the social worker was gone. That was the last time I saw him.

Huey never picked up my son, and that's when I knew that Huey had gone off again. That night was horrible. All the kids were sick. My son and I were sick. There was a bad flu going around. It was horrible. So I went to sleep. At seven the next morning, I got a call from a woman I knew, Lessie Hamilton, who had trained me as a nurse.

"Have you talked to the emergency room?"

"Huey's in the emergency room?" I asked.

"Just call the emergency room, now."

I hung up the phone and called the emergency room. They put me on hold for a long time. I told them I was looking for Huey Newton, my husband. Is he in the hospital? The doctor said, yes, he's dead. He had been shot down by a young drug dealer in West Oakland on Tenth and Center. Five minutes later all the phone calls started flooding in. My phone rang nonstop.

I called my family and we went down to the hospital. I was with my son, and we were walking really fast. I had just attended a crack conference at Glide Memorial Church in San Francisco, so I had this sweatshirt on that said, "Crack is Hell, Don't Buy, Don't Sell." Huey had been moved into the morgue. I didn't see him until they moved him into the mortuary. Then mentally, I moved into a whole different zone and dealt with all the small details, like how Huey wore his hair and how his sideburns had to be trimmed.

I had no insurance, no money, so people started donating money to bury Huey. In the newspaper, they put the address of a bank on Telegraph Avenue in North Oakland where people could walk in and offer small donations. Some were two dollars. There were five-dollar checks or twenty-two dollars in cash with a small note attached. You could tell some of the checks were from elderly people. No big checks, but it all amounted to ten thousand dollars collected in a matter of days. Sometimes I like to look at those checks and the cards. It was really beautiful. In the end, the people buried Huey.

Before the funeral, I remember watching television. It was so odd watching my husband's blood running down the street as the fire department hosed the crime scene. There were his sneakers, his new sneakers. His jacket. I don't know why the sneakers stood out, but they did. They were white, and he was kind of proud of them. Since he wouldn't let me spend money on him, in the end he dressed kind of shabby.

The funeral was big. Melvin and his wife and David put it all together. Melvin's house was central headquarters. There were a lot of people. It seemed surreal. People were kind. The Allen Temple Baptist Church at Eighty-third and East Fourteenth Street was packed with thousands of friends and supporters. I did respect the fact that Huey didn't want to be buried, so I had him cremated. Then I rode around with his ashes in the trunk of my car for a long time, just to be near him, for so long I eventually forgot he was there. Now his ashes live at home. Someday we'll sprinkle them over Oakland.

Huey cut to the chase. There was no game-playing with Huey. You didn't have to guess, and there was no saying yes if he meant no. If you asked Huey a question, you had to be prepared for the answer.

After Huey's death, I began working as a nurse in the field of addiction medicine. If someone like Huey would walk in, I'd ask if they were ready to stop. *Here are the tools to help you stop, but you've got to want it, a proven twelve-step program that can change your life if you work with the tools of the program. But are you ready to go to any lengths?* That's what it's going to take, and you have to have that gift of desperation. Huey didn't have it. He desperately didn't want to be sober. Though he was attracted to a simple home life, it was boring to him. You've got to want it. It's not an easy program of recovery, but it's a simple one—one day at a time.

CHAPTER 20

THE SPIRIT OF THE PANTHER

Huey's funeral sparked new interest in continuing the struggle and new movements. People who were there were saying this couldn't be the end; this should be the beginning of something new. Thousands of people who came together felt that the funeral and the surrounding days served as a propitious moment to reconnect with old comrades and activists from around the country. Fredricka Newton, Elaine Brown, and I created the Huey P. Newton Foundation in response to this clarion call to carry on with the ideas and the work that was left behind by Huey Newton and the Black Panther Party.

Police misconduct is rampant all across the country. Police community relations are very, very bad. Racial profiling, police killings, and corruption within police departments still exist. The issues of education, especially in the Oakland schools, have developed into antagonistic contradictions between the people and the state. These are the same problems that Huey P. Newton and the Black Panther Party addressed over forty years ago.

Our legacy today is the original ten-point program of the Black Panther Party. Some of our community service programs are sorely needed today. Some of the issues were housing, education, health care, and jobs. We were involved in the antiwar movement while the government spent billions of dollars on a war economy and neglected domestic programs. The issue of drugs and black-on-black crime plagued our communities.

Huey's murder was directly related to drugs, and he was constantly plagued and troubled by either drugs, alcohol, or both. It was in some nightclub, speakeasy, or after-hours joint where most of the violence perpetrated by Huey took place. I don't remember there ever being a time in Huey's adult life when he wasn't in some way abusing drugs or alcohol, to the very end of his life. It was a demoralizing and degrading decline, running around on the street as a crack addict, asking people for money. He was powerless over drugs and alcohol, hopelessly addicted.

Most chemically dependent people can't accept the fact that they cannot gain control and deal with their own addiction. Huey was no exception. In the beginning of the recovery process, accepting the fact that one has a problem is the most important phase. Huey was in constant denial, unwilling to go to any lengths to stay sober. Ironically, people like Richard Pryor tried to help Huey by sending him to a recovery program. Huey would go into such programs for a few days or weeks and then leave. He always ended up back on the street using drugs and alcohol. In order to deal effectively with recovery, you have to accept the fact that you are addicted and that you do not have the power to fix yourself. Anyone can get sober. Staying sober is the solution.

The last time I talked to Huey was at his brother Melvin's house, a month or so before Huey was killed. We met there, and I went to the liquor store with him to buy a lottery ticket. We were talking along the way. He'd heard about my entering a recovery program. He staunchly stated that he was not interested in being in any recovery program, and that as a matter of fact, he didn't even like being around people who were not using drugs and alcohol. I saw that as another way of denying the solution to his problems.

My response was simply, "Huey, like everything else you do, when you're ready, you'll get back into a program and deal with your problem."

"I don't see it as a problem. I'm doing what I want to do."

Demetra Gayle recalled that Huey did try to get into recovery a couple of times.

> A few months before he died, I saw him on TV. It was a public service show. Somebody was interviewing him. I could just tell he was sober. It was my "clean-dar." You know the difference if he's not high. I said to myself, "Oooo, Oooo, Huey's sober." I ran and made a lunch date and got together with him. We sat in a booth. I came clean with him and told him how I felt about our years together as family members. "It was hard talking to you. You talked over my head. Then I saw that you were clean on the TV show, and I just wanted to get with you, shake hands and see what you're up to."
>
> He seemed to like it. He was happy. I don't know what he was up to, writing or something. He seemed to appreciate that I was treating him like a regular person, taking time out to get together and honor him. He didn't look as nice as he did when he was with my sister, but he looked okay. He was casually dressed. He looked like he was taking care of himself. His hairline was starting to recede. It was the same old Huey. He relapsed and he went back to using, but at that particular span of time, he was clean.[186]

Ultimately, Huey never overcame the first stage of denial, which is to agree, believe, and accept that you are powerless over drugs and alcohol and cannot help yourself. Huey was not willing to do that. And as a result, it cost him his life. After that day, I never saw him again. A month later, on the morning of August 22, 1989, Huey was murdered on the streets of West Oakland.

In the earlier days, Huey talked a lot about the concept of reactionary suicide versus revolutionary suicide. His definition of reactionary suicide was when someone's life is taken by a set of reactionary conditions, whether it's by a crime in the community, getting involved in drugs, or committing suicide out of depression. Huey called all of that reactionary suicide because it was a set of reactionary conditions that drove a person to self-murder.

Revolutionary suicide, on the other hand, is when one takes their own life in their own hands and tries to determine a positive outcome while being under some form of systematic oppression. Maybe there's a chance, however slight, that your life and death can bring about a positive result in terms of the transformation of society.

Huey's definition of revolutionary suicide is a popular concept today. We now often hear the term "suicide bombers." The actions of those men who flew the airplanes into the twin towers of the World Trade Center might be considered by some to be acts of revolutionary suicide. They made the decision that they would not die a simple reactionary death, but that their deaths would have meaning, and that they would die as martyrs who would then go on to live in paradise.

It's ironic that Huey's own life became such a degrading, painful, and out-of-control situation that he himself met the kind of reactionary suicide that he talked about so often in his analysis. It was prophetic in some ways, because Huey certainly did have choices. Huey had a doctorate in philosophy, but what good was a PhD or his intellect when he was addicted to drugs and alcohol? It was a very sad and painful time for everybody who loved Huey because of what he stood for and the sacrifices he made. He figured that he could handle his drug addiction, but his willpower wasn't enough, and in the final analysis he was just another crack addict. He was alienated and lost his self respect. He was reduced to a pitiful state of incomprehensible demoralization.

Huey was murdered on the street by a young drug dealer with whom he had an encounter early in the morning. He was killed by a culture of drug violence, where this fratricidal insanity permeates the black community. Huey's was just one of thousands of deaths that happen over something as pathetic and insignificant as twenty dollars' worth of rock cocaine.

The Huey P. Newton Foundation was started in 1993, implemented in order to preserve our history, to implement cultural and history programs consistent with the ideas and theories of its namesake, Huey P. Newton. Fredrika Newton is the president. Elaine Brown is vice president. I'm a founding member, executive director, and treasurer.

The foundation's purpose is to honor the legacy of the Black Panther Party and its leader, Huey P. Newton, by preserving the history and educating the public about the relevance of our movement. Guided by Huey's writings and teachings, we produce knowledge.

Huey was a very complex man; there was the old Huey, the new Huey, the young Huey, and the Huey who was ever changing. I once said to Huey, "I think I know you better than most people do."

"Don't ever say that," he corrected me, "because I don't even know myself. The man I went to bed as last night was not the man who woke up this morning."

Most leaders, most human beings have problems. Everybody comes with baggage. That's the limitation of humanity. Huey had all kinds of negatives. He would admit that although he was supremely violent, he was also supremely kind.

He was a balanced man with both the capacity to love and the capacity to disagree. No more, no less. Huey understood more about dealing with his personal fear than most men, yet he never seemed to exemplify fear. But he would tell you, "I'm motivated by fear of people. I'll do to people exactly what I imagine they'll do to me if the tables were turned. That's what motivates me. I'm motivated by fear." So although Huey had the capacity to be violent, he also had the capacity to be very gentle, kind, and giving.

Huey was later diagnosed as being bipolar and manic-depressive. Unfortunately, we didn't recognize it at the time. None of us understood the severity of his drug addiction and alcoholism. He took Ritalin, he used cocaine, smoked weed, he drank cognac and gin. You couldn't do anything more than Huey. If you drank a pint, he'd drink two pints. He'd get into contests to see who could drink the most. Huey was an extreme man. After all, he was the guy who stood up and jacked rounds into a shotgun, standing in front of the police, daring them to take his life. He was like that about everything. Huey's life had become totally unmanageable. He was powerless over drugs and alcohol.

People in the Black Panther Party had an incomplete understanding of drug addiction. They generally saw Huey when he wasn't drinking or using. To them, he was a brilliant leader. But when he abused drugs and alcohol, he could be violently insane and totally out of control. We never had the awareness that he needed to be in a recovery program, that we should have done everything we could to get him hospitalized. We always thought that Huey Newton could handle it. He could drink eighteen straight shots and never stumble. He could sniff an ounce of cocaine all by himself and in a couple of hours still be walking around communicating ideas. We thought of Huey as the essence of somebody who was in control. But in reality, he was a madman, and we enabled him. Since we were all ignorant of the disease of alcoholism and drug addiction, we never intervened. Had we intervened, Huey probably would have listened. He was good at accepting criticism. If we caught him the day after, coming down, when he was sane, when he wasn't crazy or manic, with the right people who cared, who he respected and loved, I think we might have saved him. I would like to have been a part of that, but at the time, I was just as far out as he was. I needed help, too.

Eventually I made it to a recovery program. Huey and I had a dialogue about it, but he was still out there. Simply put, I was trying to get it together and he wasn't. Even when I was using, I never wanted to be anywhere near Huey when he was on drugs. I never used drugs with him. He and my wife and son would sit up in my house and use drugs, while I wouldn't, even though I was an addict, too. Huey was too crazy. I couldn't stand to be around him. It was too unnerving. I couldn't trust him. I was afraid of him, because I didn't know what he was going to do when he was high on drugs.

One night, toward the end, Huey came to my house, banging on the door.

"Lemme in! Lemme in!"

"Who is it?"

"It's me! Lemme in!" Huey was running, and he had only one shoe on.

"What are you running from?"

"The cops are after me!"

My mind warped. I couldn't believe it. I was shocked. Huey Newton running from the cops?

"The police are chasing me, let me in, they're after me."

I felt dishonored and disgraced. Huey Newton, running from the cops. They're chasing him. He's on drugs. He's hiding.

My own personal drug addiction, living on the street with a total loss of self-respect, with no place else to go, by reaching bottom, I finally made it to a drug program. And by the grace of God, I lived and I'm here to tell the story. That's what saved my life.

"I have no doubt," Huey wrote, "that the revolution will triumph."

And the people of the world will prevail, seize power, seize the means of production, wipe out racism, capitalism, reactionary intercommunalism, and reactionary suicide. The people will win a new world. Yet when I think of individuals in the revolution, I cannot predict their survival. Revolutionaries must accept this fact, especially the Black revolutionaries in America whose lives are in constant danger from the evils of colonial society. Considering how we must live, it is not hard to accept the concept of revolutionary suicide.

The great, more immediate problem is the survival of the entire world. If the world does not change, all its people will be threatened by greed, exploitation, and violence of the power structure in the American empire. The handwriting is on the wall. The United States is jeopardizing its own existence and the existence of all humanity. If Americans knew the disasters that lay ahead, they would transform this society tomorrow for their own preservation. The Black Panther Party is in the vanguard of the revolution that seeks to relieve this country of its crushing burden of guilt. We are determined to establish true equality and the means for creative work.

When scholars call our actions suicidal, they should be logically consistent and describe all historical revolutionary movements in the same way. Thus the American colonists, the French of the late eighteenth century, the Russians of 1917, the Jews of Warsaw, the Cubans, the NLF [National Front for the Liberation of Southern Vietnam], the North Vietnamese—any people who struggle against a brutal and powerful force—are suicidal. Also, if the Black Panthers symbolize the suicidal trend among Blacks, then the whole Third World is suicidal, because the Third World fully intends to resist and overcome the ruling class of the United States. Is the government of the United States suicidal? I think so.

With this redefinition, the term "revolutionary suicide" is not as simplistic as it might seem initially. In coining the phrase, I took two knowns and combined them to make an unknown, a neoteric phrase in which the word "revolutionary" transforms the word "suicide" into an idea that has different dimensions and meanings, applicable to a new and complex situation.

My prison experience is a good example of revolutionary suicide in action, for prison is a microcosm of the outside world. From the beginning of my sentence, I defied the authorities by refusing to cooperate; as a result, I was confined to "lock-up," a solitary cell. As the months passed and I remained steadfast, they came to regard my behavior as suicidal. I was told that I would crack and break under the strain. I did not break, nor did I retreat from my position. I grew strong.

The concept of revolutionary suicide is not defeatist or fatalistic. On the contrary, it conveys an awareness of reality in combination with the possibility of hope—reality because the revolutionary must always be prepared to face death, and hope because it symbolizes a resolute determination to bring about change. Above all, it demands that the revolutionary see his death and his life as one piece. Chairman Mao says that death comes to all of us, but it varies in its significance: to die for the reactionary is lighter than a feather; to die for the revolution is heavier than Mount Tai.[187]

NOTES

CHAPTER 2

1. Melvin Newton, personal interview, conducted by Lewis Cole and David Hilliard. Oakland, CA 1993.
2. Bobby Seale, personal interview, Tuesday, June 29, 2004. Oakland, CA. conducted by Zimmerman & Hilliard.

CHAPTER 3

3. Huey P. Newton, *Revolutionary Suicide* (New York: Harcourt Brace Jovanovich, 1973), 92.
4. Ibid., 94.
5. Seale interview.

CHAPTER 4

6. Newton, *Revolutionary Suicide,* 76.
7. Ibid., 110.
8. Ibid., 111.
9. Ibid., 113.
10. Seale interview.
11. Melvin Newton interview.
12. Newton, *Revolutionary Suicide,* 113.

CHAPTER 5

13. Melvin Newton interview.
14. Ibid.
15. Seale interview.
16. Newton, Revolutionary Suicide, 115.
17. Seale interview.
18. Ibid.
19. Newton, *Revolutionary Suicide,* 127.
20. Seale interview.
21. Ibid.

CHAPTER 6

22. Newton, *Revolutionary Suicide,* 139.
23. Seale interview.
24. Newton, *Revolutionary Suicide,* 142.
25. *Black Panther,* Vol. 1, Issue 1, April 25, 1967. Page 2.
26. Newton, *Revolutionary Suicide,* 146.

CHAPTER 7

27. Seale interview.
28. Ibid.
29. Ibid.
30. Ibid.
31. *Ramparts,* 1967.
32. Newton, *Revolutionary Suicide,* 150.

CHAPTER 8

33. Newton, *Revolutionary Suicide,* 173.
34. Ibid., 176.
35. Edward Keating, *Free Huey!* (Berkeley, CA: Ramparts Press), 21-23.
36. Newton, *Revolutionary Suicide,* 178.
37. Keating, *Free Huey!,* 24.
38. Newton, *Revolutionary Suicide,* 179.
39. Ibid., 181.

CHAPTER 9

40. Newton, *Revolutionary Suicide,* 184.
41. Ibid.
42. Ibid.
43. Melvin Newton interview.
44. Ibid.
45. Newton, *Revolutionary Suicide,* 184.
46. Ibid., 195.

47. Ibid., 204.
48. Ibid., 205-06.
49. Ibid., 207.
50. Keating, *Free Huey!*, 32.
51. Newton, *Revolutionary Suicide*, 210.
52. Keating, *Free Huey!*, 69.
53. Newton, *Revolutionary Suicide,* 319.
54. Ibid., 232.
55. Ibid., 240.

CHAPTER 10
56. Huey P. Newton, private papers.
57. Ibid.
58. Ibid.
59. Ibid.
60. Newton, *Revolutionary Suicide,* 129.
61. Huey P. Newton, private papers.
62. Eldridge Cleaver, *Post Prison Writings & Speeches* (New York: Random House, 1969), 29.
63. Huey P. Newton, private papers.
64. Ibid.
65. Lee Lockwood, *Conversation With Eldridge Cleaver; Algiers* (New York: McGraw-Hill, 1970).
66. Newton, *Revolutionary Suicide,* 329.
67. Ibid., 330.
68. Ibid., 331.
69. Stokely Carmichael, tape of Carmichael press conference, April 5, 1968.

CHAPTER 11
70. Taped cassette interview between Charles R. Garry and Charles Perry, May 5, 1968.
71. Newton, *Revolutionary Suicide,* opening tribute, ii.
72. Ibid., 328-29.
73. Ibid., 330.
74. Huey P. Newton, *Hidden Traitor,* unpublished manuscript, 41.
75. Ibid., 42-43.

76. Ibid., 43.
77. Ibid., 43-44.
78. Ibid., 46.
79. Transcription of television show, KGO-San Francisco.
80. Transcription of tape recorded conversation by Cleaver between Huey Newton and Eldridge Cleaver (unbeknownst to Huey).
81. Newton, *Hidden Traitor,* 47.
82. Ibid., 49.
83. Ibid.
84. Ibid., 50.
85. Ibid., 52-53.
86. Ibid., 54-55.
87. Ibid., 56.
88. Ibid., 57-58.
89. *Black Panther,* April 24, 1976, p. 2.
90. *Black Panther,* February 18, 1976, p. 15.

CHAPTER 12
91. Newton, *Revolutionary Suicide,* 249.
92. Ibid., 256.
93. Ibid., 264.
94. Ibid., 289.
95. Ibid.
96. Ibid., 292.

CHAPTER 13
97. Newton, *Revolutionary Suicide,* 291.
98. Audrea Jones-Dunham, personal interview, July 9, 2004. Telephone interview, Oakland, CA/Philadelphia, PA.
99. Newton, *Revolutionary Suicide,* 294.
100. Huey P. Newton, *The Penthouse,* unpublished manuscript, 19.
101. Ibid.
102. Jones-Dunham interview.
103. Donald Freed, personal interview, July 16, 2004. Telephone interview. Oakland, CA

104. Newton, *Revolutionary Suicide*, 299.
105. Erik Erickson, *In Search of Common Ground: Conversations with Erik H. Erikson and Huey P. Newton* (New York: Norton, 1973).
106. Jones-Dunham interview.
107. George Robinson, personal interview, July 8, 2004. Telephone interview Oakland, CA/Los Angeles, CA
108. Freed interview.
109. Newton, *The Penthouse*, 34.
110. Ibid,. 36.
111. Ibid., 38.
112. Newton, *Revolutionary Suicide*, 304.
113. Ibid., 311.
114. Pat Richartz, personal interview, July 13, 2004. San Jose, CA. Conducted by Zimmerman and Hilliard.

CHAPTER 14
115. Freed interview.
116. Robinson interview.
117. Personal interview, Ericka Huggins, June 24, 2004. Oakland, CA. Conducted by Zimmerman and Hilliard
118. Ibid.
119. Ibid.
120. Ibid.
121. Ibid.
122. Ibid.
123. Ibid.

CHAPTER 15
124. Newton, *Revolutionary Suicide*, 324.
125. Ibid., 327.
126. Ibid.
127. Huggins interview.
128. Ibid.
129. Ibid.
130. Robinson interview.
131. Ibid.

132. Huey P. Newton, *The Narcotics "Cover,"* unpublished manuscript, 104-06.
133. Ibid., 111.
134. Ibid., 112.
135. Huey P. Newton, *Exile*, unpublished, 126.
136. Ibid., 118.

CHAPTER 16
137. Huey P. Newton, *Escape to Cuba*, unpublished manuscript and personal notes.

CHAPTER 17
138. Newton, *Escape to Cuba*.
139. *CoEvolution Quarterly*, Fall 1977.
140. Ibid.
141. *Black Panther*, Feb. 18, 1978, p. 13.
142. *CoEvolution Quarterly*, Fall 1977.
143. *Black Panther*, Feb. 18, 1978, p. 13.
144. *CoEvolution Quarterly*, Fall 1977.
145. Ibid.
146. Ibid.
147. Ibid.
148. *Black Panther*, Feb. 18, 1978, p. 13.
149. *CoEvolution Quarterly*, Fall 1977.
150. Ibid.
151. Ibid.
152. Ibid.
153. Demetra Gayle, personal interview, July 14, 2004. Oakland, CA, Conducted by Zimmerman and Hilliard.
154. *CoEvolution Quarterly*, Fall 1977.
155. Ibid.
156. *Black Panther*, Feb. 18, 1978, p. 14.
157. Ibid., 15.
158. Ibid.
159. Ibid.
160. *Black Panther*, July 1977.

CHAPTER 18

161. Huey P. Newton, *Resumed Hostilities,*
     unpublished manuscript, 140.
162. Ibid., 142.
163. Ibid.
164. Ibid., 143.
165. Ibid., 141.
166. Triloki N. Pandey, personal inter-
     view-July 7, 2004. UC Santa Cruz
     campus, conducted by the
     Zimmermans and David Hilliard.
167. Ibid.
168. Ibid.
169. Ibid.
170. Ibid.
171. Ibid.
172. Ibid.
173. Ibid.
174. Ibid.
175. Robert Trivers, telephone interview,
     June 21, 2004. Oakland, CA, con-
     ducted by the Zimmermans and
     David Hilliard.

176. Ibid.
177. Ibid.
178. Ibid.
179. Ibid.
180. Ibid.
181. Ibid.
182. Ibid.
183. Ibid.
184. Gayle interview.

CHAPTER 19

185. Source for this entire chapter is
     Fredrika Newton, personal inter-
     view, January 8, 2005. Oakland CA,
     conducted by Kent Zimmerman.

CHAPTER 20

186. Gayle interview.
187. Newton, *Revolutionary Suicide,* 6–7.

INDEX